CYPRUS
THE SEARCH FOR A SOLUTION

CYPRUS

THE SEARCH FOR A SOLUTION

DS54.9.H36 2005
Hannay, David, Sir.
Cyprus : the search for a
solution
London ; New York : I.B.
Tauris ; New York :
Distributed in the United

David Hannay

I.B. TAURIS
LONDON · NEW YORK

Published and reprinted in 2005 by I.B.Taurus & Co. Ltd
6 Salem Road, London W2 4BU
175 Fifth Avenue, New York, NY 10010
www.ibtauris.com

In the United States of America and Canada distributed by Palgrave Macmillan, a
division of St Martin's Press, 175 Fifth Avenue, New York, NY 10010

ISBN: 1 85043 665 7
EAN: 978 1 85043 665 2

A full CIP record for this book is available from the British Library
A full CIP record for this book is available from the Library of Congress

Library of Congress catalog card: available

Typeset in Bliss by A. & D. Worthington, Newmarket, Suffolk
Printed and bound in Great Britain by TJ International, Ltd, Padstow, Cornwall

Contents

To my wife, my children and my grandchildren
who uncomplainingly put up with my absences
even after I was meant to have retired.

Preface

When I was first approached in February 1996 to ask whether I would be prepared to take on a new, part-time job as the British government's Special Representative for Cyprus, I had some idea of what I was being let in for, but not that it would last for seven years. Although I had never actually set foot on the island, I had, like many other British diplomats, bumped into the Cyprus problem from time to time during the 36 years of my professional career in the Diplomatic Service, which had ended the year before with my retirement from the post of UN ambassador in New York. I had been involved in the negotiations for a trade agreement between the European Community and Cyprus when Britain joined the EC in 1973; I had subsequently participated in the negotiations that developed this agreement into a customs union and, more relevant than either of these two experiences, I had a ringside seat for the last major attempt by the United Nations to negotiate a comprehensive settlement in 1992 and the subsequent, equally abortive, effort to agree a major package of Confidence-Building Measures on the island which had finally run into the sands in 1994.

So I could not be said to be unaware of the singular intractability of the problem, nor of the capacity of the main players to spin out any negotiation until the Greek Kalends, nor of their preference for playing the blame game over making any serious effort to get to grips with the core issues in an attempt to reach a settlement. Why did I say yes? Partly, I suspect, out of a reluctance to quit entirely the scene of international diplomacy in which I had spent the whole of my professional life. Partly also, like a mountain climber drawn towards an unclimbed peak, simply because it was there. The Cyprus problem was certainly an unclimbed peak, said by many – particularly by those who had tried to climb it and failed – to be un-climbable; so there was an element of irresistible challenge. And then there were less personal reasons. The commitment given by the European Union in 1995 to open accession negotiations with

Cyprus, divided or not, within six months of the end of the Inter-Governmental Conference which was drawing up the Amsterdam Treaty (in 1997), meant that we were sliding towards a parting of the ways which might either consolidate the division of the island or lead to its entering reunited into the European Union. It also had the potential to lead to a serious crisis in the relations between Turkey and the European Union and thus to a threat to the peace and stability of the Eastern Mediterranean. So the case for making a further determined attempt to reach a settlement was a serious one.

Seven years later, after two failed attempts to reach the summit, the second of which, at least, got agonizingly close, it was time to recognize that even if that peak was going, one day, to be climbed – and I do not join the ranks of those others whose efforts failed, in saying that it cannot be – it was not going to be climbed by me and almost certainly not for some considerable time to come. A secondary question then arose. Did it make sense to write down, while events were reasonably fresh in the memory, the story of the negotiations? Would anyone be interested in an account of a negotiation that failed, itself only the latest in a whole series of failed negotiations to settle the Cyprus problem? But there were arguments that pointed the other way. Cyprus may well be a place, like other scenes of long-running disputes – Northern Ireland springs to mind – that suffers from a surfeit of history. It does not, however, suffer from a surfeit of properly recorded and reasonably objective historical works. Indeed it is almost entirely lacking in them. Most of what has been written about Cyprus has been the work of members of one or other of the two embattled communities – or peoples (but that is part of the story that belongs to a later stage). As such they are at best distorted by that prism, at worst little better than polemic and propaganda. And the non-Cypriots who have ventured into the field seem to have fallen prey to the same distortions, often appearing as little more than apologists for one side or the other. So, for someone who has always been a student of history, it was tempting to try to redress this balance a little. Not that I have any illusions that what I write will be regarded by many on the island or in the region as objective. It is an occupational hazard for anyone who gets involved in attempts to resolve the Cyprus problem to be considered by both sides as being irremediably prejudiced against them and in the pocket of the other side. The same is all too likely to be the fate of any such person who tries subsequently to set out the record.

There is another reason for setting all this down. The Cyprus negotiations between 1996 and 2003 were complex enough in themselves, but they were made even more complex by the inter-relationships between two other entities, the United Nations, which was centre stage throughout the efforts to get a settlement, and the European Union, accession to which was an important motivating factor for the two parts of Cyprus and Turkey. So this was far from being a classical, bilateral international dispute, to be addressed within the framework of the relations between a limited number of nation states. It was rather a very modern negotiation, a kind of three-dimensional game of chess. Since neither United Nations diplomacy nor that involving the European Union is particularly well or widely understood, I believe that it could be useful to examine the anatomy of this negotiation from that point of view and not just as another chapter in the weary saga of attempts to settle the Cyprus problem.

So much for the author's motives; now some more practical points. This book is not, nor does it attempt to be, a history of Cyprus, even during the period described, although a chapter on the historical background is included to situate the negotiations that took place within their context. That chapter is neither an original product, nor is it the fruit of deep historical research, but the minimum needed to assist comprehension of the negotiation itself. So the book describes the anatomy of a negotiation, not the history of Cyprus. Being written very shortly after the events described, the author has had no access to any classified documents from the archives of governments or other parties. The documents referred to or cited in the book are all either formally in the public domain or else so widely and fully described in the press as to amount to the same thing. The opinions and judgement in the book are the author's own and no one else's, least of all those of the British government.

As often where two cultures and two languages are present there is a problem over the spelling of the names of people and places. I have opted for the versions most commonly used in the language in which the book is written, English. Since the two chief Cypriot protagonists, Glafcos Clerides and Rauf Denktash, both often used anglicized versions of their own names I feel in good company.

I have decided, for obvious reasons and despite the risk of appearing ungrateful, not to mention by name all those with whom I worked during this negotiation and without whose wisdom and advice it would not have got even as far as it did and this book would not have existed. It goes without saying that my thanks to them are profound.

CYPRUS: Adjustments to the status quo in the island proposed in the second revision of the Annan Plan tabled in February 2003

1:690,000

Upon entry into force of Foundation Agreement:

Turkish Cypriot constituent state

Greek Cypriot constituent State

Areas of Territorial Adjustment

After entry into force of the protocol to the Treaty of Establishment

Turkish Cypriot constituent state

Greek Cypriot constituent State

Parts of SBAs to become part of The United Cyprus Republic

corresponding maximum level of property reinstatement:

- per c-component State:- 10%
- per village or municipality 20% except in Agialousa/Yeni Erenköy, Agia Trias/Sipahi, Melangara/Adacay and Rizokarpaso/Dipkarpaz

Refer to pages 207-11

Rizokarpaso
Dipkarpaz

Agialoussa
Yeni Erenköy

Agios Andronikos
Yeşilköy

Famagusta

Varosha

Limnia
Mormenekşe

Peristerona
Alanıcı

Prastio
Dörtyol

Acheritou
Güvercinlik

Achna
Düzce

Pyrga
Pirhan

Pergamos
Beyarmudu

Asha
Paşaköy

Lysi
Akdoğan

Agia
Dikeskaya

Arsos
Yiğitler

Pyla
Pile

Larnaka

Tymvou
Kırklar

Louroujina
Akıncılar

NICOSIA

Potamia

Kyrenia

Lapithos
Lapta

Kondemenos
Kılıçaslan

Skylloura
Yılmazköy

Larnakas
Kozan

Dtkomo

Dhios
Tepebaşı

Agia Marina
Gürpınar

Morphou
Güzelyurt

Gatolakkos
Algıçköy

Katokopia
Basaliköy

Kormakiti
Koruçam

Peristeronari
Taşköy

Agia Irini
Akdeniz

Syrianochori
(Yeni Güzelyurt)

Yayla

Soli

Limassol

Lefka
Lefke

Gaimu
Onnerli

Kato Pyrgos
Günebakan

Kokkina
Erenköy

Pafos

The boundaries and names shown and the designations used on this map do not imply any official endorsement or acceptance.

1

The Historical Background: 1960–1996

The historical background to any international dispute is invariably an integral part of the dispute itself, and understanding that background and its implications for the present and for the main protagonists in negotiations for a settlement is essential to the search for a solution. Nowhere are these propositions more true than in Cyprus, whose peoples often seem weighed down by the accumulation of historical folk memories and by the received, but far from accurate, accounts of their past experiences. This chapter does not pretend to be a full, academically researched account of the modern history of Cyprus. It is more a series of snapshots taken, mainly over the last 50 years, of the principal milestones and turning points in what has been an often fraught and unhappy process. The focus is on events and developments that directly or indirectly influenced the present situation and the attitudes of the two sides when they returned to the negotiating table, first in 1997, then in 1999 and for the third time in 2002.

The story of Cyprus, from classical times down to its independence in 1960, was one of domination by outside powers. The mainly ethnically Greek population often enjoyed a fair degree of autonomy in the management of their own domestic affairs, and this was the case even when Cyprus was part of the Ottoman Empire from the sixteenth to the late nineteenth century, but for most of the time Cyprus fell under the broader sway of outsiders, whether Greeks in classical times, or Romans or the Byzantine Empire or the Latin crusaders or the Venetian Republic or the Ottoman Empire or, most recently, Britain. This history of external domination has left its mark on all Cypriots; it has contributed to the feeling, widely prevalent on both sides of the island, that Cypriots are not masters of their own destiny, that their fate will inevitably be decided by forces situated outside the island. This long sequence of external masters left a population less mixed and multicultural than might have been expected. So, while there are various small minorities, Latins (essentially Catholic descendants of the Crusaders), Armenians and Maronites, the population of the island emerged at the time of independence as roughly 80 per cent Greek and 18 per cent Turkish. The two communities lived scattered all over the island and inter-mingled geographically, with no substantial mono-ethnic enclaves; but socially and politically they were separate (with almost no evidence, for example, of inter-communal marriage) and gradually became more so under the pressure of events.

The last decade of colonial Cyprus (1950–60) was a period of turmoil and violence on the island. Many of the dragons' teeth of the subsequent dispute were sown during that period. The Greek Cypriots prosecuted a guerrilla war, both in the Troodos Mountains and in the towns, against the British colonial power and the police (many of whom were Turkish Cypriots, appointed by the British colonial authorities once the troubles had started). While casualties were not high by the standards of other similar struggles, the residue of bitterness on all sides was considerable. The objective pursued by the Greek Cypriots and by their unchallenged leader, the head of the Greek Orthodox Church in the island, Archbishop Makarios, was at the outset *enosis*, union with Greece, but gradually, as it became clear that this was unattainable in the light of the attitudes of both Greece and Turkey, it switched grudgingly to independence. However, the military leader of the armed struggle, General George Grivas, a former Greek army officer, never made that switch. The Turkish Cypriots began by putting their faith in the British colonial power, both to resist the political pretensions of the Greek Cypriots and to protect them against the attacks and harassment of their Greek Cypriot neighbours. But, as they became steadily more aware of British inadequacies in both respects, the Turkish Cypriots turned towards a reliance on Turkey as their ultimate protector and towards a willingness to use force themselves. Thus relationships between the two communities steadily deteriorated during this period. The British, for their part, zigzagged between the options of keeping the island under colonial tutelage in perpetuity for geo-strategic reasons and a traditional gradualist approach to self-government, finally dumping the whole problem in the laps of the Greeks and Turks, in return for the establishment of two Sovereign Base Areas to meet their strategic needs in an otherwise independent Cyprus. This legacy would haunt British policy in the future, as all in the region convinced themselves that Britain's involvement was solely intended to preserve its hold on the Bases. The Greek and Turkish governments were gradually drawn deeper and deeper into this morass. At various times the options of *enosis* and of *taksim* (partition or 'double enosis', with the northern part of the island becoming a part of Turkey) had some attraction to each of them. But once they realized the risk that they could be drawn into open hostilities or at least into a proxy war between them in Cyprus, they drew back, and effectively imposed an independence settlement on the two distinctly unenthusiastic Cypriot communities.

The longer-term consequences of this troubled decade were complex and highly destabilizing. The British ended up distrusted and disliked by both sides. Unlike in many other post-colonial situations they did not benefit from a post-independence honeymoon with the Greek Cypriots. The Turkish Cypriots considered that the British had let them down and never again fully trusted them. Surprisingly, given that the main characteristics of British policy in that period were muddle, fudge and indecisiveness, both sides credited the British with incredible deviousness and subtlety. Neither the Greek nor the Turkish Cypriots much liked the situation they found themselves in following the settlement, and neither felt any sense of ownership of or loyalty towards it. (Indeed throughout the 1960s President Makarios openly described the creation of the state of Cyprus as a step on the road to enosis.) It was something imposed on them by Greece and Turkey and by the indifference of Britain. Greece and Turkey in the short term drew a deep sigh of relief at having escaped from a dangerous corner but they did little to help make the newly independent bi-communal Cyprus work; and, in the case of Greece, once the military regime of the colonels took over in 1967, they actively set about undermining the settlement and once more promoting enosis. A further development from that period was that the United States began to take an interest in Cyprus, but largely from the point of view of avoiding an open conflict between two NATO allies, Greece and Turkey, and the consequent weakening of NATO's southern flank. Predictably the Soviet Union became interested too, with the precise aim of weakening that southern flank, an objective it pursued by lending largely unquestioning support to Makarios.

Three international treaties, the Treaty of Guarantee, the Treaty of Alliance and the Treaty of Establishment, between them effectively limited and constrained the exercise of Cyprus's sovereignty. The 1960 Cyprus constitution is difficult to categorize in any of the commonly known definitions; it was neither federal nor confederal; it was perhaps

closer to a unitary structure, but it contained elaborate checks and balances between the powers exercised by the leaders of the two
communities as president and vice-president and between the other
representatives of the two communities. It could only ever have worked
smoothly with a high degree of cooperation between the two sides; in the
hands of people who were in no way motivated to try to make it work, it
provided a recipe for deadlock and frustration. The Treaty of Guarantee
forbade secession or the union of Cyprus with any other state; it gave to
the three guarantor powers (Greece, Turkey and the United Kingdom)
the duty to consult together to preserve the territory and the constitutional order of the newly established state of Cyprus and, if such
consultation did not lead to agreement on the steps that needed to be
taken, it permitted each of the guarantor powers to intervene unilaterally
with a view to restoring the status quo ante. The Treaty of Alliance
provided for a small military force composed of a specified number of
Greek and Turkish troops, with a tripartite headquarters, to be stationed
on the island. This treaty was never implemented. The Treaty of Establishment was the basis for the United Kingdom's retention of sovereignty
over 99 square miles of Cyprus in the two Sovereign Base Areas of Akrotiri and Dhekelia.

This potentially dysfunctional set of arrangements lasted for only
three years before a major crisis derailed it. In 1963 the Turkish Cypriots
withdrew from participation in the institutional structures of the state.
The proximate cause of this withdrawal was a dispute over fiscal matters.
But disagreements between the two communities went deeper than that.
The Greek Cypriots believed that this was part of a systematic campaign
by the Turkish Cypriots to frustrate the proper working of the state and
so lead to partition. In response they threatened to push through (uncon-
stitutionally) a number of constitutional amendments that would have
removed the Turkish Cypriot veto. From this time on the security situation deteriorated steadily, with extensive harassment, particularly of
Turkish Cypriots by Greek Cypriots and of Greek Cypriots by paramili-
tary nationalists, with numerous atrocities committed by both sides and
with the much less numerous Turkish Cypriots tending to abandon their
houses scattered in villages and towns where Greek Cypriots were in a
majority and to group themselves together in enclaves where they could
better defend themselves. Both sides formed militia forces, the Greek
Cypriots EOKA B, the Turkish Cypriots TMT. The Cyprus National
Guard, the Republic's army, was entirely Greek Cypriot in composition

and accordingly partisan. It was at this time that the United Nations first became directly involved in Cyprus, with the deployment in 1964 of a small UN military force which, however, was unable to do much to improve the security situation. The Security Council continued, following the breakdown of the 1960 constitution, to treat what was now effectively a Greek Cypriot administration as the properly constituted government of the Republic of Cyprus. A number of appeals were made to the guarantor powers to intervene but, prior to 1974, no such intervention took place, although in 1967 the Turks were only dissuaded from intervening militarily at the very last moment by a brutally forceful demarche from the then president of the United States, Lyndon Johnson.

This time of troubles, from 1963 to 1974, marked all the players in the Cyprus problem and profoundly influenced the attitude of those who participated in the subsequent attempts to reach a settlement. Throughout that period, and even more so after 1974, the Turkish Cypriots believed that the constitution had simply been hijacked in 1963 by the Greek Cypriots and that it therefore no longer had any validity. They bitterly resented the fact that the United Nations (and other international organizations such as the European Union, the Council of Europe and the Organization for Security and Cooperation in Europe which followed suit) continued to treat the Greek Cypriots as the sole government of Cyprus. Denktash in particular was prone to argue that until that recognition was reversed, either by recognizing the Turkish Cypriots on an equal but separate basis or by derecognizing the Greek Cypriots, there could be no solution to the Cyprus problem. The refusal of the UN to do this led both Turks and Turkish Cypriots to suspect the Security Council and the whole international community of being biased against them, and it also caused them to take a restrictive view of the use of the UN secretary-general's good offices. In addition the Turkish Cypriots acquired a conviction that UN peacekeepers could not protect them from Greek Cypriot harassment. The Greek Cypriots for their part regarded their recognition as the sole government of Cyprus as the jewel in their crown and used their position in the various international organizations to outmanoeuvre the Turks and Turkish Cypriots and to build up defences against the latter's secession and attempts to achieve international recognition. They came to believe that the Turks had always wanted to annex Cyprus for its strategic value and that the Turkish Cypriots' complaints about their plight was merely special pleading to provide cover for this policy. The British, disinclined from the outset to allow themselves to be dragged back into Cyprus, came to see the United Nations as a preferable instrument for conflict prevention and resolution than the Treaty of Guarantee.

The Greek Cypriot coup d'état in July 1974 triggered off a series of events that profoundly altered all the parameters of the Cyprus problem. The coup, which was actively encouraged by the military regime in Athens, then in an advanced state of decay, resulted in the forcible over-throw of Makarios and the installation as president of Nikos Sampson, a former guerrilla fighter with an unsavoury reputation. It was followed by a short but bloody civil war with his Greek Cypriot political opponents, particularly members of AKEL, the Greek Cypriot communist party, and by some high-profile attacks on Turkish Cypriot enclaves. Within days the Turks invaded Cyprus and in two stages occupied about one-third of the island, finally stopping their operations along the present Green Line which crosses Cyprus from east to west. During this military phase the outside powers, the US and the UK in particular, avoided intervening and did little more than wring their hands, calling for restraint on all sides. Sampson's regime had collapsed (as did that of the military in Athens) and, after some delay, during which Glafcos Clerides as president of the National Assembly was acting president, Makarios returned. Many Greek Cypriots from the north of the island fled south and many Turkish Cyp-riots from the south fled north or took refuge in the British Sovereign Base Areas. In 1975 this ethnic cleansing was regularized by an agreement that enabled the practical arrangements for the population exchange to be completed but did not legally recognize the exchange. Only a few Greek Cypriots and some Maronites, the former mainly living in villages in the Karpas Peninsula (the 'pan-handle') in the north-east, remained in the north and even fewer Turkish Cypriots remained in the south. Thus in 1975 the geo-political configuration of Cyprus as we now know it came into being, with two virtually mono-ethnic states separated by a buffer zone guarded by UN peacekeeping troops.

These traumatic events scarred all parties in the dispute. The Greek Cypriots had lost control of one-third of what they regarded as their country, and the part most agriculturally fertile and developed for com-mercial and tourist purposes at that. They were determined to recover at least some of the territory lost. Moreover many tens of thousands of Greek Cypriot refugees had abandoned their property in the north and were left destitute; they and successive Greek Cypriot governments were determined to get this property back in any settlement and regarded getting compensation for its loss as an unacceptable alternative. These property claims were eventually taken up in a series of private cases brought before the Council of Europe's European Court of Human Rights, where the first case was won in 1998. The Greeks had discovered just how disastrous meddling in Cyprus's internal politics could prove for them and for the Greek Cypriots. They had also discovered that if Turkey did intervene militarily, there was no way in which they could effectively resupply their own and Greek Cypriot National Guard forces in Cyprus and thus withstand the superior military might of Turkey. Turkish aircraft could be over Cyprus within a few minutes of takeoff; by contrast, by the time they had made the long trip from Rhodes or Crete, Greek aircraft had only about 30 minutes' endurance over the island before needing to refuel.

The Turkish Cypriots saw their view that only Turkey could be relied upon when the chips were down vindicated. They were also confirmed in their prejudices towards the Greek Cypriots as people who were determined at least to dominate Cyprus by force and at worst to expel all Turkish Cypriots from the island. The Turks, whose military operations had gone rather less smoothly than had appeared to the outside world, were determined never again to be put in the position of having to mount an opposed, amphibious landing in order to protect the Turkish Cypriots. The Turkish military now had a massive troop presence (even today numbering about 35,000) in the north and, as the Greek Cypriots recovered from their defeat and began to acquire ever more sophisticated equipment, found themselves having to deal not only with Turkish Cypriot security concerns but with their own too. They also became convinced that the British Sovereign Base Areas (of which the key airport at Akrotiri was now embedded in the Greek Cypriot part of the island) meant that Britain would always take the side of the Greek Cypriots in any dispute. The outsiders had seen that a smouldering ethnic dispute could burst into flames, which only narrowly avoided spreading into hostilities between two NATO members; they were all the more convinced of the need to work under the aegis of the UN for a settlement to the Cyprus problem; but their alarm was not sufficient to incline them to overcome their reluctance to get drawn into direct involvement.

From 1974 onwards a UN peacemaking process of some kind or another was under way, with successive special representatives of the UN secretary-general working with the two sides on the elements of a comprehensive settlement or, during some periods, on confidence-building measures designed to reduce the tension on the Green Line and to pave the way for a settlement.

In 1977 and 1979 High-Level Agreements were reached, the first between Makarios and Rauf Denktash, the second, following Makarios's death, between Denktash and Spyros Kyprianou. These agreements were only thin skeletons of a settlement, not the real thing. But they did establish a framework for a solution based on a bi-communal, bi-zonal federation. The demand for a federation was a Turkish Cypriot one (they had in 1975 named their own part of the island the Turkish Federated State of Cyprus, i.e. not at this stage claiming independence from the state of Cyprus). By conceding federation the Greek Cypriots effectively recognized that the bi-communal unitary state of 1960 had gone beyond recall and that in the future Cyprus would need to consist of two units, with the Turkish Cypriots having a considerable range of responsibilities. But attempts to move beyond this conceptual breakthrough were systematically frustrated by the obstinacy and hesitations of both sides when it came to fleshing out the agreed framework.

In November 1983 Denktash and the Turks proclaimed, through a unilateral declaration of independence, that the north of the island was the Turkish Republic of Northern Cyprus (TRNC). The United Nations Security Council condemned this move and called on UN members not to recognize the new state. None did; and, to this day, only Turkey recognizes the TRNC. The 1983 declaration considerably complicated the search for a settlement. By giving Denktash, backed by Turkey, a status that was unnegotiable with the Greek Cypriots and with the whole of the international community, it introduced a new, potentially insoluble, element. And over time it also led directly to the further isolation of the Turkish Cypriots, as their unrecognized claim gave rise to problems ranging from the trade with the European Union to participation in international sporting competitions and to international arrangements for civil aviation. It therefore contributed to the widening prosperity gap between north and south and to the increasing dependence of the northern economy on Turkish subsidies.

In 1992 Boutros Boutros-Ghali's Set of Ideas brought together the elements of a comprehensive settlement. This document, which was negotiated at a series of meetings in New York between George Vassiliou and Denktash, went far beyond the 1977 and 1979 High-Level Agreements, on which it was based, but still fell short of a comprehensive, self-executing settlement. In any case it was never agreed, both sides still having difficulties with it when negotiations were suspended for the Greek Cypriot presidential elections in early 1993. The narrow victory of Glafcos Clerides, who campaigned against the Set of Ideas, meant that the negotiations for a settlement then lapsed. Instead the UN tried, through 1993 and 1994, to get agreement on a major package of Confidence-Building Measures, the most significant of which would have led to the return of the tourist ghost town of Varosha to the Greek Cypriots and to the reopening of Nicosia Airport to trade and passenger transport with both sides of the island (the airport, being in the UN buffer zone, was contiguous to both north and south). These negotiations also failed to come to fruition; as ever in Cyprus, having swallowed the elephant, the two sides strained at the gnat, agreeing to the principle but failing to agree on the practical arrangements necessary to implement a deal.

Before we reach the period covered by the present book, one further development needs to be noted. In 1990 the Greek Cypriots applied for Cyprus to become a member of the European Union; in 1995 this application was, in principle, accepted as being valid by the European Union, a date for opening negotiations being set at six months after the EU's Inter-Governmental Conference which met in Amsterdam in June 1997. The Turkish Cypriots challenged the legality both of the application and of the European Union's acceptance of it and refused point-blank Clerides's invitation to join a common Cypriot negotiating team.

2

The Players

Any diplomat facing a complex and extremely long-running international dispute such as the Cyprus problem and hoping to help move it towards solution needs to recognize and take account of the importance of personalities and of the interaction between them for any such effort. But he or she also needs to recognize that personalities are not all-important, that even the strongest and most dominant characters are not entirely free agents, and that national and sectoral interests, the weight of history, the flow of events outside those directly related to the problem, will influence the outcome every bit as much and sometimes more than the actions and views of the individual players. This was certainly the case with the Cyprus problem, which from the outset had never anywhere near made it into the first league of world problems demanding a solution and which remained for everyone except the inhabitants of the island a second-order problem – one which it was desirable to solve but which failure to solve would not be a life or death matter.

As I made my way around the Cyprus circuit, two other things struck me about the personalities involved. The first was the unevenness of the importance of personality in the different capitals. On the island the two leaders were precisely that, the virtually unchallenged determinants of Greek Cypriot and Turkish Cypriot policy and the real players in negotiations if negotiations ever could be got under way. In Athens the significance of the foreign minister's role in the determination of Cyprus policy was considerable, but, given its history in Greece as a national issue, far from absolute. In Ankara opacity was invariably the order of the day. It was never at all clear where Turkey's Cyprus policy was being decided or who was at any one time playing the key role in deciding it. It was often tempting to believe that the answers were nowhere and no one, and that policy was largely being decided by default, falling back, for lack of agreement on any new policy, on the old one. Certainly personality played some role – Bulent Ecevit's sincerely held belief that he had solved the Cyprus problem in 1974 weighed like a dead hand on the policy-making process so long as he was prime minister – but not, it seemed, a crucially important one compared with the institutional and historical influences.

The second impression was how tiny and how hermetically sealed was the circle of those in each of the four capitals who had any real say in the making of Cyprus policy. All four were democracies, but the public debate on Cyprus in each of them was ill-informed, formulaic and chauvinistic. Negotiations to resolve the Cyprus problem had been going on for so long and so fruitlessly that most commentators, journalists and their readers had become bored and cynical, unwilling to look at the issues with a fresh eye or to challenge conventional wisdom. Indeed many journalists, especially on the island, seemed to consider it their patriotic duty to follow the long-established partisan line and to denounce any politician who dared to suggest that any aspect of it might be re-examined. Within the bureaucracies, and in particular within the foreign ministries in Athens and Ankara, Cyprus was an important and sensitive subject but not an attractive one, not one to be chosen from a career development point of view. Most officials kept their distance and concentrated on less static, less entrenched areas of policy. In Cyprus itself the problem was an all-consuming obsession but far too politically charged for officials or diplomats to have much say in the matter.

Two sets of inter-relationships between the principal players were of critical importance – those between Greeks and Greek Cypriots on the one hand and those between Turks and Turkish Cypriots on the other – but they were, by their nature, singularly difficult for an outsider to penetrate or to comprehend fully. None of the players was prepared to discuss these inter-relationships freely, and much effort was devoted by all concerned to concealing from prying eyes and ears, including from their own public, the content of their mutual discussions and the view each took of the other. Both pairs also devoted a considerable effort to sustaining what was often a fiction, or at least only a half-truth, namely that their views at any given time and on any given issue were identical. The relationship of the Greek government and the Greek Cypriots was burdened by history – by the perception that in the 1950s the Greek government had traded in the aspirations of the Greek Cypriots for better Greek–Turkish relations and that in 1974 the military regime in Athens had overthrown the democratically elected president of Cyprus by force and thus precipitated the events that led to over one-third of the island being controlled by Turkey and to the ethnic cleansing of 1975. Any suggestion that the Greek government was giving less than wholehearted support to the Greek Cypriots or was meddling in Greek Cypriot internal politics was therefore dynamite, both in Athens and in Nicosia. Indeed the official mantra quoted often by both Greek and Greek Cypriot politicians and journalists was 'Cyprus decides; Greece supports'. Add to this that throughout the period of negotiations the government in Nicosia was on the right of the political spectrum while the Greek government was a socialist one and there was plenty of scope for friction and submerged tension.

The relationship between the Turkish government and the Turkish Cypriots was rather different, although not entirely devoid of similar tensions. The primacy of Denktash in determining not only Turkish Cypriot but Turkey's policy on the Cyprus problem was longstanding. Any challenge to it, as there had been when Prime Minister (and subsequent President) Turgut Özal tried to settle the Cyprus problem, brought about an immediate sharp rise in the temperature but had, hitherto at least, always ended in victory for Denktash, who at any point in time had as high, if not higher, opinion-poll ratings on the mainland as any Turkish politician.

Strangely enough the personal relationships between the Greek Cypriots and the Turkish Cypriots, and between their two leaders, Clerides and Denktash, were of less significance than those other two symbiotic pairs of relationships. It was true that Clerides and Denktash personally got on well together, respected each other, reminisced about their time practising law in colonial Cyprus and rather wistfully looked at each other as the only ones from that period left standing. But that did not translate into any beneficial effects at the negotiating table. Denktash was no more flexible dealing with Clerides than he had been in the 1992 negotiations with his predecessor Vassiliou, whom he disliked and distrusted. And while Clerides initially thought that face-to-face negotiations with Denktash were the key to unlocking a deal, he came to believe, once they had started, that there was little point in negotiating directly with Denktash, as the ultimate decisions would be taken in Ankara. So neither the ups and downs in Clerides's and Denktash's view of each other, nor the fact that, almost alone of Cypriot politicians on either side, they never made personally offensive remarks about each other, played much of a role in determining the outcome of the efforts to get a settlement.

The Greek Cypriots

The 1960 constitution of Cyprus was full of checks and balances between Greek Cypriots and Turkish Cypriots, in particular between the Greek Cypriot president and the Turkish Cypriot vice-president; but once, after 1963, the Turkish Cypriot dimension and participation had been removed, what remained was an executive presidency whose powers and influence were greater than in almost any other democratic state in the world. The president was elected for five years; there was no limit on the number of times he could be re-elected; he had no vice-president (the president of the National Assembly stood in if the president was absent or incapacitated); he had no prime minister and appointed all the ministers (who did not need to be elected members of the legislature); it was the norm to rule without a majority in the Assembly; he was the negotiator for the Cyprus problem.

The holder of this powerful office for all but the last two weeks of the period covered by the present book was Glafcos Clerides. He had been a prominent figure in Greek Cypriot politics from before the establishment of an independent Cyprus; he had been president of the National Assembly at the time of the 1974 coup and had stood in for the first president, Archbishop Makarios, until the latter returned to the island and resumed office; he had been the Greek Cypriot negotiator for the Cyprus problem when that post had been separate from the presidency; he had been elected president for a first time in 1993 and for a second time in 1998, on both occasions by a tiny majority of around 1 per cent; he was the leader of the Democratic Rally, a centre-right, nationalist party, which throughout his presidency was either the largest or the second largest in Greek Cypriot politics; he was in his late 70s, passing his 80th birthday about half way through his second term of office. He was short, rotund, bandy-legged, with a twinkle in his eye, an infectious laugh and a complexion that bore witness to his love of the sea and swimming. He was not much interested in the day-to-day minutiae of government, which he left to his ministers, and not at all in economic matters, and he found everything to do with the European Union puzzling and not particularly enthralling.

His passion was the Cyprus problem, about which he was subtly and encyclopaedically knowledgeable, reflected in his multi-volume autobiography, *My Deposition*. He understood very well that the Greek Cypriots had made major mistakes, with disastrous consequences, when they had hijacked the Republic in 1963 and when they had precipitated the hostilities in 1974. He was determined to learn and to apply the lessons from those mistakes. As time wore on, as the residue of his second term of office grew shorter, and as the negotiations intensified, he became ever more committed to achieving a positive outcome, although never at any price. The Clerides one met in his office, invariably over a working breakfast, could be tetchy and irritable if he thought things were not going well or that he was being put under pressure, but generally he was a fluent and flexible interlocutor, abreast of every twist and turn of the negotiations. The Clerides one met on his boat on a swimming expedition, with none of his ministers or officials present, was a perfect host, full of stories drawn from his time in the RAF during the war, when the bomber of which he was a crew member was shot down over Germany (an MRI scan in the last months of his presidency picked up only one piece of Second World War shrapnel, much to his doctor's relief), and from his long political career, loving to gossip about personalities and addressing the negotiations only in a tangential and non-specific way.

Clerides's negotiating team was small, the inner core consisting of his attorney-general Alecos Markides and his under-secretary and eminence grise Pantelis Kouros. Markides was a skilled and assiduous lawyer who was equally capable of using his legal knowledge to frustrate or to facilitate progress in the negotiations; during the proximity talks the accent was on the former, during the final year of negotiations very much on the latter. Behind a gruff and often glowering exterior, he nursed a burning ambition to be president himself. There were also three semi-detached figures: Ioannis Kasoulides, who was the president's spokesman at the outset and then his foreign minister, George Vassiliou, Clerides's predecessor as president and later Cyprus's chief negotiator with the European Union, and Michalis Papapetrou who was spokesman during the crucial phases of the negotiation. Kasoulides (who also nursed presidential ambitions), Vassiliou and Papapetrou were a good deal more outward-looking and cosmopolitan than the normal run of Greek Cypriot politicians and realized how tight a rope the Greek Cypriot politicians were walking if they were to be accepted into the European Union even without a settlement of the Cyprus problem. Kasoulides was capable of wearing either hawkish or doveish plumage; Vassiliou was an imaginative and committed dove and was a close confidant of Clerides; Papapetrou, an enthusiastic participant in bi-communal meetings with Turkish Cypriots, was also a dove – even if compelled by his role as spokesman to appear hawkish in public – although much less close to Clerides than the other two and a less experienced politician.

For the last two weeks before the negotiations ended in March 2003 Clerides gave way to Tassos Papadopoulos, the incoming president, who had handsomely won the presidential election in mid-February. Papadopoulos, another lawyer, had also figured prominently in most phases of Greek Cypriot history pre- and post-independence. He had at one stage served as Clerides's deputy negotiator on the Cyprus problem before taking the role over from him. He had a reputation as a hardline rejectionist, a reputation that he did everything possible to live down once he had reached agreement with the communist party (AKEL) to support his presidential candidature and during the campaign itself. In my own dealings with him, both over the years when he was deputy leader, then leader of DIKO (a centre-right nationalist party formerly led by Spyros Kyprianou), and in the short period after he was elected president, Papadopoulos was always exceptionally careful to avoid saying anything which would enable him to be categorized as a rejectionist. But he was less careful in his public comments aimed at a domestic audience and it was not too difficult to gauge that he was less committed to making the compromises necessary to achieve a successful outcome than Clerides.

To the extent that the Greek Cypriot president was accountable to anyone it was not to his parliament but rather to the National Council, which grouped together the leaders of the political parties represented in the Assembly and past presidents of Cyprus (i.e. Spyros Kyprianou, until his death in 2002, and George Vassiliou). This peculiar body (set up outside the constitution) had no other function than to advise the president on the conduct of negotiations on the Cyprus problem and did not have powers of decision unless it was unanimous. And given that Clerides could normally rely on the leader of his own political party (Nikos Anastasiades) and on Vassiliou to back him up, the chances of his ever being overruled were minimal. But since any settlement reached would need to be endorsed subsequently in a referendum, the views and involvement of the party leaders, even those politically opposed to Clerides, were important and could not easily be ignored. The National Council was also remarkably leaky, with the result that, however hard Kofi Annan and Alvaro de Soto might work to keep a news blackout over the details of the negotiations and however well Clerides might try to cooperate with this policy, it never worked; and, within minutes of Clerides briefing the National Council, some version of the briefing, usually several versions, spun this way and that to suit the views of the leaker, was in the hands of the media. In theory Clerides could leave the National Council behind when the negotiations took place outside Cyprus (this option obviously did not exist when they were in Nicosia) but in practice it was not an attractive course to take; the members of the National Council left behind in Nicosia were all too likely to spend their time sniping at the president on the basis of inaccurate press reports. On most occasions, therefore, they went along, a handicap but a necessary one.

The key players in the National Council, apart from the president himself and his team and the leader of his own party, were the leaders of the three biggest parties, Dimitris Christofias of AKEL, the communist party, Spyros Kyprianou (later Tassos Papadopoulos) of DIKO, and Vasos Lyssarides (later Yannakis Omirou) of the socialist party KISOS, formerly EDEK. Of these, Christofias was by a long way the most important politically. The reason was simple. Come wind, come rain, AKEL clocked in approximately one-third of the vote in any Cyprus election, and it voted as their leader told it to, like the unreconstructed Marxist-Leninist party that it was. So, if AKEL opposed a settlement, it would not be easy to muster a majority in a referendum (an integral part of all settlement plans from the 1992 Set of Ideas onwards) in favour of one. Traditionally AKEL had been the most doveish of the Greek Cypriot parties, with links to a Turkish Cypriot sister party (Talat's CTP). But the party had been out of office and deprived of the perquisites of office since 1993, and gradually the determination to reverse that came to prevail over any spirit of moderation on the Cyprus problem. Christofias, the architect of the alliance with Papadopoulos (which brought him, along the way, the presidency of the National Assembly), gradually hardened his position in the settlement negotiations, resisting Clerides's efforts to enlist his support. Papadopoulos's views have already been described. As to Lyssarides, who had been Makarios's doctor, he was a flamboyant and quixotic rejectionist, the strength of his views only tempered by his close links with the Greek governing party, PASOK, which was, of course, throughout the latter part of this period far from rejectionist. Once Omirou took over the leadership and particularly during the period up to December 2002 when he was being promoted as a coalition candidate to succeed Clerides with the electoral support of the latter's party, there ceased to be problems in the National Council from that quarter.

Outside the president, his negotiating team and the National Council, there were really no other significant players on the Greek Cypriot side. The ministers were completely cut out of the action. The foreign ministry and the diplomatic service (apart from Kasoulides and his private secretary) were told little of what was going on and were left to wage the endless worldwide campaign to resist Turkish and Turkish Cypriot efforts to enhance the TRNC's status. There was one other important factor, the media, most definitely part of the problem, not part of the solution. It is a safe bet to say that no place on earth has a greater concentration of newspapers and of television and radio stations than the southern part of the island of Cyprus – six daily newspapers, five national television stations and about 50 radio stations, all serving 600,000 people. And all of them were writing and broadcasting almost exclusively about only one subject, the Cyprus problem. Given the paucity of news on that topic, the media were driven to making most of it up as they went along. Issuing rebuttals of their latest fictional extravagances was grist to their mill. To some extent such saturation coverage and such an unprofessional attitude to reporting were self-defeating. Anyone who handled the Cyprus problem just had to grow an extra skin, preferably several. But, watching from the depths of one of Denktash's sofas as a gaggle of Greek Cypriot journalists called in to cover one's call on Denktash, put offensively worded questions to him and then scribbled out feverishly the equally offensively worded replies, was to feel that one was in the presence of two of the most prominent obstacles to reaching a settlement.

The Turkish Cypriots

The powers of the Turkish Cypriot president were, on paper at least, less than those of his Greek Cypriot counterpart, but in practice his position was even more dominant and less constrained. The Turkish Cypriot constitution, which bore some superficial resemblance to that of Turkey itself, in fact, largely due to the personalities involved, operated quite differently. So what appeared on the surface to be a parliamentary system, with a prime minister and a government based on a coalition enjoying majority support in the legislature, in reality operated as a presidential system, with all decisions relating to the Cyprus problem in the hands of Denktash who, like Clerides, was the negotiator. If one added to that the unwritten code by which Denktash was the main and often the sole Turkish Cypriot interlocutor of both the Turkish government and the Turkish military, one ended up with a situation in which Denktash called all the shots. And although, when he wanted to play for time or to avoid responsibility, he would often say that he would have to consult his government or parliament, or that the matter in question was for the government and not for him to decide, this was no more than a façade: when an important matter arose on which he wished to take a position no such procedures were invoked or applied.

Rauf Denktash had been president throughout the nearly 20-year existence of the TRNC and before that he had been president of the Turkish Cypriot federated state. He bestrode north Cyprus like a colossus, and indeed, despite his modest stature, he did embody that image. A massive torso was topped by an expressive and dominant face with a large nose (about which he was capable of making jokes, particularly when comparing it to that of Papadopoulos whose nose had been likened to Cyrano de Bergerac's). Like Clerides, although some years after him, he had been trained as a lawyer in Britain and had practised in colonial Cyprus, with the interesting distinction that whereas Clerides tended to defend Greek Cypriot guerrilla fighters, Denktash prosecuted them on behalf of the British authorities. He had an almost unstoppable flow of idiomatic and forceful English which he would unleash on any new visitor in the form of a lengthy history lesson retailing all the sufferings of the Turkish Cypriots and all the iniquities of the Greek Cypriots. With those who had progressed beyond that opening salvo (which tended to be repeated for several visits before it was accepted that something closer to a dialogue might be more useful) he would launch himself with enthusiasm into a rumbustious and aggressively conducted debate during which, however, he always remained polite, correct and controlled, with bursts of humour often breaking through. As a host at his residence near Snake Island, a few miles west of Kyrenia, he could be extremely hospitable, though relaxed was hardly a word one would use even there, except when he was talking about photography or was conducting a guided tour of his collection of budgerigars, parrots and small animals, kept in a menagerie behind the house. Like Clerides he had a remarkable supply of engaging personal reminiscences – of being in Trafalgar Square on VE Day, of his escape from house arrest in Ankara in the 1960s (when the Turks regarded him as a dangerous firebrand), of his return to Cyprus in a small boat, leading to his arrest and deportation by the Makarios government. There was, however, a darker side to Denktash: his isolation from anyone who might have stood up to him, his vindictiveness towards anyone among his own people who criticized him and towards Greek Cypriots, both collectively and individually.

Most of those who had dealt with Denktash in the past had reached the conclusion that he simply did not particularly want a settlement of the Cyprus problem or at least not one short of a wholesale capitulation by the Greek Cypriots. I came to share that view. The basic case that he made for a completely new start, with genuine political equality for the Turkish Cypriots, was a compelling one. But the language he used to describe it and the proposals he put forward to bring it about were not even remotely negotiable, and his forthright condemnation and misrepresentation of proposals designed to achieve these objectives by less direct methods than he favoured suggested that he did not really believe them to be attainable. Moreover the Greek Cypriot fear that his ultimate aim was secession and permanent partition of the island was no mere figment of their imagination. It often seemed to me that Denktash's own preferred solution was that north Cyprus should become part of Turkey. He clearly did not trust his successors, whoever they might be, to hold to the firm line he had established, and he certainly did not trust Turkish governments, either present or future, to do so either. So the only way to lock the door and throw away the key was through annexation. Unfortunately for him this was the one solution that no Turkish government with a concern for its international standing and aspirations to join the European Union could contemplate. So he was forced to make do with what he regarded as second best, although that did not stop him hankering after his ideal solution or trying to edge his way towards it.

Another feature of Denktash's handling of the Cyprus problem, which it took me longer to understand, was his fundamental unwillingness to negotiate at all with the UN or with those backing its efforts. There was never any question of his responding with some flexibility to private probing about where areas of common ground with the Greek Cypriots might exist. It gradually dawned on me that the only people he ever negotiated with were the Turks themselves. With them he showed great agility and manipulative skills. His objective was to enlist in advance the backing of the Turkish state for whatever position he was going to take in the negotiations and, once he had it, to camp on that position and refuse to budge. He thus validated the views of those who said that it was only in Ankara that a solution to the Cyprus problem could be found.

Denktash's negotiating team was as exiguous as that of Clerides but it lacked the bureaucratic underpinning which the Greek Cypriots undoubtedly had and which enabled them to produce large amounts of material for the legislation in a new Cyprus at short notice when the final stage of the negotiations got under way. Denktash's main adviser was Mumtaz Soysal, a Turkish academic and politician who had briefly served as foreign minister in the early 1990s. Soysal was about as hard a liner as you could get on the Cyprus issue, and was viscerally opposed to Turkey joining the European Union, and so reinforced Denktash's prejudices on both these matters. In addition he was inclined to inject his own particular brand of vitriol into joint negotiating sessions with the Greek Cypriots. The other member of the Turkish Cypriot negotiating team was Ergun Olgun, Denktash's under-secretary. His background was in business and not in politics, and a spell at a university in the United States had somewhat widened his horizons. But he was still very much his master's voice, at least until a very late stage in the negotiations when his involvement in the joint working group drawing up the international obligations and domestic legislation for a reunited Cyprus began to open his eyes to the benefits that the Turkish Cypriots could get under the Annan Plan. Apart from those three and because of Denktash's refusal to countenance any hint of opposition to his policies from those around him, there was really little else that could be described as a negotiating team, as became all too apparent when Denktash went into hospital in New York in October 2002. Olgun remained with him and Soysal retired to Ankara, thus leaving effectively a vacuum where the Turkish Cypriot pillar of the negotiations was supposed to be.

Denktash had no National Council of party leaders to hobble him as Clerides did. The prime minister, Dervish Eroglu, and his UBP party, which had the largest number of seats in the Turkish Cypriot Assembly but not a majority, had even more negative views on the Cyprus problem than Denktash. Their coalition partners in the early stages of the negotiation were the centre-left TKP led by the doveish Mustafa Akinci, a former mayor of Turkish Cypriot Nicosia and a man determined to work for a compromise settlement. But he had little influence on the government's policy and none at all on Denktash's. When the TKP was removed from the government following disagreement over Denktash's decision to walk out of the negotiations in November 2000, it was replaced as junior partner in the coalition by Denktash's party, the DP, led initially, and again at the end of 2002, by his son Serdar. The main Turkish Cypriot critic of Denktash's intransigence was Mehmet Ali Talat, whose centre-left CTP was in opposition throughout the period of negotiations, and who kept up a drum-beat of well-directed comments, but for a long time with little impact, not least because of his uneasy relationship with Ankara. It was only in 2002, when the establishment of a non-political movement under the leadership of Ali Erel of the Turkish Cypriot Chamber of Commerce, designed to rally support for a settlement and for joining the European Union, provided a focus and an umbrella for the opposition's activity, that serious pressure on Denktash began to mount. The centre-left parties did particularly well in the municipal elections that year, winning the mayoralties in three of the largest towns in the north, Nicosia, Famagusta and Kyrenia. This was followed at the end of the year and early in 2003 by a series of huge (by Turkish Cypriot standards and numbers) public demonstrations in support of the Annan Plan and membership of the European Union. For the first time in the history of the TRNC Denktash found himself faced with a serious opposition.

This pattern was to some extent reflected in the Turkish Cypriot media, who were in any case a good deal more deferential and submissive than their colleagues in the south. For a long time support for Denktash's policies in the press was general and unquestioning, with only one notable dissenter, *AVRUPA* (later renamed *AFRIKA* after attempts to close it down), a courageous voice crying in the wilderness and subjected to continuous harassment by the authorities. But, as opposition to Denktash's rejectionist policies mounted in Turkish Cypriot society in general during 2002, so too did criticism in the press, with the main daily paper *KIBRIS* coming out in support of the Annan Plan, and with the whole tone of the media becoming more critical of Denktash and Turkey.

Greece

The Greek corner of the quadrilateral was the one where the players were the least directly and the least intensively engaged in the process of the Cyprus negotiations. This partly reflected the desire of the Greek Cypriots to avoid the impression that they were other than fully masters of their own fate, and of the more mature nature of Greek Cypriot democracy. Also, historical experience had made both Greeks and Greek Cypriots wary of too close a Greek involvement in Cyprus affairs. But this detachment at times reflected a calculation that Turkey was internationally at a disadvantage in a whole number of ways as long as the Cyprus problem was unresolved, so that it was no skin off Greece's nose if it remained that way, and that continuing deadlock would be easier to handle than the awkward compromises that a settlement would require. Those who took a pessimistic view of the chances of getting a settlement tended to be in that camp. Against that view, and in complete contrast to it, were those who believed that it was in Greece's interest to bring about a strategic shift in the relationship with Turkey and to achieve a lasting and solidly based rapprochement with that country. This school of thought was all too well aware that without a settlement of the Cyprus problem any such rapprochement was bound to remain incomplete, limited in scope and fragile.

The Greek prime minister throughout the period of these negotiations was Constantinos Simitis. Very early on in his premiership, at the beginning of 1996, the Imia crisis between Greece and Turkey over conflicting claims to an uninhabited islet in the Aegean had jeopardized his hold on power. This had reinforced his natural caution about any high-risk moves involving Turkey, but it had also reminded him of the capacity of the disputes between Greece and Turkey to blow off course his own prime objective of making Greece into a modern, prosperous European state with sound finances. His tendency, therefore, was to stand well back from the Cyprus problem, waiting and watching to see how others fared in their efforts towards a solution, neither hindering nor greatly helping them. Insofar as he could, he avoided giving prominence to Cyprus in his dealings with other European leaders and he avoided also getting too personally involved in the rapprochement with Turkey. He deliberately left these issues to his two successive foreign ministers who held diametrically opposite views both on Cyprus and on the relationship with Turkey.

At the beginning of the period covered by this book the Greek foreign minister was Theodoros Pangalos. For him Cyprus was not so much a problem to be solved as a piece on the larger chessboard of Greek–Turkish relations to be manoeuvred for tactical advantage in this wider game and deployed as a grievance when necessary. This approach very much cut with the grain of traditional Greek foreign policy and the views of the majority of Greek diplomats. Pangalos's deputy, Ioannis Kranidiotis, himself of Greek Cypriot origin, who continued in that position when George Papandreou took over as foreign minister, had less clearcut views and gradually came to appreciate that a settlement might be achievable on terms consistent with Greek and Greek Cypriot interests. How far this dawning support for settlement negotiations might have carried him we shall never know, since he died tragically in a freak aeroplane accident in 1999, but he would have been a key player in the tricky interface between Greece and the Greek Cypriots.

Papandreou, who took over as foreign minister following Pangalos's resignation in early 1999, was no Cyprus expert at the outset, but he had clear views about the strategic interest for Greece to have a better relationship with Turkey, and he well understood that Cyprus could be either an obstacle or a source of momentum towards achieving that objective. Immediately he immersed himself in the subject and went to considerable trouble to ensure that he saw all those on the Cyprus circuit whenever they visited Athens, on one occasion even breaking into a hectic round of electioneering in the midst of a general election to find an hour to talk things over with me. Meetings with Papandreou were invariably both agreeable and valuable. He would concentrate hard on what his visitor had to say and engaged directly with any suggestions he might make. His own softly spoken contributions set out Greek positions in firm, clear but conciliatory terms. There was never any doubt that he saw a Cyprus settlement as being in Greece's interest and that he would do what he reasonably could to bring one about. His handling of his frequent contacts with his Turkish counterpart, Ismail Cem, and of his visits to Cyprus both bore witness to his determination to play an active and positive role.

Fortunately, and somewhat surprisingly given the historical record, Cyprus remained a largely bi-partisan issue in Greece throughout this period. I used to see either the opposition New Democracy foreign affairs spokesperson, Dora Bakoyanni (until she became mayor of Athens), or the leader of the opposition, Costas Karamanlis, whenever I visited Athens, to brief them on what was going on. They too were supportive of the UN's efforts to get a solution and wary, but not critical, of the Annan Plan as it gradually emerged and evolved. It was clear that they would have been only too happy if the Cyprus problem had been resolved before the next opportunity for them to regain power arose at the general election of 2004.

Turkey

In none of the four key capitals was it more difficult for an outsider to discover how and where the real decisions on Cyprus policy were taken than in Ankara, and in none was it more difficult to be sure who was a real player, who an adviser and who merely a spectator. Even well-informed Turks had difficulty reading the runes. For much of the period (1996–2002) the government of Turkey was in the hands of a succession of fractious, fractured coalitions whose component parties had differing views on almost every subject under the sun and thus had the greatest difficulty formulating policy on any of them. In many cases, of which Cyprus was one, this difficulty in formulating policy led to paralysis and to falling back by default on existing policy, however inadequate that might be to the needs of the current situation. Right at the end of the period (from November 2002 until March 2003) and during the crucial phase of the negotiations, the new AK party, following its crushing general election victory, was in office as a single-party government, albeit with two successive prime ministers, Abdullah Gül and Recep Tayyip Erdogan. But the attitude and behaviour of the Turkish 'establishment' (a word which I think better and more neutrally conveys the complex and interconnected structure of the military, the bureaucracy, the diplomatic service, opinion formers in the academic and journalistic world and big business than does the phrase 'the deep state' which is often used) was not welcoming to the new government and this led to considerable tension and a disconnect between what the politicians were saying and what was actually happening in the decision-making machinery of the state.

Of the Turkish prime ministers during this period, none was at ease with the Cyprus problem and none was prepared to engage in serious and detailed discussion of it with their foreign visitors to Ankara or on their own visits overseas. Necmettin Erbakan took a straight nationalist line, Mesut Yilmaz was taciturn in the extreme, and Ecevit's view that he had settled Cyprus in 1974 hardly offered an easy entry into a serious discussion. Gül and Erdogan were different (and Gül actually had a good deal of practical experience of grappling with the Cyprus problem from his time as minister responsible for Cyprus in the Erbakan/Ciller government). Their public posture 'no solution is no solution' and their readiness to approach the Annan Plan with an open mind were strongly positive developments. But they had the greatest difficulty, and received little help from the establishment, in grappling with the complexities of the settlement negotiations in the short time allowed to them after their election victory. Every one of these prime ministers had to take account of Denktash's views, which reached them both directly and through the establishment and which were unfailingly negative and a complicating factor.

The successive foreign ministers, Tansu Ciller, Ismail Cem, Sükrü Sina Gürel, Yasar Yakis and Abdullah Gül, were a good deal closer to the everyday action on the Cyprus problem than were the prime ministers, and it was their officials in the foreign ministry who provided the information and the advice. But they too showed considerable reluctance to engage in serious discussion with outsiders on the subject. It was just too difficult politically, too sensitive and too complex to be easy or attractive to handle. In the seven years I spent dealing with Cyprus, during which I frequently saw each of these ministers (with the exception of Yakis, whom I did not meet in his brief tenure), I can count the occasions on which discussion really got to grips with the essentials on the fingers of one hand. Cem's reluctance to involve himself in the Cyprus problem extended even to his frequent and often fruitful dealings with the Greek foreign minister. Papandreou tried again and again to address the issues, including those which directly concerned Greece and Turkey – for example the number of Greek and Turkish troops that should remain in Cyprus after a settlement – only to be systematically fended off or treated to generalities. Gürel's brief tenure was particularly unproductive since his views on Cyprus were those of Denktash, only more so.

So that left as interlocutors (once the military became completely incommunicado to overseas, non-military visitors on this or any other subject in 1997) the small group of senior officials in the foreign ministry who dealt directly with Cyprus and Greek–Turkish relations. Throughout the period the under-secretary at the ministry (whom in the British system we would call the permanent under-secretary and who, in the absence of any junior ministers, came directly underneath the foreign minister) became more and more expected to handle Cyprus in a hands-on, detailed way. So an intensive dialogue developed with successive holders of that office, Onur Oymen, Korkmaz Haktanir, Faruk Logoglu and Ugur Ziyal. Of these, the dealings with Ziyal, who was there during the most intensive phase of the negotiations, were particularly useful. He was hard-hitting but straightforward and ready to look for solutions as well as problems, but always had what was best for Turkey at the forefront of his mind. He was for the UN and for all those supporting its efforts a crucial point of contact and often the only fully authoritative exponent of Turkish policy on Cyprus. Carrying the burden of the run-up to the war in Iraq at the same time as the Cyprus endgame, he was under tremendous pressure.

Below the under-secretary there was a departmental team headed by officials at the equivalents of British deputy secretary and under-secretary rank. Many of those who held these jobs had spent a substantial proportion of their professional lives dealing with Cyprus issues, often shuttling between postings to the Turkish embassy in north Nicosia (a massive establishment, given the scale of the Turkish financial support programme and military presence in the north of the island, but one cut off from all normal diplomatic intercourse by the fact that Turkey did not recognize the Greek Cypriot government and no one else recognized the

TRNC to whom the Turkish embassy was accredited) and the Cyprus section of the foreign ministry. They tended either to be faithful mouthpieces for Denktash's views or to have a rather short tenure of their jobs.

For a long time Cyprus was something of a non-subject in both Turkish politics and the media. As a national issue government parties and the opposition both tended to stand shoulder-to-shoulder in defence of the status quo and of whatever formulation of it Denktash was putting forward at the time. The media had concluded that nothing much was going to come of the UN's efforts to get a solution on Cyprus and that this need not worry Turkey too much. After earlier decades in which Cyprus had been a prominent issue for the Turkish media they were slow to recognize that it was about to become so again. All that changed considerably during 2002 when the negotiations moved into a higher gear and awareness began to dawn of the problematic inter-relationship between Turkey's EU aspirations and its Cyprus policy, and even more so with the advent of the new AKP government which seemed genuinely committed to working for a solution in Cyprus. The only parliamentary opposition following the November 2002 elections, the CHP, who regarded themselves as the true heirs to the Atatürkist tradition, immediately became hardline critics of the government's attempts to negotiate a solution and of the Annan Plan. The media, on the other hand, broke out into a thoroughly pluralist debate on Turkey's interests in Cyprus and on how best to protect and forward them, with views challenging the conventional wisdom surfacing for the first time for many years.

3

The Issues

Throughout the period covered by this negotiation, and indeed for more than 20 years prior to it, there had been little dispute that four core issues would need to be resolved if there was to be a comprehensive settlement of the Cyprus problem. These issues – governance, security, territory and property – were at the heart of each of the successive negotiations that took place under the aegis of the United Nations in the period after the Greek Cypriot coup of 1974, the Turkish military intervention that followed it, the division of the island along a ceasefire line (the Green Line) and the subsequent transfer of populations, with almost all the Greek Cypriots living north of the line being transferred to the south and almost all the Turkish Cypriots living south of the line being transferred to the north. These events fundamentally changed the parameters within which any negotiation would take place. In place of an island where Greek Cypriots and Turkish Cypriots had lived mingled in close proximity in some 300 towns and villages, there was now an island divided into two zones, each with a largely mono-ethnic population.

In addition to these four core issues there were others to which one or the other side attached the greatest importance and insisted they too would need to be resolved if there was to be a settlement. For the Greek Cypriots these included what was to be done about those Turkish citizens who had come to the north of the island since 1974 (often referred to disobligingly as 'settlers'), many of whom had meanwhile been granted Turkish Cypriot citizenship. For the Turkish Cypriots the issues of the status of their state (the TRNC), which had been unilaterally proclaimed an independent sovereign state in 1983 but not recognized as such by any country other than Turkey, and sovereignty were of fundamental importance. And for both, the question of continuity between any new Cyprus and the state of affairs that had preceded it, both in the south and the north of the island, were of extreme significance and sensitivity, the

Greek Cypriots insisting at the outset on a simple amendment of the 1960 constitution, the Turkish Cypriots demanding a legally new entity. To these other issues came to be added that of the accession to the European Union of a reunited Cyprus which was clearly going to require specific provisions going beyond the usual transitional arrangements and temporal adjustments, if any settlement of the Cyprus problem (which would, of necessity, contain provisions not easily reconcilable with EU law and practice) was not going to be undermined by accession and the application of the *acquis communautaire* (the body of exisiting EU legislation which a new member state has to accept on its accession).

No review of the main issues would, however, be complete without reference to two intangible but nevertheless real fears, which can be thought of as the twin nightmares of the two peoples of the island. For the Greek Cypriots the nightmare was of a settlement that somehow enabled the Turkish Cypriots subsequently to secede from the new Cyprus and achieve the international recognition that had hitherto eluded them. For the Turkish Cypriots, the nightmare was that, however carefully political equality and balance was nailed down in the settlement itself, the Greek Cypriots would somehow succeed in dominating the institutions of a new Cyprus and would in effect hijack them, as the Turkish Cypriots believed they had done successfully in 1963. No solutions to the core issues and to the additional problems referred to above were going to be sufficient unless it also proved possible to banish or at least to diminish these twin nightmares.

Governance

The Cyprus that gained independence in 1960 was endowed with a system of governance that virtually defies categorization. It could perhaps be described as a bi-communal but unitary state, which required a high degree of consensus to work because of the extensive veto powers given to the minority Turkish Cypriot community. The system rapidly became deadlocked over a fiscal issue in 1963, prompting the Greek Cypriots to move to amend the constitution unilaterally, at which point the bi-communal system as such ceased to operate. One of the few points about which both sides agreed was that it made no sense to revert to this 1960 system. Two successive High-Level Agreements reached between the two sides in the late 1970s planned to replace that system by a bi-zonal, bi-communal federation, but the subsequent negotiations in the 1980s and early 1990s never enabled agreement to be reached on the specifics of how that should be done.

Despite the fact that the switch from a unitary to a federal state had originally been a reluctant concession by the Greek Cypriots to the Turkish Cypriots, the former stood by the concept even when the Turkish Cypriots in 1998 upped their demands and insisted on a confederation. This difference over a federal v. a confederal system was a constant feature of the negotiations that began in 1999, with all Turkish Cypriot proposals after that date being based on a confederal model and all Greek Cypriot proposals rejecting that and continuing to be based on a federal model. The terminology is arcane but important. In the language of the Cyprus problem 'federal' came to signify a single recognized state, devolving a high level of autonomy to two subordinate entities, whereas 'confederal' meant two recognized states pooling 'their' sovereignty on a limited range of issues, mainly foreign policy related. In the event this was a less significant aspect of the negotiations than it might have been following the tacit acceptance of the United Nations' suggestion in July 2000 that the whole question of labels be set on one side, to be addressed only at the end of the negotiations. In reality, while there were major differences in the approach to governance of the two sides, there was a strong element of semantics about the argument over labels. The 1992 Set of Ideas, while labelled a federation, contained a number of confederal elements in it, and the same was true of the proposals that emerged during the 1999–2003 negotiations (the Swiss precedents, which played some role in shaping these latter proposals, are equally ambiguous, Switzerland having a federal government but being entitled a confederation).

The failure to reach agreement on the specifics of a bi-zonal, bi-communal federation during the 1992 negotiations led by Boutros-Ghali masked the fact that there was much common ground established at that time which it was possible to carry forward into the subsequent negotiations. It was not seriously disputed that the central government would have responsibility for a rather limited number of subjects, some of which would in any case, after EU accession, be a matter for decision at the European rather than the national level, nor that all matters not specifically allocated to the central government in the settlement would fall to be decided by the separate governments of the two zones, nor that any future change in that allocation would need to be made by common agreement of the Greek Cypriots and the Turkish Cypriots. Nor was there wide disagreement over the actual powers to be given to the central government. It was also not seriously disputed that the executive would need to be made up of an appropriate balance of Greek and Turkish Cypriots, which would ensure that the representatives of one community could not force decisions through against the wishes of those of the other; that there should be a bi-cameral legislature with an upper house split equally between the two communities and a lower house which reflected at least to some extent the difference in population size of the two communities; and that there should be a supreme court on which both communities would be equally represented.

But, apart from these areas of potential convergence, there were plenty of others in the field of governance where the positions were sharply divided. The Turkish Cypriots wanted an explicit veto in every institution of government – executive, legislative and judicial – and only paid lip service to the need to reflect in some institutions the greater population of the Greek Cypriots; the fact that the 1960 constitution had, at least in part, been shipwrecked by excessive rigidity did not seem to concern them. The Greek Cypriots wanted to ensure that deadlocks would not occur, crippling the central government, and pushed for a strong reflection of their numerical superiority. The Greek Cypriots would have liked to have had electoral arrangements that involved some cross-voting of Greek Cypriots for Turkish Cypriot candidates and vice-versa in an attempt to get away from a two-states mentality after a settlement. This idea was anathema to the Turkish Cypriots who feared it could lead to effective domination of Turkish Cypriot elections by Greek Cypriots. The Turkish Cypriots wanted a rotating presidency in which they would have had an equal share or alternatively a co-presidency, between their leader and that of the Greek Cypriots. The latter considered that their numerical superiority entitled them to the presidency, if not all the time, at least for the greater part of it. Both sides were extremely reluctant to envisage any non-Cypriot judges (and certainly not British ones) on the Supreme Court, while recognizing that the equal number of Greek and Turkish Cypriot judges which was common to all approaches was only too likely to lead to deadlock and thus to render the Supreme Court nugatory as a potential tie-breaking instrument when there had been deadlock elsewhere in the system.

All these and many other issues of governance arose during the negotiations and were hotly contested. But of the four core issues this was probably the least contentious and the one over which there was the most obvious potential for compromise. In particular, discussion of the rotating presidency brought out into the open the undesirability of having a strong executive president (and vice-president) as had been the case in the 1960 constitution. One possible solution was to have a purely honorific president (and vice-president) with no executive authority at all, as was the case in constitutions as diverse as those of Ireland, Israel and Germany, but that risked replicating the problems one level down, if you then vested strong executive authority in a prime minister (and deputy prime minister). Another possibility was to have a collective executive with a frequently rotating honorific presidency, as was the case in Switzerland. On other issues, the possibility of cross-voting, theoretically attractive though it was in breaking down the barriers between the two sides, gradually faded away. And the recognition of the need for non-Cypriot judges on the Supreme Court, thus enabling that institution to work as a tie-breaker, gained ground. In every case and in every institution the crucial issue was the decision-making process and in particular the scope for one or other side to block a decision it did not like. This tension between equality and rigidity ran through every discussion and was predictably hard to resolve.

One specific decision-making process came to bulk larger as the negotiations continued, that of determining the position the new reunited Cyprus would take in European Union discussions and decisions. It was clear that a mechanism would be needed to prepare such positions on a daily basis and that it would need to cover matters falling under the responsibility both of the central and of the component state governments. The possibility of disagreements over such questions had to be provided for, with abstention in Brussels being a conceivable approach for all except the very few European Union decisions that required a positive vote from all member states. On this issue a constructive contribution was made by the Turkish Cypriots, advised by a group of Belgian academics of ethnic Turkish origin, who were able to draw on the mechanisms applied in the Belgian federal system.

Security

The special nature of the security problems of Cyprus was recognized from the outset of its existence as an independent state. It was reflected in the 1960 Treaties of Guarantee and Alliance. The Treaty of Guarantee was signed by the three guarantor powers (Greece, Turkey and the United Kingdom) and committed them to uphold the independence, security and constitutional order of Cyprus, to consult together about any threats to these objectives and to act together if they could agree on a course of action; if not, each of the three had a unilateral right of intervention. The Treaty of Alliance provided for the establishment of a joint military headquarters of Cypriots, Greeks and Turks and provided for set numbers of Greek and Turkish troops to be permitted to remain on the island. It also established a Cypriot National Guard with provisions for Turkish Cypriot participation. The Treaty of Guarantee was invoked by Turkey in 1974 when it intervened militarily following the Greek Cypriot coup against Archbishop Makarios. The Treaty of Alliance remained a dead letter, in that the joint headquarters was never established. Following the 1963 withdrawal by the Turkish Cypriots from the government, the National Guard became mono-ethnically Greek Cypriot. Although the Greeks and Greek Cypriots from time to time argued that the Treaty of Guarantee was no longer in force, since Turkey had in their view exceeded and abused the limited right of unilateral intervention, the general opinion was that, neither treaty being time limited, both remained in effect.

Clerides had made proposals, before and during the period covered by this book, for the complete demilitarization of Cyprus. Under these proposals all Greek Cypriot and Turkish Cypriot armed forces would have been disbanded, all Greek and Turkish troops would have been withdrawn from the island and Cyprus's security would have been guaranteed either by the UN Security Council or, in some versions, by the European Union. These proposals had been rejected both by the Turkish Cypriots and the Turks, who made it clear that any solution must include the maintenance of the Treaty of Guarantee, including Turkey's right of unilateral intervention, and of the Treaty of Alliance, which permitted Turkish troops to remain in Cyprus. For the Turks and Turkish Cypriots these treaties were a sine qua non of any settlement, the only bankable guarantee of its political provisions. While Clerides continued for public and political purposes to maintain his own proposals, he had, by the time the negotiations began in 1999 (and even more so by the time they resumed in earnest at the beginning of 2002), recognized that they could not provide the basis for a solution. He was reluctant, however, to give up entirely the possibility of diluting or time limiting the Treaty of Guarantee in some way or another, and he did not want to see any Greek or Turkish troops on the island, being as insistent on the withdrawal of the former as of the latter in the light of his experience of the involvement of the Greek military in the 1974 coup.

Although security was a critical issue for the Turkish Cypriots – their basic guarantee that the numerically superior Greek Cypriots would not overturn the political balance contained in a settlement – it soon became clear that this was an issue principally to be negotiated by the Turks. Turkey had a substantial military force on the island (usually reckoned at about 37,000, although it fluctuated around that number from time to time). Turkish officers commanded the modest number of Turkish Cypriot troops. And, while protecting the security of the Turkish Cypriots was certainly part of their mission, it was by no means the whole of it. Their greatest concern was the threat Cyprus could represent to Turkey's own security if the island was ever to fall into the hands of an unfriendly power (and for these purposes not only the Greek Cypriots but the Greeks fell into that category). Turkish rhetoric frequently described Cyprus as a 'floating aircraft carrier' or a 'dagger pointing at Turkey's heart'. This Turkish sensitivity about their own security tended to grow rather than diminish with time as the geo-political significance of Ceyhan, the oil terminal which already exported oil from northern Iraq and which was destined to export oil and possibly in due course gas from the Caspian region, increased. While the Turks could almost certainly contemplate a considerable reduction in their troop strength on the island in the context of an otherwise satisfactory political settlement to the Cyprus problem, they would not accept complete withdrawal, and they were adamant that the Treaties of Guarantee and Alliance had to remain, undiluted in any way. They recognized the advantage to them of the disbandment of all Greek Cypriot and Turkish Cypriot armed forces (the former being much more numerous and better equipped – the Greek Cypriot National Guard, for example, having more tanks than the British army, although not all of them fully operational), and of a mandatory arms embargo on military supplies to the island. One further dimension of the security question lay in the obscure but important politico-military nexus of relationships in Turkey. The Turkish armed forces regarded themselves as the saviours of the Turkish Cypriots. They were certainly not prepared to be cast at some future date in the role of having 'lost north Cyprus'.

The firmness of the Turkish attitude on the security issue did not leave much scope for negotiation – a fact recognized by all concerned, including the Greek Cypriots. That left one major element of the security equation, the question of an international military presence on the island, its provenance, size and mandate. It had always been emphasized by the

Greek Cypriots that if they were to make major concessions to the Turks and Turkish Cypriots on this issue of security (as the Turks and Turkish Cypriots would have to do over territory and property), it was essential that there should be a robust international military presence on the island. At first they had flirted with the idea of a NATO force (which had the advantage of including as members all three guarantor powers) but this became politically impracticable for them following NATO's intervention in Kosovo which was deeply unpopular with the Greek Cypriots in general and in particular with AKEL, the Greek Cypriot communist party whose support (as it had a rock-solid 33 per cent of the electorate) was important for the endorsement of any deal in a referendum. They had also flirted with the idea of an EU force but no such force yet existed and in any case the rapid reaction capability being earmarked by the EU was not intended for the territorial defence of a member state. Neither of these two options was even remotely likely to be acceptable to Turkey. That left no alternative to the UN, but even that was not likely to be uncontentious.

The small existing UN force was strung out across the island along the Green Line. However, following a settlement, including as it would have to a territorial adjustment to the line dividing the two parts of the island, that would no longer be appropriate. A UN force would have to be deployed island-wide, able to underpin a settlement wherever and whenever necessary. This would certainly require a larger force with a quite different mandate from the present one. The Greek Cypriot demand was for a much larger force with a strong mandate; the Turkish Cypriots and Turks wanted a smaller one with a weaker mandate. Although in reality in no circumstances could such a force be expected to take a confrontational role towards either Greek or Turkish troops, there are still many gradations in even a fairly classical peacekeeping mandate. In this case, as the mandate would be an integral part of a negotiated settlement agreed by the parties, such gradations would need to be negotiated in detail in advance by all concerned, not just promulgated by the Security Council. There was also the question of a civilian police element to any peacekeeping force which was highly desirable if, as seemed likely, there was to be no central police force but merely two separate Greek Cypriot and Turkish Cypriot forces operating in the two component states, perhaps with a central 'FBI'.

Territory

When hostilities ceased in 1974 and the situation was stabilized along a ceasefire line that divided the island from east to west into two zones (with one tiny Turkish Cypriot enclave at Kokkina in the far west), the proportion of territory under Turkish Cypriot control was a little more than 36 per cent of the territory of the 1960 Republic of Cyprus, and the proportion of territory under Greek Cypriot control was a little over 63 per cent of that territory. The proportions of coastline controlled by the two sides was 57 per cent by the Turkish Cypriots against 43 per cent by the Greek Cypriots. These figures contrasted with population figures drawn from an earlier British census of broadly 80 per cent Greek Cypriots against 18 per cent Turkish Cypriots (the remaining 2 per cent being accounted for by minorities such as Armenians, Maronites and Latins). Not surprisingly, in the light of these figures, it was accepted as axiomatic by all concerned, including the Turkish Cypriots, that any settlement would have to include a territorial adjustment to the benefit of the Greek Cypriots.

During the negotiations for a settlement that took place in 1992 under the aegis of the UN Secretary-General Boutros-Ghali, the UN proposed a map setting out an adjustment that would have divided the territory in the rough proportions of a little over 28 per cent to the Turkish Cypriots and a little under 72 per cent to the Greek Cypriots. Neither side accepted that map, but the United Nations Security Council endorsed it, and it was a reasonable supposition that in any subsequent negotiations the overall proportions would not vary significantly. The proposed 1992 boundary, like the ceasefire line itself, was an extremely irregular one, with considerable scope for minor adjustments to take account of geographical features and pre-1974 population patterns. However, any major shift, for example in the name of greater simplicity, risked throwing out of kilter the overall equation. The Boutros-Ghali map involved the return to the Greek Cypriots of the town of Morphou in the west (but not of the main part of the citrus orchards around it, which would have remained Turkish Cypriot), and the return of the tourist ghost town of Varosha in the east, but not of the contiguous old city of Famagusta. Those were the only major centres of population involved in any adjustment.

The Greek Cypriot position was to push for a substantial territorial adjustment in their favour but not to be too specific about the geographical details until the matter came to the negotiating table. They spoke of eventual figures for the Turkish Cypriot zone as low as 25 per cent, knowing that this was unnegotiable. They let it be known that a key parameter for them in any territorial settlement was the proportion of the Greek Cypriot refugees expelled from the north who could be returned to the adjusted territory, and that this would affect their attitude both to the territorial proposals and to the property issue. They attached great importance to including in the Greek Cypriot zone at least some part of the Karpas Peninsula, the unicorn's horn or 'pan-handle' in the north-east corner of the island, which contained both a religious site of significance in the monastery of Apostolos Andreas at the tip of the peninsula and also a residual Greek Cypriot population which had remained behind after the population transfer of the 1970s. So the Greek Cypriots very deliberately sought to link the three related issues of territory, property and the right to settle in the north, realizing that only if their people were satisfied overall with this package would they be willing to accept any one part of it.

As to the Turkish Cypriots they refused to contemplate even the most informal discussion of the territorial issue until the very last stage of the negotiations and until their preconditions on recognition and sovereignty had been met. For Denktash the equation was simple. He knew that he would gain substantially from the governance and security aspects of a settlement, both of which would be resolved on a basis which met most of the Turkish Cypriots' longstanding demands. On each of the other core issues, territory, property and the linked issue of the right of Greek Cypriots to reside in the Turkish Cypriot component state, he knew he would have to make concessions. These concessions would make it clear that the new Cyprus would not only be bi-zonal but also, to some modest extent, bi-communal, whereas his own ideal outcome was to pocket gains on governance and security while not conceding anything inconsistent with his preferred two-state solution. Hence his approach was to de-couple the three issues and present unyielding positions on each (such as his proposal for settling all property claims by compensation and allowing no Greek Cypriot returns to the north). It was the exact opposite of, and irreconcilable with, the Greek Cypriot approach. And, in his unending negotiations with Ankara, he was able to depict any concession in the worst possible light, as likely to lead to Greek Cypriot dominance or to weaken the Turkish military position or both.

So on territory the Turkish Cypriots did put forward some vague and rather complex criteria for determining a territorial adjustment, but the trouble about these criteria was that they could mean either quite a lot or nothing at all, depending on how they were interpreted and applied on the ground; so this was not likely to prove a very useful path to pursue, and in any case, the Greek Cypriots refused from the outset to pursue it.

There was one wild card in the territorial equation, of which all concerned were in practice unaware until a very late stage in the negotiations, and that was the British Sovereign Base Areas. These two areas, which had been excluded under international law from the 1960 Republic of Cyprus, occupied 99 square miles of the island. They were effectively in the south of the island, and thus embedded in any Greek Cypriot zone, although the Eastern Sovereign Base Area was in fact also contiguous with the Turkish Cypriot side of the Green Line. Should the United Kingdom be ready to cede some of its territory, this would, modestly but significantly, affect the overall equation and could bring some increase of territory to both constituent states.

The proposition that the territorial issue could only be settled right at the end of the negotiation was broadly shared by all concerned, but the refusal of the Turkish Cypriots even to discuss the matter cast some doubt on whether they intended ever to allow that moment to arrive. And no one involved was in any doubt as to the difficulties of reaching agreement peacefully at the negotiating table on an adjustment to boundaries that had been established on the battlefield. This last concern was, however, considerably alleviated when the Turkish general who had commanded the Turkish troops during the military operations in 1974 and who had gone on to become president of Turkey, General Kenan Evren, said publicly in 2002 that it had always been clear to the Turks that they had taken more of the island than they needed in 1974 and that now was the time to think of giving some of it back.

Property

None of the four core issues was more complex and none was more sensitive than the question of property – what was to be done about the property rights and claims of Greek Cypriots displaced from the north of the island and of Turkish Cypriots from the south. According to UN assessments almost half of the population of Cyprus lost properties as a result of the intercommunal strife or military action between 1963 and 1974; roughly three times as many Greek Cypriots as Turkish Cypriots were affected. The solution to the problem had been made infinitely more difficult by the extreme positions staked out by the politicians on either side, with the Greek Cypriots asserting that every single Greek Cypriot with a valid claim to property in the north should have the right to return to it, and the Turkish Cypriots asserting that no such right would be recognized, that no returns would take place and that all claims should be settled by global property exchange and/or financial compensation.

The technical complexity of the property issues was such that both sides did agree on one thing, namely that individual claims could not be settled in the negotiations themselves and that details could not, in this field, be spelled out. There would have to be a property board or commission to implement whatever terms were agreed in the settlement. Both sides also recognized that part of the problem would be resolved as a result of the territorial adjustment, since Greek Cypriots who wished to return to their property in the area adjusted should be able to do so in a reasonably straightforward manner, it being assumed that Turkish Cypriots would not wish to remain in territory coming under Greek Cypriot administration but would choose to move to the territory of the Turkish Cypriot component state. But there was, of course, no agreement on the size of the territorial adjustment and thus also no agreement on how much of the property problem would be solved in this relatively painless way.

Beyond that point there was nothing but fundamental disagreement. The Greek Cypriots did recognize that the idea of all those Greek Cypriots displaced returning to the north was unrealistic and, given the large number of Greek Cypriots who had lived in the north prior to 1974, not really compatible with a bi-zonal solution in which the Turkish Cypriots were masters in their own house for a wide range of policies. They believed that, in any case, relatively few Greek Cypriots from the north, many of whom had completely rebuilt their lives over the past 30 years and who were now reasonably prosperous and well established in their new homes, would choose to go off and live in what would be a Turkish-Cypriot-administered component state. They were also prepared to contemplate a range of tight quantitative and transitional arrangements, including a moratorium on returns in the early years after a settlement, which would limit the number of Greek Cypriots who would be permitted to return to their properties in the north. Such an approach had begun to be discussed in the 1992 negotiations when it had been known as the 'fishing net' and they were prepared to resume that discussion. What they would not accept was an approach that extinguished any right of return from the outset and offered only one option, financial compensation. That was precisely the position of the Turkish Cypriots who stated flatly that all property claims must be settled by compensation and refused to contemplate any right of return, however tightly circumscribed. They placed great weight on the precedent of the population transfer between Greece and Turkey in 1923–24 which had been conducted on this basis and were unwilling to recognize that both the political climate and international jurisprudence had moved on since then and that legitimizing ethnic cleansing by force was not an approach likely to commend itself to the international community, let alone to the Greek Cypriots. And because the Turkish Cypriots were only prepared to discuss the details of compensation mechanisms if it was agreed in advance that this would be the sole method of resolving all property claims, it was not even possible to address these highly technical issues, despite both sides being in agreement that such mechanisms would be required.

There was a wild card in the property core issue too. This took the form of a test case brought by a Greek Cypriot refugee from the north, Mrs Titina Loizidou, before the Council of Europe's European Court of Human Rights. Mrs Loizidou won her case in 1996 when the court found that she had been wrongfully dispossessed of her property in the north by Turkey (not by the Turkish Cypriots whom the ECHR did not recognize) and in 1998 awarded her a large sum in damages with interest. As soon as this case, in which Mrs Loizidou had had the support of the Greek Cypriot government, was won, a large number of similar cases were instituted before the ECHR. The case had important and damaging implications for Turkey and was also relevant to the settlement negotiations. If the Turks, as for a long time they did, refused to pay damages, they risked eventual suspension from the Council of Europe on human rights grounds with serious collateral damage to any hope they might have of convincing the European Union that they had fulfilled the Copenhagen criteria for membership. The implications for a Cyprus settlement were less direct but no less important. It was in effect crucial that any property settlement negotiated should be accepted by the European Court of Human Rights as invalidating the base for bringing individual legal proceedings before the Court. It was a great deal less likely that they would do this if the settlement simply extinguished any right of return and offered compensation rather than providing alternative remedies for those who had lost their property.

Status

No issue was raised more frequently by Denktash than that of status, and he never made any secret of the fact that he regarded getting satisfaction on this matter a precondition for negotiating on the four core issues. He continued to take this line despite the call in Security Council Resolution 1250, on which the negotiations were based, for there to be no preconditions, and he continued to take it even after receiving at least partial satisfaction in Annan's clarificatory statement of 12 September 2000.

In the eyes of Denktash, and on this point he had full Turkish support, a fundamental error and a grievous wrong had been perpetrated when the United Nations, and in particular its Security Council, had continued after 1963 to recognize the Greek Cypriot government of Cyprus as the properly constituted representative of the 1960 Republic of Cyprus despite the absence of any Turkish Cypriots from its counsels. And the fact that other international organizations such as the Council of Europe and the European Union and every member of the United Nations apart from Turkey did likewise merely rubbed salt in the wound and compounded the original error. In this view the error had to be corrected in one way or another before there could be an even-handed negotiation on the future of Cyprus and a settlement. Since Denktash was certainly not offering to return the Turkish Cypriots to the positions they had held under the 1960 constitution, there were, in theory, two ways this could come about. Either the international community could recognize the TRNC as an independent sovereign state, which was Denktash's and Turkey's strong preference, or it could, as it were, derecognize the Greek Cypriots. Neither course was even remotely likely to occur. The Turkish government had been trying for nearly 20 years to get recognition for the TRNC and had so far failed to find a single country ready to do so. And although Denktash sometimes spoke of intermediate options, some form of 'acknowledgement' of the TRNC's status stopping short of formal recognition, or recognition for a brief moment – half an hour was sometimes mentioned – before a new reunited Cyprus came into being, his subsequent public statements invariably undermined any confidence that he was really seeking to find an acceptable way round the problem and that there was any real distinction between the intermediate options and going the whole hog.

This was in any case ground on to which neither the Greek Cypriots nor the international community was prepared to venture, and with good reason. For the Greek Cypriots their title to the leadership of the 1960 Republic was quite simply an existential issue on which they believed they could not afford to compromise. For others the Turkish Cypriot case seemed less than compelling, whatever thoughts they might have about the rights and wrongs of what had happened in 1963. It ignored the fact that the problem of recognition had been precipitated in the first place by the Turkish Cypriots absenting themselves from the institutions of the 1960 Republic and subsequently by their decision to abandon in 1983 the status of Turkish Cypriot Federated State (of Cyprus) and to opt for full independence. It glossed over the fact that the TRNC, which did not have its own currency, could not assure its own security and depended on large subsidies from Turkey to pay its public servants, fell some way short of the normal criteria for recognition, even if the Security Council had not formally closed off that option which was also inconsistent with the 1960 Treaty of Guarantee. And above all, it, rightly or wrongly, conveyed more than a suspicion that the ultimate aim was not that of preparing for a new reunited Cyprus but rather for the subsequent secession of the northern part of it.

That status was an issue in the negotiations could not be denied. But it was one which could only be resolved in the context, and within the framework, of a comprehensive settlement. Such a settlement would need to anchor the political equality of Greek Cypriots and Turkish Cypriots in practical constitutional provisions within an indissolubly reunited Cyprus, including measures that would ensure that its two component states could handle internationally those areas of policy for which they were responsible.

Sovereignty

In a number of ways the question of sovereignty was one that overlapped with that of status. The attitudes of the two sides were similarly in stark contradiction and deeply entrenched, and for some of the same reasons.

For the Greek Cypriots sovereignty resided in the new federal state of Cyprus alone (and before it in the 1960 Republic of Cyprus whose constitution they were, however, prepared to see abrogated and replaced by a completely different, federal one). They were not ready to contemplate any explicit division of sovereignty between the federal state and the two constituent states (such as can be found in the Swiss constitution where it is stated that the cantons are sovereign insofar as their sovereignty is not limited by the Federal Constitution) although they recognized that a constitution that was silent on the issue of sovereignty would actually amount to that. And they recoiled in horror from phrases such as that sovereignty 'emanated' from the component states to the federal state. Their reasoning was similar to their concerns over recognition and over any use of the word 'peoples' as opposed to 'communities' to describe Greek Cypriots and Turkish Cypriots, namely that the door was being opened to secession by the north of Cyprus from a reunited Cyprus. The Turkish Cypriot position on the sovereignty issue was the mirror image of the Greek Cypriot one; it was absolutely essential that the sovereignty of the two component states be explicitly stated and that it be made clear that any sovereignty possessed by the federal state should come from the component states.

One possibility was to avoid any reference to sovereignty at all in the settlement and the new constitution for a federal Cyprus (and also, necessarily, in the constitutions of the component states) but that was not easy to envisage given the importance that both sides attached to it, albeit in an entirely contradictory manner.

Continuity

The question of continuity ran like a thread between the other two issues of status and sovereignty and contained scope for meeting and reconciling some, but by no means all, the positions put forward by the two sides on those other issues. During the nearly 40 years since the original breakdown of the 1960 constitution and even more so since the hostilities in 1974, the subsequent transfer of populations and the Turkish Cypriot unilateral declaration of independence in 1983, the two sides had lived quite separate existences, legislating, taking executive decisions and negotiating (in the Turkish Cypriot case almost exclusively with Turkey) international agreements. There could be no question of simply foisting the corpus of legislation, decisions and agreements of one side on to the other but nor did it make sense to think of starting from scratch for the new Cyprus. Some way had to be found of legitimizing the past acts of both sides and of deciding what needed to be the dowry in the form of legislation and international agreements for the new reunited Cyprus. About the need for this there was no real disagreement between the two sides, particularly between those on each side who understood the legal technicalities (and both Clerides and Denktash were trained lawyers). But even a largely technical operation of this sort was fraught with all sorts of wider implications. Such an approach did involve a degree of recognition (post facto only, after any settlement was agreed and ratified by referendum) of the existence and legitimacy of the institutions of the TRNC, and it also involved a recognition of the genuine equality of the two sides.

Both the technical aspects of the continuity issue and its wider implications were present in the minds of all concerned and, in particular, of
the UN team trying to assemble the elements for a comprehensive settlement. It was for this reason that they rightly attached such importance to
the effort to mount a joint negotiation in a working group or groups of the
raw material needed to achieve continuity, and why they and others drew
such negative conclusions when this effort was frustrated (until October
2002), delayed (until December 2002) and eventually aborted (in March
2003) by action on the Turkish Cypriot side.

Turkish citizens in north Cyprus

In 1974 the Turkish Cypriots, roughly 18 per cent of the population of
Cyprus, found themselves in control of 37 per cent of the territory of the
1960 Republic. In the years that followed, this partial vacuum was filled
by a substantial inflow of immigrants from mainland Turkey, many of
whom were subsequently given Turkish Cypriot nationality; both tendencies were actively encouraged by the Turkish Cypriot administration.
Given that the newcomers were frequently moving into property that had
previously belonged to Greek Cypriots, that they came to represent a
quite substantial demographic shift in the make-up of the population of
north Cyprus, and that those who obtained Turkish Cypriot nationality
also influenced the politics of the north, this issue, although never formally categorized as one of the four core issues, was an emotional and
sensitive one on both sides, a kind of time bomb ticking away among the
other, more openly recognized issues.

On the Greek Cypriot side, where these immigrants were pejoratively
referred to as 'settlers', the political discourse of all the main parties
encouraged an extreme approach. Most Greek Cypriot politicians would
publicly take the line that all the 'settlers' should simply be sent back,
lock, stock and barrel to Turkey. Privately they would recognize that
many of the immigrants having married Turkish Cypriot wives, now
having families born and brought up in Cyprus and having spent quite as
long in Cyprus as a normal European country would require before
naturalization could be granted, could not, in human rights terms, simply
be shipped back to Turkey. On the Turkish Cypriot side the view taken
was that this was none of the Greek Cypriots' business; the Turkish
Cypriots should control their own nationality and citizenship laws without let or hindrance. But this view masked considerable differences within
northern Cyprus, where the scale of the immigration and the social and

cultural contrasts between the immigrants and the indigenous Turkish Cypriots gave rise to considerable tensions.

This issue was not only the object of fundamental disagreement between the two sides; its actual scope was hotly disputed. The Greek Cypriots habitually quoted extremely high figures for the scale of immigration and of the grants of Turkish Cypriot nationality, without being in a position to validate them. Figures in excess of 100,000 immigrants, a large proportion when it is recalled that the figure for the indigenous Turkish Cypriot population was in the region of 180,000, were bandied about. The Turkish Cypriots, insofar as they were prepared to discuss the matter at all, tended to play down the problem. Denktash asserted in the negotiations that Turkish Cypriot citizenship had been granted to only 30–35,000 immigrants, a figure that was soon admitted, even by its author, as a substantial underestimate.

For all these reasons it was unlikely that a settlement would be reached without this issue being addressed in some way or another, but equally unlikely that it would be resolved in a scientific and objective fashion. More likely was the establishment of a fairly arbitrary figure for those who could be regarded as Turkish Cypriots and who could remain as citizens of the new Turkish Cypriot constituent state, and some rather tough rules about the Turkish citizens above that figure and about future immigration from Turkey.

The European Union dimension

During the 1992 negotiations over the UN's Set of Ideas the European Union dimension did not loom large. Although the Greek Cypriots had by then submitted an application to join the European Union, the Commission had not yet delivered its formal opinion on it, and accession negotiations had therefore not started. The whole enlargement timetable was still obscure. It was therefore simply assumed that it would be a reunited Cyprus that would in due course conduct accession negotiations, and that the outcome, if successful, would be ratified by referendums in the two component states. Any EU problems would be ironed out in the accession negotiations. Like every other aspect of the 1992 negotiations none of this was ever actually agreed by the two sides.

By the time settlement negotiations resumed at the end of 1999, the whole situation had changed quite dramatically. The Greek Cypriot application had been endorsed by the Commission, accession negotiations had been opened with them in 1998, and the Turkish Cypriots had rejected all attempts to persuade them to associate themselves with these negotiations. Moreover the Greek Cypriots were rattling through the accession negotiations at a steady pace; it was already clear that no serious technical obstacles were going to arise that would impede or delay their conclusion, and that Cyprus would be in he first wave of any accession package or packages. And the Helsinki European Council had stated categorically that a settlement was not a precondition for membership, having previously fended off attempts by the Turks and Turkish Cypriots to argue that accession by a divided island was either illegal or should be stopped until there was a settlement. The timetable for enlargement was also by then much clearer and any analyst could see that an end-2002 date for the conclusion of EU accession negotiations was likely.

It was becoming evident therefore that the settlement and EU accession negotiations were no longer going to be sequential but were far more likely to be simultaneous. This prospect posed all sorts of unprecedented problems, both technical and political. The technical problems related to the fact that the Commission had not had the chance to do all the preliminary work in the north of Cyprus that was necessary to prepare for actual negotiations and for the adaptation of Turkish Cypriot legislation to the *acquis communautaire*. Numerous attempts were made by the Commission to put such work in hand informally but all were rebuffed by Denktash who would not allow European experts access to his administration without prior recognition. He persisted in believing that this gave him a lever to secure formal recognition and refused to recognize that this was a serious miscalculation. So the technical work in the north remained as a kind of over-hang to the settlement negotiations which might, and probably would, need to be completed after any agreement was reached.

The political problems were more serious. Some, including those related to the very different levels of economic development between the north and the south (per capita GNP in the north being somewhere around 20–25 per cent of that in the south) were susceptible of fairly straightforward treatment with existing European Union policies and instruments. It was clear that north Cyprus would have to be classified differently from the south under the structural funds and thus would receive much higher subsidies from the EU budget. But, beyond these relatively straightforward issues, were much trickier ones arising from the fact that a number of the necessary elements of any negotiable settlement package would not be in conformity with the *acquis communautaire*. Measures to allay Turkish Cypriot concerns about an immediate and irresistible influx of Greek Cypriots buying property and businesses in the north would be necessary and would not be in conformity with full freedom of movement of people, capital and establishment. Would the concerns require long EU transitional periods or would they perhaps require full derogations (much more difficult for the EU to swallow)?

One thing gradually became clear. Neither the UN nor the EU could afford to allow these issues to be settled in one set of negotiations and then reopened in the other. For the UN to permit that was to open itself to accusations of bad faith, for the EU to do so was to run the risk of being saddled with the blame for wrecking a UN settlement that had been agreed. So the stage was set for an unprecedented level of coopera-tion and concertation between the two organizations and the two negotiations; but achieving that was less easy than asserting the need for it. The handling of these issues was further complicated by a Greek Cypriot tendency to try to use the *acquis communautaire* as a kind of battering ram with which to demolish attempts to find ingenious and flexible solutions to Turkish Cypriot concerns in the settlement negotia-tions and have them accepted by the EU. Fortunately the Commission, the ultimate guardians of the *acquis communautaire*, were alert to this threat and proved well capable of heading it off.

In addition to all these practical aspects the European Union dimen-sion also affected the political climate on both sides of the island quite fundamentally and to an increasing extent as time wore on and as actual enlargement came closer. For the Greek Cypriots, while Clerides's quite genuine desire to reach a settlement of the Cyprus problem before he quit the political scene in February 2003 played an important role in ensuring some flexibility in their negotiating position, an even stronger incentive was the need to avoid being seen as the awkward or obstructive party in the settlement negotiations. As the European Union and its member states signalled ever more clearly and insistently their preference for the accession of a reunited Cyprus rather than a divided one, this factor became more prominent. (These causal links are hard to prove, because they are so hotly denied by those most directly concerned, but it is diffi-cult to see why else, during the last year before their terms of accession were settled by the European Union, the Greek Cypriots showed more flexibility on a wider range of issues than at any previous stage of the 30 years of negotiation.) Sadly the Turks and Denktash chose to ignore all this and even to deny it, asserting that the EU had handed the Greek

Cypriots their EU accession on a plate. They thus, yet again, passed up an important opportunity.

On the Turkish Cypriot side, what had always been a widespread but vague feeling in favour of joining the European Union as part of a re-united island and following a settlement, came gradually into sharper focus as a high proportion of Turkish Cypriots, but not unfortunately their leaders, came to realize that the simultaneous denouements of the settlement and the EU accession negotiations presented a once-and-for-all opportunity to get a settlement on terms favourable to them and at the same time to find a way out of their dead end of impoverishment, isolation and economic stagnation. This was the background to the massive Turkish Cypriot public demonstrations at the end of 2002 and early in 2003 in favour of acceptance of the Annan Plan and of joining the European Union.

4

1996: Getting a Show on the Road

The beginning of 1996 marked one of the lowest points in the international effort to find a comprehensive solution to the Cyprus problem, which stretched back to 1963 when the post-colonial constitutional settlement first broke down and when the drift towards inter-communal violence, and eventually open hostilities, began. A UN-led attempt to negotiate a comprehensive settlement – Boutros-Ghali's 1992 Set of Ideas – had run into a brick wall when Clerides had won the February 1993 presidential election in the south of the island on a platform rejecting Boutros-Ghali's proposals. A subsequent UN-led attempt to find an oblique approach to a settlement through a number of major Confidence-Building Measures – the most significant of which would have led to the reopening of Nicosia Airport, stranded unused since 1974 in the buffer zone between the ceasefire lines, and the return to its Greek Cypriot owners of the ghost town of Varosha, a holiday resort just south of Famagusta – had also run into the sands, wrecked by a combination of Turkish and Turkish Cypriot obsession with the minutiae of the policing of the areas in question and Greek Cypriot lack of enthusiasm for measures that they saw as giving more benefits to the other side than to themselves and in particular as undermining the barriers to trade between the north and the European Union.

In parallel with these two major setbacks, Cyprus's application to join the European Union was making steady progress. Not only had the application itself been accepted by the European Union, despite the continuing division of the island, but the Commission had given a positive formal opinion opening the way to accession negotiations, and the European Union had committed itself in 1995 to engaging in such negotiations no later than six months after the conclusion of the Inter-Governmental Conference then under way to prepare the European Union's institutions for enlargement, a formula which pointed towards a date somewhere between late 1997 and early 1998. The EU dimension of the Cyprus problem was thus becoming more prominent than it had ever been in the past. And, while it was possible to hope that it would act as a catalyst towards a comprehensive settlement, it was equally feared that it would lead towards the definitive partition of the island, to a major crisis in the relations between the European Union and Turkey, itself another applicant for accession, albeit on a much slower track than Cyprus, and to a sharp rise in tension in the Eastern Mediterranean.

Faced with this unpromising scene, none of the main players seemed inclined to make much of an effort. The two Cypriot leaders, Clerides and Denktash, had reverted, with some relief, from grappling with issues of substance to the tactical manoeuvring they knew so well and which avoided the need to make any hard choices or to reach and defend compromise solutions. The United States, after a failed attempt in 1995 by Richard Beattie, the Presidential Special Representative, to broker secret talks between the two sides and to find a formula which would park Denktash's status demands and enable the EU accession negotiations to proceed on a joint basis, had lapsed into a passive mode. The United Nations, deeply discouraged by several years of hard slog with nothing at the end to show for it, was extremely hesitant about undertaking any new initiative; and in any case the UN Secretary-General's then Special Representative, Joe Clark (former Canadian foreign and prime minister), who had put an impressive effort into the 1993–94 negotiations over Confidence-Building Measures, was in the process of bowing out.

In addition to these strictly Cyprus-related matters, the relationship between the two mother countries, Greece and Turkey, was going through a particularly rough patch. Actual hostilities had only narrowly been avoided during a dispute in January 1996 over an uninhabited islet (known in the different languages as Imia or Kardak), situated between Greece's Dodecanese archipelago and the Aegean coast of Turkey. The dispute, which had shown every sign of slipping out of the control of the two countries and their prime ministers (in Greece the newly installed Constantinos Simitis and in Turkey Tansu Ciller) was damped down after some active diplomacy by outside powers, in particular by the United States in the person of Richard Holbrooke, the Assistant Secretary of State for Europe; but it had demonstrated yet again how fragile the relationship between these two NATO partners was and how real were the threats to international peace and security in the Eastern Mediterranean. Moreover it led to Greece unilaterally blocking implementation of the European Union's financial commitment to Turkey, part of the

March 1995 agreement establishing an EU/Turkey Customs Union. By thus forcing the EU collectively to renege on its commitment, the Greek government both exacerbated its own relationship with Turkey and seriously complicated the handling of the important links between the EU and Turkey.

This was the picture when I was approached at the end of February 1996 by Jeremy Greenstock, the Political Director in the Foreign and Commonwealth Office (and subsequently, from 1998 to 2003, the United Kingdom's Permanent Representative to the United Nations in New York) on behalf of Malcolm Rifkind, then foreign secretary, to ask whether I would be prepared to take on a new part-time post as British Special Representative for Cyprus. We talked the idea through at a number of meetings subsequently and I agreed to take on the appointment, which was publicly announced by Rifkind at a press conference on 23 May.

The mission

The fashion for mission statements was by then getting into its swing, although it was only to reach its full development when the Blair government came to power the following year. We managed to avoid one on this occasion. But we did not duck the need to agree in advance the parameters of what I was setting out to do.

The first point firmly established was that although the decision to appoint a British Special Representative for Cyprus marked a distinct raising of our national profile in attempts to resolve the Cyprus problem, there was to be no question at any stage of initiating or pursuing a solo British or even a UK/US approach to the problem. The task was to put more clout into the United Nations efforts. We agreed that Britain's significant but historically fraught relationships with all concerned over the Cyprus problem meant that any initiative with a British label on it would be doomed from the outset, and that, in any case, only the United Nations was likely to be acceptable to all concerned as a vehicle for settlement negotiations.

Secondly, the enlargement of the European Union, the modalities of which were not at that stage clear, was a major objective of British foreign policy and must in no way be delayed or damaged by developments over Cyprus. It was already obvious that, whatever approach was eventually chosen by the European Union, Cyprus would be in the first wave of acceding countries.

Thirdly, while getting a settlement in Cyprus before it joined the European Union was a clear objective, indeed the basic raison d'être of my appointment, it was not to be pursued in such a way as to put at risk Britain's close and steadily developing relationships with the countries in the region most directly involved (Cyprus, Greece and Turkey).

Apart from these three clear guidelines, which were all constraints on the handling of the job, I was not given, nor did I at that stage seek, much guidance. It was evident that the best way to proceed and the most promising basis for making progress would be largely dictated by the views of other players. It made no sense for Britain to draw up blueprints or design negotiating fixes on its own. As to the constraints, at no stage did I feel uncomfortable with them and on no occasion did I seek to have them varied. I was naturally aware that both what they prescribed and what they did not prescribe had implications for the negotiation of a settlement and were in different ways unsatisfactory to one or other or several of the regional players. The Turks and Turkish Cypriots would have preferred us to agree that it was legally and politically impossible for a divided Cyprus to enter the European Union; the Greeks and Greek Cypriots would have wished us to be bound to the precise letter of whichever of the many Security Council resolutions most faithfully reflected their own position at a given point in time. But either of those approaches would quite simply have brought the whole attempt to get a negotiated settlement to a standstill, so the temptation to contest the constraints or to accept additional ones was not very compelling.

First reflections

While it certainly made no sense to settle down at the outset to devise blueprints for a settlement or negotiating fixes, it made equally little sense to set off on a voyage of discovery to the region without having done a good deal of background reading and reflected carefully on previous attempts to get a settlement, the lessons to learn from them and the traps to be avoided. The historical background was, unusually, the most difficult to grapple with. There is astonishingly little published material about Cyprus that is not distorted by the views of the author, who tends to be on one side or the other of a deeply contentious and embittered argument. Even the British, the foreigners with probably the largest and deepest experience of Cyprus and not usually short of well-trained historians, seemed to have shied away from a scene where their experience had perhaps been too painful and too recent to encourage objective research.

Those who did tackle the issue had all too often gone the other way and became hopelessly subjective apologists for one view or the other.

The negotiating background was a good deal easier to come to terms with, largely thanks to the admirable reporting practices followed by the United Nations Secretariat in their reports to the Security Council on the different attempts they had led to achieve a settlement; large slabs of carefully marshalled factual material, interspersed with brief and succinct but unemotional sections of judgement, were precisely what was needed. And of course I had actually experienced in New York as British Permanent Representative to the UN, though more as a bystander than as a participant, the two most recent rounds of negotiations on the Set of Ideas and the Confidence-Building Measures, and had got to know some, but by no means all, the principal actors with whom I would have to deal.

This preparatory phase, which lasted from March to May of 1996, left me with some clear impressions to be tested on the ground when I began my travels. The first of these was the high quality and continuing value of Boutros-Ghali's 1992 Set of Ideas, painstakingly pieced together over the preceding years by his Special Representative on the island, Oscar Camilion, and the leading official in the UN Secretariat responsible for Cyprus, Gustave Feissel.

The proposals had been endorsed by the Security Council soon after the negotiations had been suspended in 1992, and established a bi-zonal, bi-communal federation with extensive autonomy for the two component parts, with a substantial territorial adjustment to the benefit of the Greek Cypriots set out in a map attached to the proposals, with limited returns of Greek Cypriot property owners to the north, and with security resting on a continuation of the Treaty of Guarantee, a reduced Greek and Turkish troop presence and an international peacekeeping force. Those proposals were no mere skeleton, having been fleshed out in quite a detailed way. While Clerides had rejected the Set of Ideas as such in his 1993 election campaign, he seemed to have fewer objections to its individual parts. And Denktash's position was that he could accept 90 per cent of what had been proposed, even if he was a bit coy about coming clean on what matters made up the remaining 10 per cent. So the case for ensuring that any new initiative did not just start from scratch, but rather sought to build on what was already on the table, seemed very strong.

At the same time, the Set of Ideas appeared to have some serious shortcomings. Its treatment of the important issue of the reunited island's membership of the EU was, not unnaturally, since it had been put together at a very early stage in Cyprus's candidature, rather sketchy and increasingly inadequate as time passed and this issue came to bulk larger both in complexity and political sensitivity. Also the Set of Ideas, although it went well beyond a skeleton or framework agreement, still fell well short of a fully operative, self-executing and comprehensive settlement. Given the genesis of the breakdown of the 1960 constitution in a dispute over the implementation of fiscal provisions, the propensity of both parties in Cyprus to contest even the tiniest detail in an agreement or piece of legislation and to see an unrequited benefit to the other side and loss to themselves in the most arcane of provisions, and given also their tendency to prevaricate and to spin out any negotiations on such points, it did seem to me that a more comprehensive approach would be needed on the next occasion.

Another salient point seemed equally clear and that was the importance of some external impetus and also external expertise if any progress was to be made. That was not to suggest that a reversion to the methods used in the late 1950s, when the original independence settlement was effectively stitched up by the two motherlands, Greece and Turkey, and imposed on the two Cypriot parties, was either practicable or desirable. Time had moved on; neither motherland was prepared to play that role, nor was either party in Cyprus prepared to accept it. But the attitudes of the motherlands towards any settlement negotiations remained important. Long and bitter experience, however, had shown that the two Cypriot parties, left to themselves, would get nowhere. Their preference for tactical manoeuvre over substantive engagement on the core issues was longstanding. Neither had been willing, in putting forward its own proposals, to take any real account of the interests and sensitivities of the other side; both sides had a pathological fear of making substantive concessions, which they believed would be pocketed by the other side and then become the starting point for future negotiations and yet more concessions. And then there was another less tangible but no less real factor. This was the deeply held belief of most Cypriots that in the end the outcome would not be determined by the Cypriots themselves but by various outside forces. It was this factor that went some way towards explaining the degree of irresponsibility that often imbued policy making on the island. All this pointed towards the need for the United Nations to resume the central role it had played in previous attempts to reach a settlement, but also for the UN to be backed up by the main external actors with experience of Cyprus and a stake in the prospects for a settlement – the United States, the United Kingdom, the European Union and Russia being the most obvious but not the only ones – and for those external actors not to allow themselves to be played off against each other, as had often occurred in the past.

These thoughts led on to another – the need at some stage to find a time frame that would genuinely constrain and compel the decision making of all the main parties to the negotiation. One, but only one, of the reasons why negotiations had already continued off and on for more than 30 years without any outcome was that they had been conducted in an open-ended time frame. Not only was the current situation of each of the Cypriot parties too comfortable to push them towards the difficult compromises required – the Greek Cypriots with their internationally recognized position as the sole representative of the Republic of Cyprus, their prosperity and their gradually advancing EU candidature; the Turkish Cypriots with the overwhelming military superiority and security derived from the presence of Turkish armed forces and the flow of subsidies provided by Turkey to palliate the deficiencies of the economy in the north of the island and the negative effect on it of the impediments to exports to the EU – but the absence of any time line, let alone a deadline, meant that it was always easier to call for more time to negotiate and to put off indefinitely tough choices or compromises. And on this point, if none other, there had invariably in the past been an unholy alliance between the two Cypriot parties. There was no immediate answer to this deadline problem in 1996, although, well down the road, it was already clear that there could be one in the form of the conclusion of the EU's enlargement negotiations.

All these considerations did not take account of arguably an even more important dimension, the personal one. Was there a real prospect of getting the two Cypriot leaders to the negotiating table; and, once there, could they reasonably be expected to negotiate with some flexibility and in a spirit of give and take? In neither case could a positive answer be assumed. Clerides had won office campaigning against the Set of Ideas, and he had, at the end of the road, played his part in ensuring that the Confidence-Building Measures got nowhere. But since then, in a series of informal meetings with Denktash, under the aegis of the UN Deputy Special Representative, Feissel, in the autumn of 1995 he had pushed hard for a framework approach based on reaching trade-offs on the most sensitive core issues, leaving the detail to be filled in later. While the method was unlikely to work, the signal was at least encouraging. From Denktash no such encouragement had emerged. Successive UN negotiators, including two UN secretaries-general – Pérez de Cuéllar, who had himself done a stint as Special Representative for Cyprus before becoming secretary-general, and Boutros-Ghali – had despaired at Denktash's inflexibility and had effectively concluded that he was not interested in a settlement, from which he had decided that he had more to lose than to gain. There was no reason to hope for a fundamental change or help from that quarter. This meant that, as so often in the past, the key was likely to be in Ankara and not in the north of the island.

A first round of contacts

Within a month of my appointment I was able to make visits to Cyprus and then to Athens and Ankara and thus to begin to build up at first hand a picture of the challenges and opportunities that accompanied any effort to mount a new negotiation for a settlement. The challenges comfortably outnumbered the opportunities.

As my Cyprus Airways flight came in to land at Larnaca, I realized, with some trepidation, that the waiting press, about whose cannibalistic tendencies I had been liberally warned in advance, might latch on to the fact that I had never previously set foot in the island. I decided I was certainly not going to start off by obfuscating. I need not have worried. The Cyprus press accused me of any number of crimes and conspiracies over the next seven years, but they missed this glorious opportunity to suggest that here was another in a string of ignorant foreigners set on telling them how to handle their affairs. Driving up through the somewhat lunar landscape that separates Larnaca from Nicosia I was able to grasp the division of the island, with the northern Kyrenia Range, adorned with Turkish and Turkish Cypriot flags and the obligatory quotation from Mustafa Kemal Atatürk, looming out of the heat haze on the right and on the left, less easily visible, the Troodos Mountains and the ugly but burgeoning sprawl of Greek Cypriot Nicosia. A later walk along the Green Line, where it runs through Nicosia, with the ruined shops and cafés left as they were when the shooting stopped in 1974, made the point even more cogently.

My arrival was greeted with two auguries. It rained. That, on a day celebrated by the Greek Orthodox Church as the anniversary of Noah's flood, was apparently an auspicious sign. The second was a good deal less so. A Greek Cypriot conscript was shot dead by a Turkish sentry in the dried-up river bed that formed the ceasefire line between the two sides, quite near the offices of the British High Commission. Later in the summer there were some ugly incidents at the Famagusta end of the ceasefire line when Greek Cypriot protesters broke through their own police cordon and brushed aside the UN troops in the buffer zone, leading to some shooting by Turkish Cypriots and two Greek Cypriot fatalities. All this was a timely reminder, if one was needed, that the situation was not quite as comfortably stable as it was often depicted. And the incidents were of course grist to the mill of the extremists on both sides who were quick to point out how foolish it was even to contemplate a settlement.

My meetings in Nicosia fell into what was to become a scarcely varying pattern of my visits there. A working breakfast with Glafcos Clerides and his close advisers at the presidential palace (formerly the British colonial governor's residence but hardly recognizable from those days as a result of the damage done to it in 1974 by the tanks of the Greek Cypriot National Guard in support of the coup against President Makarios), then a meeting with the foreign minister, then a call on the president of the National Assembly, and contacts with other party leaders, who together made up the National Council, which advised the president on the conduct of negotiations on the Cyprus problem. On the Turkish Cypriot side, after crossing the Green Line at the old Ledra Palace Hotel checkpoint, there was a meeting and working lunch with Rauf Denktash in his presidential palace (formerly the residence of the British district commissioner for colonial Nicosia, also hardly recognizable, although not for the same reason, having been greatly extended to accommodate the centre of Turkish Cypriot governance). This was followed by contacts, either social or working, with party leaders, some in government, some in opposition, and with civil society and activists on both sides. This required some fairly careful navigation round a complex protocol course reflecting the fact that while the British government recognized and dealt with Denktash as the leader of the Turkish Cypriot community (but not as president of the TRNC), we did not have official dealings with his government and ministers, and could not therefore call on them in their offices. This caused irritation but no major problems. The routine programme was usually completed by a bi-communal press conference at the Ledra Palace Hotel until a much later stage, when the UN's news blackout on the settlement negotiations made that undesirable.

South Nicosia

Rather as I had expected, I found no great enthusiasm anywhere in the south for initiating a new effort to reach a negotiated settlement. Clerides argued that there must first be a greater degree of common ground established on the main issues before it made sense to launch any serious negotiations, and he was not prepared to respond positively to Denktash's current objective, the holding of a face-to-face meeting between the two of them, clearly designed to boost his own status. (In the years ahead these two negotiating ploys, the prior establishment of 'common ground' and the holding of face-to-face talks, emerged several times and then faded away, and they were swapped between the two sides in a disconcerting way that did much to justify the cynicism of outside observers – in the period 2001–3 it was Denktash who was calling for common ground as a precondition to negotiation and Clerides who wanted face-to-face talks.) But Clerides was quite flexible in private on many of the component parts of what had been in 1992 the UN Set of Ideas. He was prepared to go a considerable way to meet Turkish and Turkish Cypriot security concerns and in particular did not contest the need to preserve the 1960 Treaty of Guarantee which had been the basis of the Turkish military intervention in 1974. In those early contacts I floated past him, without provoking much of a reaction either positive or negative, the possibility that the rotation between Greek Cypriots and Turkish Cypriots of the posts of president and vice-president in a reunited Cyprus – one of the issues that had remained unresolved and hotly contested at the end of the 1992 negotiations – might be easier to handle if one worked within the framework of a parliamentary rather than a presidential system, with the posts of president and vice-president being purely honorific and possessing no substantial executive powers, as was the case in countries such as Ireland and Israel (but not in the 1960 Cyprus constitution).

In a theme that would become familiar over the years, Clerides argued that Denktash's approach was fundamentally negative and that the key to any negotiation lay in Ankara and a shift in the Turkish government's attitude. I could not, and never tried to, fault that analysis, which I shared anyway. But I noticed that it was accompanied by a deliberately pessimistic and not terribly well-informed view of the prospects for bringing about a shift in Turkish policy. Over the years it was brought home to me what a major handicap it was that the main Greek Cypriot players and their Turkish counterparts never met (other than the occasional content-free handshake at a multilateral meeting such as an OSCE Summit or, later, at EU meetings) and that there was therefore no opportunity to break down the barriers of suspicion and mutual misunderstanding, let alone to discuss the core issues of a Cyprus settlement. And neither had a diplomatic mission in the other's capital. So instead each side appeared to rely on an interpretation of the other's position based on reading press summaries and speeches, with the most extreme and populist expression of the situation being invariably assumed to be true. Worse still, all four of the main regional players (Greece, Turkey, Greek Cyprus and Turkish Cyprus) spent the largest part of almost any meeting telling you about the defects of the other side's position and explaining why these ruled out any chance of a successful negotiation, and tended to avoid to the maximum degree possible any discussion of their own position.

North Nicosia

A mere ten-minute drive across the city, through the zigzag barbed wire barriers of the Green Line, past pictures of Greek Cypriot martyrs, past too the bullet-pocked façade of the Ledra Palace Hotel, now adorned with the drying underwear of British UNFICYP troops quartered there, I settled down to what was to be the unvarying fare of my early meetings with Denktash: the history lesson. (After a few years I must have been considered an old enough hand to have graduated from this, although, when accompanying a new visitor, for example Joyce Quin when she was minister for Europe at the Foreign and Commonwealth Office, there was no escaping it. In her case I timed it at 49 minutes before Denktash drew breath and allowed his visitor to speak for the first time.)

The history lesson usually began in about 1878 when Cyprus ex-changed Ottoman for British rule. It was filled with bitter complaints of British betrayals, leaving the minority Turkish Cypriot community to the tender mercies of the Greek Cypriots. It continued with a long history of Greek Cypriot perfidy, focusing in particular on Archbishop Makarios's hijacking of the 1960 constitution when the Turkish Cypriots walked out of the government in 1963, and on the folly of the international commu-nity thereafter in accepting the Greek Cypriots as the sole representatives of the Republic of Cyprus. There would be some vivid passages on the atrocities committed against the Turkish Cypriots from 1963 to 1974 and a rather insistent invitation to visit the mass graves outside Famagusta. The inner circle of the inferno was then completed with an onslaught on the European Union and the illegality and iniquity of its decision to treat as valid the Greek Cypriot application for membership. The purpose of the history lesson was not just to let off steam, though it certainly had that effect, but it was also designed to bring home to the visitor the view that the Turkish Cypriots had been the victims of an unparalleled series of historic blunders and that there was not the slightest chance of a settlement to the Cyprus problem until those blunders were reversed and the wrongs righted. Only when the Turkish Cypriot state was recognized as such (a slightly softer version used the word 'acknowledged', but probing tended to reveal that there was no real difference between the two formulae), when all property claims on either side had been eliminated and handled through compensation alone, and when a new Cyprus based on the absolute equality of the two communities reflected in a right of veto over every decision, however minor, had been agreed, would it be possible to address such issues as a territorial adjustment and the question of security.

I did my best, without making much of a dent on my interlocutor, to explain that whatever one's view of the historic rights and wrongs – and not all of Denktash's analysis was wide of the mark; for example his strictures on the way Turkish Cypriots had been treated in the first decade of Cypriot independence – it was not within my power or my remit to reverse decisions taken by the international community over the recognition of the continuing legitimacy of the Republic of Cyprus, and anyway, as it was simply not going to happen, waiting for it to do so meant never finding a solution that would improve the Turkish Cypriots' lot. On a more positive note I tried to get it across to him that Cyprus's EU application offered a real opportunity to negotiate a comprehensive settlement that would fill in the disagreed parts of the 1992 Set of Ideas in ways consistent with the Turkish Cypriots' vital interests and that the very strong desire of the EU member states to see a reunited rather than a divided Cyprus join the Union offered considerable possibilities if only the Turkish Cypriots would come to the negotiating table and, once there, show some degree of flexibility.

Athens

My early visits to Athens were to some extent handicapped by the decision of the Greek foreign minister, Theodoros Pangalos, to have nothing to do with me. This decision was rooted in some rather sharp disagreements between us over Europe's relationships with Turkey and Cyprus during the period (1985–90) when I had been Permanent Representative to the European Union and thus often, towards the end of Council meetings, left by the foreign secretary to hold the fort. As a result my talks in Athens were with the secretary-general of the foreign ministry, an old friend, Alecos Filon, and with the able and very experienced junior minister Ioannis Kranidiotis. Kranidiotis was in fact of Cypriot origin, his father having been the first Cypriot ambassador to Athens following independence. Not surprisingly his knowledge of the Cyprus problem was encyclopaedic, and, while at the outset he was far from convinced of the case for making another serious attempt to reach a settlement, as time passed he became more and more committed to such an effort.

The Greek position at this stage was to pay lip service to the need to resume negotiations for a Cyprus settlement and to the central role of the United Nations, but to avoid making any major effort to bring that about and, above all, to avoid getting at cross-purposes with Clerides who, as we have seen, was similarly unenthusiastic. They too cast doubt on the readiness of Denktash and the Turks to engage in good faith in such a negotiation or to be ready to make the necessary compromises if they did so. Greek–Turkish relations were in poor shape following the crisis at the beginning of the year over Imia, and there was absolutely no give in the Greek blockage of the funds which the EU had committed itself to disbursing to Turkey as part of the deal over a customs union reached in 1995. Pangalos himself was much given to periodic intemperate rhetorical onslaughts on Turkey which poisoned the atmosphere, and he clearly preferred to have Cyprus as an additional grievance to nurse rather than to put any effort into having its problems resolved.

Ankara

My first visit to Ankara in late June coincided with the latest in a series of governmental crises that had arisen since the leaders of the two centre-right parties, Mesut Yilmaz and Tansu Ciller, had decided to take turns as prime minister. While the deal had not quite yet been stitched up, Ciller was known to be contemplating what the whole of the Ankara establishment regarded as a diabolical alliance with the leader of the then largest Islamist party, Necmettin Erbakan. It was hardly the best moment to get the Turks to concentrate on the problem of Cyprus, a subject which in any case invariably caused them a great deal of difficulty if there was to be any question of moving away from a stalwart defence of the status quo.

It nevertheless proved possible to have some useful and interesting contacts. The top official in the foreign ministry dealing with Cyprus and Greece, Inal Batu, had been Turkish ambassador to the UN when I had been in New York and we knew each other well. Over a private dinner he expressed extreme pessimism about the prospect of getting any likely government in Ankara to negotiate a settlement on Cyprus, and he clearly had the greatest doubts about Denktash's willingness to do so. He asked whether there was any chance of trading a unilateral Turkish Cypriot ceding of territory in return for international recognition of the Turkish Cypriot state. I said I did not really think so. The idea was just the old scheme for partition that had been rejected so often in the past and which was in any case not consistent with Security Council resolutions and the 1960 Treaty of Guarantee. Moreover any attempt to achieve such a trade-off would inevitably lead into a discussion of other issues such as property claims and the return of refugees. Would it not make more sense to deal with all this in a comprehensive settlement, which would in addition support rather than undermine Turkey's ambition to become a member of the EU?

When I saw the foreign minister, Imre Gonensay (destined in fact to be out of office within a week), we discussed Cyprus's application to join the European Union, which the Turks argued was illegal under the terms of the 1960 Treaty of Guarantee (a view not shared by us or other members of the European Union). I decided that if I was not to be accused later of misleading them, I needed to be frank about Cyprus's EU prospects. So I said that, in my view, if Denktash and the Turks continued to take a negative attitude towards negotiating a Cyprus settlement, then it was pretty well certain that a divided Cyprus would in due course be admitted to the Union. This caused some turmoil at the meeting. No one else in Europe had told them that. I emphasized in reply that this was not an outcome that the British government favoured. Quite the reverse. Indeed my appointment had been made precisely with the objective of trying to ensure that a reunited not a divided Cyprus entered the Union. But the commitment given by the member states in 1995, at the time the EU/Turkey Customs Union Agreement was sealed, had been pretty unambiguous. And, if the blame for failing to negotiate a Cyprus settlement was seen to lie principally with Denktash and the Turks, then I believed, on the basis of a good deal of experience of Brussels and in the knowledge that enlargement of the European Union mattered more to most member states than the question of Cyprus, that a divided island would be accepted. We left it there. They were not happy. But an important penny had been left to drop. It was to take a long time to do so.

It also proved possible during these early visits to Ankara, although not later on, after 1997, when a conscious decision was taken somewhere in the Turkish governmental machine to refuse all meetings between their military and visiting diplomats, to have some contact with the Turkish general staff. This was valuable not only because the influence of the military in Turkey on political decision making remained considerable, if singularly obscure in its precise significance, but because there were a number of issues relating to any settlement of the Cyprus problem – the future of the 1960 Treaty of Guarantee, the nature and scale of any continuing Turkish troop presence on the island, the configuration of any territorial adjustment reducing the Turkish-Cypriot-controlled part of the island to the benefit of the Greek Cypriots – that directly concerned the Turkish general staff in its purely military functions. My interlocutor was General Cevik Bir, the deputy chief of the Turkish general staff, whom I had met in New York in 1993 when he commanded the ill-fated UN peacekeeping forces in Somalia. Our discussions, although never even approaching negotiation, were useful. Bir made it clear that while he could certainly conceive of circumstances in which Turkey's and the Turkish Cypriots' vital security interests could be assured with a substantially reduced Turkish troop presence on the island, the Treaty of Guarantee must remain in force, undiluted; and a necessary precondition of even contemplating a reduced troop presence was prior agreement on a political settlement that gave the Turkish Cypriots proper political equality.

On the Treaty of Guarantee I was able to assure Bir that in the view of the British government its continuation was an essential component of any settlement. And I also assured him that we saw no future in pursuing a 'security first' approach to the negotiations, which had temporarily found favour in Washington and London in 1995. But I warned him that there was equally no future in an approach that envisaged a political settlement being reached ahead of Turkey making any commitments on security, including the removal of a substantial proportion of their troops from the island. All the issues would need to be dealt with in a single, comprehensive settlement if there was to be the balance required by all concerned. Clearly, with no actual negotiating process under way at that stage, there was not much more to be said. But the fact that, when a negotiating process did get under way, and most particularly in the later stages of that process in 2002–3 when actual settlement proposals were on the table, there was absolutely no direct contact between the UN negotiators and the Turkish military, must have undermined the chances of an agreement. Above all it meant that every aspect of the UN-led negotiation only reached the Turkish military through a filter controlled by Denktash or by Turkish foreign ministry officials.

One other meeting during that first visit to Ankara was worthy of note. On the British ambassador's sunny terrace, I had a long, agreeable but completely unproductive lunchtime discussion of Cyprus with Bulent Ecevit, who had been prime minister of Turkey in 1974 when the Turkish military interventions in Cyprus took place. Ecevit at this time was simply a backbench member of parliament, his party (DSP) being out of office and thought likely to remain so for the foreseeable future. Ecevit's view, which he continued to repeat when he was catapulted back into the prime minister's office in 1999, was that the Cyprus problem had been settled by him in 1974 and that nothing remained to be done except for the rest of us to come to terms with that. I tried to explain why this approach was a little simplistic: that because the best efforts of Turkish diplomacy over the preceding 15 years had not produced a single country that recognized the Turkish Cypriot state and because there had meanwhile been a large number of Security Council resolutions saying that the status quo was unacceptable and contrary to international law, it was a little unrealistic to argue that the matter was settled, and that a number of developments over the next few years, particularly in regard to Cyprus's EU candidature, were likely to evolve in a way that would not be to the benefit of Turkey or the Turkish Cypriots unless a serious effort were made to reach a settlement. To no avail. Ecevit's own view did not shift much, if at all, during the period from 1999 to 2002 when he was again prime minister.

Constructing a network

To stand even the remotest chance of achieving a comprehensive settlement there needed to be a robust and effective network of international organizations and of the states that counted for something in the regional capitals (Nicosia, Ankara and Athens). If the UN (both the secretary-general and his special representative) was not functioning fully there would simply be no settlement to negotiate, since the two Cypriot parties never had and were clearly not going to provide the negotiable material that would be needed. If the United States was not fully on board, there would be no movement in Ankara; if the EU was not supportive, the Greek Cypriots were likely to focus exclusively on completing their accession negotiations before a settlement and there was also the risk of mismatch between the terms of a Cyprus settlement and those agreed for Cyprus to join the EU; if the Russians were not at least acquiescent there would be trouble every time the matter came back to the Security Council. While there was apparently no major conflict of interest between all these parties and while all were signed up in principle to supporting an effort to get a settlement, their cooperation could certainly not be taken for granted. It was not long since the EU and the UN had stopped behaving as if the two of them lived on separate planets. US support in Ankara had on occasion been lacking in the past. Most EU member states knew little and cared less about the Cyprus problem and rated it as of low priority.

It was clear from the outset that the UN was not going to be easily persuaded that the time was approaching for another attempt to get a comprehensive settlement on Cyprus. The memories of setbacks over the Set of Ideas (1992) and the package of Confidence-Building Measures (1994) were relatively fresh. The secretary-general, Boutros Boutros-Ghali, had in particular found his dealings with Denktash a bruising experience (the feeling was mutual) and was convinced that as long as he was in power there was little if any chance of a solution. Boutros-Ghali was in any case at that stage deeply preoccupied with his own unavailing campaign to avoid an American veto and secure a second term of office as secretary-general.

The new UN Special Representative for Cyprus, Han Sung Joo, a former foreign minister of South Korea had been appointed about the same time as I had. He met Denktash's basic requirements of all new appointees to the office (in view of the fact that this was a Good Offices Mission, the agreement of both Clerides and Denktash was required before any appointment could be made) of not being a European and of having no previous experience of Cyprus. We met in July and again in December, when he came to London to see the foreign secretary. We met also in Brussels when I engineered a first contact with Hans van den Broek, the commissioner responsible for the enlargement negotiations and thus for Cyprus. Han was charming, intelligent and knowledgeable but he had some real handicaps for this particular job, the most serious of which was being based on the other side of the world in Seoul and only intermittently available for short periods in the Eastern Mediterranean region. He was also somewhat overawed by the waves of negativism and hostility habitually purveyed by the parties. I began to doubt whether he would be able to manage the job if ever we reached the point of launching a new initiative. Clearly he did too, because he stood down in the spring of 1997 when it was clear that an initiative was in the offing. All this meant that we could certainly not count on a proactive UN at the outset and that it would be up to the leading member states to press for action and to convince the UN Secretariat that this time they would put their own backs into it.

The US was as keen as Britain to get things moving again, not out of any exaggerated expectations of early results but because a negotiating vacuum in Cyprus tended to lead to an increase in tension throughout the region and because it could already see in the EU's enlargement agenda, which it strongly supported, both an opportunity and a risk of a major confrontation between two NATO allies, Greece and Turkey. So in July, on the first of many visits I was to make to Washington, I established the very close working relationship that was essential and was given firm commitments of high-level interest and support.

That the European Union was an important part of any negotiating equation was not in doubt but it was not entirely obvious how best its undoubted influence could be harnessed and deployed. The problem was complicated by the fact that the attitude of the then Greek foreign minister, Pangalos, made any calm, sensible, collective EU discussion of either Cyprus or Turkey impossible. So such collective discussion as did take place had to be managed in ad hoc groupings of the member states principally concerned (France, Germany, Italy, Spain and the UK). The common view in this group was that we all needed to be pressing the parties to come back to the negotiating table; that we should encourage the UN to begin shaping up a new initiative; that we should do what we could to find a way round the Greek veto on the EU's financial commitment to Turkey and try to keep Turkey's relationship with the EU moving forward; and that we should not be lured down the path of promoting the EU as a mediator in Cyprus, a favourite ploy of both Greeks and Greek Cypriots, given that, with Greece's membership and with Cyprus's application accepted, the EU was clearly not acceptable in that role to either Turkish Cypriots or Turks. At this stage, with the enlargement negotiations not yet started, there seemed no particular role for the Commission.

Enter the foreign secretary

At the time of my appointment in May, Malcolm Rifkind had made it clear that he would like to get involved personally in the effort to get negotiations for a comprehensive settlement under way again. Both he and the prime minister, John Major, had ensured that my appointment was properly understood and welcomed where it needed to be (in the region, at the UN, in Washington and in the main EU capitals). Now, that autumn, after two complete rounds of visits to Nicosia, Athens and Ankara and numerous contacts with the other main players, it seemed to me time to take stock and consider how best to take forward the foreign secretary's offer.

A visit to Cyprus by a British foreign secretary was by no means as straightforward or as routine a matter as bilateral official visits normally are in this age of jet travel. Oddly enough there had been no such visits in the recent past, although Douglas Hurd had visited the island when the Commonwealth Heads of Government Meeting was held there in 1994, and he had had a working lunch with Clerides and Denktash at the UN Deputy Special Representative's house in the buffer zone to discuss progress, or rather the lack of it. Prior to that a whole series of foreign secretaries had decided that visiting Cyprus was a high-risk, low-gain venture and had left it to their ministers for Europe.

Among the complications in mounting such a visit was the matter of seeing Denktash. For the visit to be worthwhile at all there had to be a proper discussion with him, but this needed to be achieved within the framework of our (and others') position on recognition, that we regarded him as the elected leader of the Turkish Cypriot community but not (as he regarded himself) as the president of the Turkish Republic of North Cyprus. Then there was the more interesting and risky question of what we should try to achieve. Should we try to bring Clerides and Denktash together and, if so, with what desired outcome? Should we try to get agreement on the broad issue of resuming negotiations for a settlement and, if so, on what basis? And, if we did neither of the above, how were we to avoid the visit being just a flash in the pan with no follow up or influence on events? It was decided that trying to get Clerides and Denktash together was unwise and as likely to set back the process in which we were engaged (of gradually building up the case for resuming negotiations) as to advance it. Denktash would be delighted by a photo-opportunity meeting to enhance his status but would set out his case in unnegotiable terms; Clerides, if he agreed to such a meeting at all, which he might well not, would push back and not thank us for bringing matters prematurely to such a point. Reaching agreement with the two sides on a communiqué or statement, however bland, was also judged likely to end in failure. The capacity of the two leaders, with their training at the London bar, to haggle over words and formulae until they were ground to dust was well proven.

So in the end an approach was chosen which would avoid these pit-falls, but still, we hoped, advance the cause for which we were working. Following the foreign secretary's meetings with the two leaders, and assuming their outcome was not totally negative, Rifkind would set out in his bi-communal press conference at the end of the visit a number of points that, together, could be said to indicate that there was a good deal more common ground than many believed there to be and therefore a good case for resuming negotiations for a settlement. While no attempt would be made to agree the wording of these points in advance with the two leaders, Rifkind would send them the text shortly before the press conference and would urge each of them to respond positively.

The visit, on 15–16 December, duly went off without a hitch. The meetings with Clerides and Denktash in fact went rather better than I had feared. Clerides, no doubt conscious that crucial decisions on Cyprus's EU candidacy were due to be taken in 1997, made it clear that he still hoped for a framework negotiation in which he and Denktash could agree on the key, substantive trade-offs, leaving the detailed legal drafting to follow. And Denktash, after the obligatory history lesson, managed to sound as if he regarded the resumption of settlement negotiations as pretty well inevitable and indeed said that he would enter such negotia-tions in a spirit of give and take. The reactions to the press conference by each side were relatively muted and limited to one or two detailed points of drafting which, since no one intended to use the text for negotiating purposes, were neither here nor there.

Moreover at separate meetings in London with the Turkish foreign minister, by now Ciller, (on 5 December) and with the Greek foreign minister, Pangalos, (on 18 December) the discussion of Cyprus was relatively positive. Ciller in particular showed a considerable grasp of the main issues, with which she had had to deal in detail when she had been prime minister during the negotiations over Confidence-Building Meas-ures. While her approach was distinctly robust, she also listened carefully to Rifkind's analysis of why a settlement on Cyprus could be of real benefit to Turkey and the Turkish Cypriots.

So, as 1996 ended, it seemed as if some progress back to the negotiating table was being made. The ten points for Rifkind's press conference indicated a broad framework within which a resumed negotiation could be situated and were as follows:

(i) The aim should be a comprehensive settlement covering all aspects of the Cyprus problem which will be based on a bi-zonal, bi-communal federation in conformity with the High-Level Agreements and Security Council Resolutions;

(ii) The federation and its constitution will reflect the principle of political equality of the two communities, as defined by the UN Secretary-General:

(i) The federation will have a single international personality. Its existence and powers will derive from separate referenda in the two communities.

(ii) There will be no right of partition or secession, nor will there be domination of the federation by either side.

(iii) The security of each of the two communities and of the settlement as a whole will be achieved by means of international guarantees and by such measures of international collective security as may be agreed by the parties.

(iv) The boundary of the two federated zones will not conform to the present ceasefire line. The adjustment should contribute to a solution of the problem of refugees.

(v) Before the end of the first half of 1997, there should be an open-ended session of face-to-face negotiations under the aegis of the United Nations aimed at securing a comprehensive settlement to the Cyprus problem. The further preparation of these face-to-face negotiations by an intensified process will start early in 1997.

(vi) The success of these negotiations will depend on the creation of genuine mutual confidence between the two sides. It will therefore be important for both sides to encourage steps designed to achieve that and to avoid any actions which will increase tension over the coming months. In particular they will work to ensure the success of UN efforts on unmanning, unloading and rules of military conduct.

(vii) EU membership should be of benefit to all the people of the island and the terms of accession will need to take account of the basic interests of each of the two communities.

(viii) The negotiation of the terms of accession of Cyprus to the EU will, if a political settlement can be reached in 1997, be conducted on behalf of the bi-zonal, bi-communal federation, taking account of the European Union's agreement to start such negotiations six months after the conclusion of its Inter-Governmental Conference.

5

1997: Missiles and Missed Opportunities

The year 1997 did not start well. Within a few days of the beginning of the year it was announced that the Greek Cypriots had signed a contract with Russia to purchase S300 surface-to-air missiles. This was only the latest in a series of arms purchases by the government of Cyprus which, together with mounting Turkish deployments, had resulted in the island being one of the most heavily armed places on earth. But this latest purchase was qualitatively rather different from previous ones and potentially more destabilizing. The missiles in question had a range sufficient to shoot down Turkish aircraft taking off from their bases in southern Turkey from where the Turks provided air cover for their troops on the island (neither they nor the Greeks stationed military aircraft in Cyprus). They therefore represented a challenge to Turkish air supremacy in the event of hostilities. And so did a further Greek Cypriot decision to construct a military airbase at Paphos in the west of the island, with hardened shelters for aircraft, which would enable Greek planes to be deployed in a time of tension.

The effect of these developments on the prospects for settlement negotiations were entirely negative and were not much mitigated by an assurance immediately given to a US envoy by Clerides that the missiles would not arrive on the island before the end of 1997 at the earliest (this was in fact no concession at all, since the missiles had not yet begun to be manufactured). The reaction in the north of the island and in Ankara was strong, and the Turkish foreign minister in particular made some extremely bellicose statements which implied, although they did not state it in terms, that force might be used either to prevent the delivery of the missiles from Russia or against them once deployed. While there were some indications that the Turkish general staff, who were no fans of the Erbakan/Ciller government, were unhappy about the strength and speci-

70

ficity of the threats made by their government, it was clear that compla-
cency about what might happen if deployment went ahead would not be
justified. Meanwhile one of the centrepieces of the Greek Cypriot negotiating position for a settlement, a proposal that the whole island be
demilitarized, was left looking distinctly forlorn, if not positively hypo-
critical. Other consequences were that the Greek Cypriots lost the moral
high ground on which they had been comfortably encamped and that
many of the diplomatic efforts of the United States, Britain and the other
European countries over the next two years had to be diverted to avoiding
deployment of the missiles rather than being focused on persuading the
Turks and Turkish Cypriots to show more flexibility at the negotiating
table.

   Discussion of these unfortunate developments with the Greek Cypriots was not easy, nor, for a long time, particularly fruitful. They argued
with some emotion that they had the right to defend themselves against
the very substantial Turkish military presence in the north of the island
and on the mainland opposite Cyprus. They brushed aside the suggestion
that they were in any way acting in a manner inconsistent with the numerous Security Council resolutions that had urged all parties to avoid a
military build-up on the island. And in private Clerides was prone to
suggest that the missile purchase was a kind of negotiating ploy designed
to bring Denktash and the Turks to the negotiating table. The trouble
was that none of these arguments were either valid or particularly convincing. Acquiring these missiles neither increased the security of the
Greek Cypriots nor did it make the Turks and Turkish Cypriots more
likely to negotiate a settlement. On the first aspect, powerful though the
missiles were, they could not hope to undermine the massive Turkish air
superiority nor did they change the facts of geography. And it was those
facts – the distance of Cyprus from Greece and its proximity to Turkey,
and the consequent impossibility for Greece to resupply or to reinforce
Cyprus in a time of hostilities, which had been amply demonstrated in
1974 – that remained unaltered by the latest arms purchase and meant
that the best form of security for the Greek Cypriots was an internationally guaranteed settlement and not the acquisition of additional weapons
systems. Moreover the nature of the new weapons system ensured that if
there ever was a Greek–Turkish military confrontation, there would be
no hope of avoiding its spilling over into Cyprus, since the Turks would
not be likely to leave such a threat to their mainland airbases untouched.
As to making the Turks more inclined to negotiate with flexibility, the

opposite was the case. Not only did the rather febrile atmosphere in Ankara mean that there was a premium on an aggressively nationalistic response, but even cooler Turkish heads were quite capable of working out that if an arms purchase such as this could be shown or be believed to have softened up their negotiating position, then there would be no end to further such purchases.

Nor did attempts by the Americans and the British to persuade the Russians to cancel or at least to delay delivery of the missiles bear any fruit. When I spoke to Vladimir Chizov, the Russian Special Representative, on a visit to London in February I got no change at all. Chizov was a well-informed and sophisticated operator and there was no reason to doubt Russian support for a new UN-led effort to get a settlement. But that support did not include reining in arms supplies in the meanwhile, and the argument that these were contrary to the spirit, if not the letter, of Security Council resolutions was met with a degree of obfuscation worthy of Soviet diplomacy at the height of the Cold War. In effect Russia had a two-track policy – support for settlement negotiations and selling any weapons the Greek Cypriots would buy – and they pursued both tracks without admitting any inconsistency between them throughout the whole period of the negotiations. This was some improvement on their Cold War policy of using the Cyprus problem politically to stir up trouble within NATO, but not much.

So there matters stood on the missiles all through 1997, and, with a presidential election looming in Cyprus in February 1998, it became clear that the missiles would neither be delivered nor cancelled ahead of that. But they hung heavily over the first attempt to get a new negotiation under way.

Another shoe drops

By the end of 1996, and following the Rifkind visit to Nicosia, it had become relatively clear that a resumption of negotiations was on the cards in 1997. But the Turkish attitude to this had not yet been clarified and that was a crucial element. In mid-February I was able to have a long discussion over a working breakfast in London with Onur Oymen, at that time the under-secretary (PUS in our parlance) in the Turkish foreign ministry. It was never very easy to understand precisely where in Ankara policy on Cyprus was made and where the decision-taking buck stopped. But it became steadily clearer as the years went by that the under-secretary was on this issue the focal point where all the threads came together. Our talk on that occasion over breakfast, although far from a meeting of minds, went quite well and Oymen said he would do his best to ensure that the foreign minister (Ciller) cleared her mind on the subject before I visited Ankara a week later and that she would see me on that occasion (as she had not done when I had last visited Ankara the previous October). He was as good as his word on both points.

Getting to see Ciller was no straightforward matter. She did not transact business at the foreign ministry but from the official residence that she had occupied when she was prime minister and where she was still installed. Nor did she see foreign ministry officials to prepare for meetings with visitors; all that was handled by Oymen, who alone appeared to have access to the residence, thus ensuring a considerable bottleneck and much delay. So we kicked our heels for some time in the Ciller anteroom before Oymen finally appeared to say that all was ready. He asked rather nervously that I should remember that she was a strong-willed person who did not like being contradicted. I said that, having worked for Margaret Thatcher for some 11 years, I did have some experience of that phenomenon. We were then ushered in, accompanied by a substantial portion of the Ankara press corps, television cameras and all. The whole meeting was conducted in their presence. Ciller said straightaway that Turkey believed that the time had come for Cyprus negotiations to resume and that it would support a UN initiative to that effect. She fired off some remarks about the need for the EU to unblock its financial commitments to Turkey and for the Russian missiles not to be deployed on the island. There was not a great deal for me to do but to agree on all these points while pointing out that none of them were in our gift.

I was also able to see in Ankara on that occasion the junior minister responsible for day-to-day relations with north Cyprus and in particular for the extensive Turkish aid programme there (thought to be running at about $200 million a year and rising, although no official figures were ever published and that did not include the cost of military support). Abdullah Gül (who became prime minister following the November 2002 general election and then deputy prime minister and foreign minister when the political impediments on his party leader, Recep Tayyip Erdogan, were lifted in March 2003) made an immediately positive impression. Smiling, intelligent and well informed, he had studied in Britain. He readily accepted that the status quo in Cyprus was neither ideal nor easily sustainable in the long term. He set out Turkey's requirements for political equality and security guarantees in a firm but conciliatory manner. And he clearly understood that Denktash was likely to be an obstacle to reaching a negotiated settlement. The political scene in Ankara, with the army increasing pressure all the time on the Erbakan/Ciller government to step down, meant that Gül's views were not, however, likely to be of much direct relevance in the period immediately ahead.

A change of cast at the UN

At the beginning of 1997 Boutros-Ghali stepped down as UN secretary-general and was succeeded by Kofi Annan. This move had implications for the handling of the Cyprus problem. Although Boutros-Ghali had responded positively to representations made to him by the US, Britain and other European countries the previous year to appoint a new Special Representative for Cyprus and to explore whether it was time to renew attempts to negotiate a settlement, it was hard to believe that his heart was in it. He had put a lot of effort into the two previous negotiations (in 1992 and in 1993–94) and had been left empty handed; and he had no confidence in Denktash's good faith, even if he did not actually block a renewed attempt. Moreover Boutros-Ghali had come to be seen by the Turks and Denktash as in some way prejudiced against them (a familiar cycle in Cyprus negotiations, which neither the Turks nor Denktash ever seemed to attribute to Denktash's own behaviour); this meant that he would not have been well placed for the periods of personal involvement in the negotiations without which no solutions would be found. Annan, on the other hand was not so marked. As a long-serving UN official, most recently as under-secretary-general for peacekeeping operations – and thus responsible for UNFICYP, the UN peacekeeping operation in Cyprus – he was reasonably familiar with the subject matter at issue, but he did not have a track record in the eyes of any of the parties.

As Annan moved towards a decision to launch an effort to resume negotiations for a settlement, he realized that he would need a special representative somewhat closer to the action and to himself than Seoul. In place of Han, he chose Diego Cordovez, an Ecuadorian with long experience at the UN during the 1980s and subsequently foreign minister of Ecuador in the early 1990s. Cordovez had played an important role in brokering the withdrawal of Soviet troops from Afghanistan when he had acted as a go-between for the Soviet Union, the United States and Pakistan. I did not myself know Cordovez well, having only met him briefly when Ecuador served on the Security Council in 1991–92, but our first contacts on Cyprus were encouraging. I naturally argued the case for an early resumption of negotiations, but I cautioned against excessive expectations of rapid progress, which seemed to me highly unlikely. The crucial thing, once some kind of process was under way, was not to drop the thread but rather to keep on following it where it would lead; experience had shown that when the thread snapped, or when the UN dropped it, it could take a frustratingly long time to pick it up again.

I also argued for a comprehensive approach, seeking to resolve all the issues definitively, in written texts; again experience had shown that a partial or interim agreement, even one as elaborate as the 1992 Set of Ideas, risked becoming stuck in mid-stream, with the well-established Cypriot proclivity for arguing the toss on even the smallest issues, then ensuring that the negotiator never actually reached the far bank of the river. But to get to a fully self-executing, comprehensive agreement would require a major technical input by the UN, including the drafting of a new constitution, of arrangements on property and security and many other matters. That would require a UN team of experts of which there was as yet no trace; and I undertook to see whether we could find a constitutional lawyer to help in this work, which indeed we did in the form of Henry Steel, a former member of the Foreign Office's legal staff who had worked on the constitution of Zimbabwe. And I urged Cordovez to develop his links with the EU Commission, which was now moving closer to the centre of the stage as the Union approached a decision to open accession negotiations with a first group of applicant countries which was bound to include Cyprus.

Holbrooke ex machina

So far the US contribution to resuming negotiations for a Cyprus settlement had been supportive but low key. The previous Presidential Special Representative, Richard Beattie, had been much involved in the attempt to set up confidential talks between the two sides in 1995 but subsequently had not had much time to devote to Cyprus, given the demands of his law firm in New York and of a number of additional tasks in the State Department given to him by the new secretary of state, Madeleine Albright. The appointment in June 1997 of Richard Holbrooke as Presidential Special Representative for Cyprus came out of the blue and, given the reputation Holbrooke had gained as the architect of the Dayton agreement ending the Bosnian crisis, it caused plenty of ripples. Quite by chance Holbrooke happened to be in London immediately after the announcement of his appointment, holed up in the house of the US deputy chief of mission which he had commandeered to enable him to finish the book he was writing about Bosnia and Dayton. So we were able to spend the better part of two days going over the ground in detail and discussing the way ahead. I had known Holbrooke from the 1970s and we had met frequently during the Bosnian crisis, although I had left the scene before the denouement at Dayton. We did not therefore start from scratch.

Most of our lengthy discussions over these two days were taken up by my briefing him. His immediate reactions were interesting, perceptive and revealing. He quickly saw that a key factor in the Turkish position would be where they stood so far as their own longstanding application to join the European Union was concerned. If that was showing signs of making progress, the motivation to focus on Cyprus and to look for ways of resolving that problem would be powerful because it was so obvious that there was a fundamental inconsistency between Turkey's ambition to join the European Union and the status quo in Cyprus. But, if Turkey's EU candidacy was getting nowhere, then the Turks were likely to camp on the status quo in Cyprus and to see no reason why they should strike the difficult compromises that a Cyprus settlement would require.

I was not able to offer much comfort. The EU Commission's mind was on other things than Turkey as they put the finishing touches to their Agenda 2000 proposals for the handling of the enlargement negotiations. The Greek government was an obstacle to making any progress with Turkey's candidacy, not even being prepared to release the customs union funds. And the incoming Luxembourg presidency of the EU was about as bad as one could get, with no particular motivation to smooth Turkey's path, and a long tradition of taking an aggressively tough line on Turkey's human rights record. In that case, Holbrooke said, we must either change the EU attitude or recognize that we were getting the component elements of the negotiation in the wrong order, trying to make progress on Cyprus itself before the Turks would be ready for it. I could not fault the reasoning. Holbrooke was also somewhat impatient with my description of the complexities of the various aspects of the impending negotiation and of the need to fit various multilateral wheels (the UN and the EU in particular) together so that they meshed and did not clash, or simply did not engage. I was, he said, obsessed with process. There must be some way of cutting through all this, of getting the key players to take the big decisions and to focus on the politics of the problem, not its technicalities.

I said I doubted if this sort of approach would work for Cyprus. It never had done in the past. The main protagonists were lawyers who knew every nook and cranny of every aspect of the problem and they were deeply distrustful of each other. I did not think there was any alternative to a painstakingly detailed approach. My private conclusion was that while Holbrooke's arrival on the scene could be a major asset in terms of negotiating clout and imaginative tactical handling, there was not likely to be a lot of teamwork involved, and keeping the UN centre stage was not something to which he was deeply committed.

Troutbeck and Glion

The new team at the UN now moved to the first stage of a new negotiation without much preparation and without much consultation with the main players. There was always a dilemma to be faced. Time spent in preparatory contacts with the parties and the two motherlands tended to be frustrating and to yield few results. No one was prepared to show their cards, as they saw it, prematurely. Instead discussion tended to focus on extraneous matters (missiles, Cyprus's EU application) and to go round in circles. Han had shown how going round the circuit, 'in a listening mode' as he described it, could after a certain time simply undermine the credibility of the whole process. So the decision to move immediately to face-to-face meetings was entirely justified. What was less so was to do that without preparing any detailed material for the follow-up to the initial meetings and without a clear idea of how the negotiations were to be pursued thereafter. Moreover it began to become evident that Cordovez was strongly imbued with the UN house culture that it was important to keep governments, including those like the US and the UK whose primary role was to give the UN effective diplomatic support, at arms' length, telling them little of what the UN was up to. In many cases this UN culture was quite understandable and indeed necessary. But in the case of Cyprus, where previous UN efforts had tended to falter because of the lack of strong back-up from member states and where the roles of the US and the UK had always been an essential factor for all the main regional players, it did not make sense and it did not produce good results.

Annan therefore invited the two Cypriot leaders to a meeting in mid-July at Troutbeck, a kind of country club in the rolling hills to the east of the Hudson River about an hour and a half's drive north of New York City. He followed that up with a further meeting in mid-August at Glion, a small resort perched among the vineyards at the far end of Lake Geneva, high above Montreux (the proximity of Glion to Montreux and Lausanne, sacred names in the diplomatic history of modern Turkey, was a source of some fascination to the Turks at least). The UN encouraged the presence of Greek and Turkish delegations, which was in any case unavoidable and therefore wise, but made it as difficult as possible for all others – and they made no attempt at all to enlist Holbrooke's presence or support.

The Troutbeck meeting started reasonably promisingly. Annan immediately struck up a good working relationship with the two leaders which he was to maintain through thick and thin over the next seven years. Clerides and Denktash, whose personal relationship dated back to their time practising law in colonial Cyprus and had survived all vicissitudes since, appeared relaxed and friendly. But Denktash quickly began to push his own personal agenda, seeking recognition of his separate and equal status not only in the negotiations themselves which had been agreed from the outset of attempts to settle the Cyprus problem many years earlier (and which was reflected in the fact that the UN negotiations were, formally, between the leader of the Greek Cypriot community and the leader of the Turkish Cypriot community) but outside the negotiations too. He asked Clerides to concede that he did not represent the Turkish Cypriots in any way, which implied that Clerides had no right to be called the president of Cyprus. Clerides, not surprisingly, declined to do anything that would undermine his legitimacy, although he made it clear that within the settlement negotiations he spoke for no one other than the Greek Cypriots.

The scene was thus set for many weary repetitions of this same dialogue of the deaf. And neither side showed any great appetite for getting to grips with the core issues, although Clerides reiterated his view that the two principals should focus on the main political trade-offs and should leave the details to be followed up later by their teams. Into this rather stagnant pool there dropped news of the publication of the EU Commission's Agenda 2000 proposals on the opening of EU accession negotiations with a number of countries including Cyprus and dealing only cursorily and in a dilatory manner with Turkey's own EU application. Both the Turks and Turkish Cypriots took this development extremely badly, although the inclusion of Cyprus within the first wave of applicants had been a foregone conclusion since 1995 when the EU's commitment to that had formed part of the deal with Turkey to move to a full customs union. Whether their reaction would have been less negative if Agenda 2000 had been more constructive about the future handling of Turkey's candidacy it is impossible to say. What is certain was that the Troutbeck meetings ended on a sour note, with no reason for optimism about the sequel at Glion.

When Cordovez debriefed to a group of special representatives at Troutbeck at the end of the meeting, he said that he and Annan had been struck by the fact that since the conclusion of the High-Level Agreements of 1977 and 1979 and through the whole long series of UN-led negotiations thereafter, the two Cypriot parties had not reached agreement on a single piece of paper. The UN felt that that sequence must be broken and that the first priority was to get agreement on a document, however brief and unsubstantial that might be. That was what they would be trying to achieve at Glion. I questioned this approach, doubting whether a largely procedural piece of paper would prove of much value and querying whether in any case it was likely to be possible to achieve agreement given the Turkish Cypriots' determination to push the issue of status before all others. I said, as did the US representative, that the most important objective in our view, now that the UN had the negotiating thread again in its hands, was not to let that drop or be broken. So if the attempt to reach agreement on a piece of paper did not prosper at Glion, we hoped that at least the UN would ensure that a process of negotiation would continue and that it would thus prove possible to get to grips with the core issues in the months ahead. As became clear afterwards, we might as well have been talking to the wall.

When the same cast assembled at Glion a month later, it soon became clear that the negotiating climate was not going to match the dazzling sunlight of a Swiss August. A private dinner with the Turkish delegation revealed Inal Batu gloomier even than when we had last talked in Ankara in June. It was evident that the new and fragile Turkish coalition government of Mesut Yilmaz, which had been formed after the military had nudged out the Erbakan/Ciller government, was in no mood to engage in a serious negotiation about Cyprus and had effectively given Denktash his head. Denktash was never a man to miss such an opportunity. From the outset of the meeting he pressed his points aggressively, in particular insisting that Cyprus's EU application must be frozen, something to which Clerides was never going to agree. Clerides himself was by this time in a very nervous state, being criticized by the Greek Cypriot press for not responding robustly enough to Denktash's rumbustious press briefings, which totally ignored Annan's plea for a press blackout while the meeting was going on. It took some private reassurance from the US and the UK to avoid a walk-out by Clerides. In the midst of all this the UN not only failed to get agreement on the piece of paper they had drafted but also made no serious attempt to salvage a follow-up process to the two meetings, apparently assuming that the atmosphere was so bad that there was no point in trying. And they did not put on the table any material relating to the core issues that might have provided a rationale for such follow-up meetings, despite considerable prompting, for the simple reason that Cordovez's team, which consisted of a single lugubrious Belgian official who knew very little about Cyprus, had not prepared anything. So there we were, back at square one. It was to take more than two years before the negotiating thread was picked up again.

European manoeuvres

The failure of the Glion meeting and the absence of any attempt to provide for a follow-up left something of a vacuum in the UN-led effort to get a settlement, a vacuum that was only partially filled by sporadic visits to the region by Cordovez. Cordovez was by now based more in Quito than New York, which meant that for most of the time he was completely removed from the scene of action, rather as his predecessor Han had been, based in Seoul. In any case the UN had decided to wait and see how Turkey's relationship with the European Union developed in the months ahead before deciding what to do next.

The European Union was faced with two tricky decisions which would have to be taken at the European Council meeting in Luxembourg in December. The first related to Cyprus. There was never any real doubt that the Luxembourg meeting would agree to the opening of accession negotiations with a number of countries and that Cyprus would figure among that number. This was not simply, as the Turks believed, because Greece was blackmailing her EU partners with the threat that they would block the whole enlargement negotiation if Cyprus was excluded from the first group, although that eventuality was a real possibility which weighed on the minds of EU governments; it was because in 1995 the European Union had, as part of the deal over concluding a customs union with Turkey, committed itself to opening accession negotiations with Cyprus six months after the conclusion of the Inter-Governmental Conference set up to agree on the institutional changes to take account of enlargement and that conference had been concluded in Amsterdam in June 1996. Much can be said in criticism of the European Union, but its track record in sticking to commitments of that sort is good. And the Turks had been unwise to doubt it. Moreover the circumstances under which the Cyprus negotiations had collapsed at Glion, with most of the blame accruing to Denktash and his failed attempt to block Cyprus's EU accession, were not likely to encourage any EU member state to reopen the commitment to Cyprus. So the question for Luxembourg was not whether to agree to open accession negotiations with Cyprus but how to do so in a way that did not preclude the Turkish Cypriots being brought into the accession negotiations and, above all, in a way that did not presume already that the Cyprus joining the European Union would be a divided rather than a united one.

The second issue facing the European Union was what to say at Luxembourg about the Turkish application. The original preference of the Luxembourg EU presidency, and perhaps also of the Commission, to say nothing at all about Turkey, was by October seen to be sheer fantasy. Not only was the Turkish government itself now, somewhat belatedly, beating on every door in Europe, but it was not realistic to think that silence on Turkey's application, when other applicants whose bids for membership had come in after Turkey's and which were even poorer and less ready economically than Turkey for membership were being given preference, would be seen as other than an outright rejection of Turkey. Unfortunately for Turkey the circumstances were far from propitious. It was only a few months since the Erbakan/Ciller government had been ousted, more by the efforts of the Turkish military than by any democratic developments in the Turkish parliament, in what was seen by most observers as a kind of 'soft' coup. Relieved though many European governments might be by the departure of a partly Islamist government, there was no way in which these events could be fitted within what were called the 'Copenhagen criteria' for EU membership. So the EU was bound to say something between 'Yes, but...' and 'Not yet'. Much thought was also being given to the calling of a European Conference, originally a French idea but now being backed with some enthusiasm by Britain too, which would bring together all the applicant countries, including those with whom accession negotiations were not going to be started straightaway, and provide for pan-European discussion of issues such as the environment, drugs, illegal immigration and security. The Conference was intended to be a kind of anteroom for EU membership, but one of its defects was that it was never very clear how easy it was going to be to use the door from the anteroom to full membership.

The Turkish lobbying campaign did not prosper. As Yilmaz wound his way round the capitals of the European Union, the traditional Turkish over-bidding, with requests for the early opening of accession negotiations, was met with increasingly negative responses. Nor did discussion of the Cyprus problem reveal any inclination by Turkey to press Denktash to work for a settlement. A heavy-handed attempt by the United States, led and orchestrated by Holbrooke, to support the campaign did not go down well. The hostility of the Luxembourg presidency was revealed in a reference by Jean-Claude Juncker, the Luxembourg prime minister, at a press conference during Yilmaz's visit there, to the 'barbarity' of Turkish police practices. By the time Yilmaz reached London on 9 December immediately before the meeting of the European Council, his usual taciturnity had lapsed into almost complete silence. He had clearly given up hope of eliciting anything useful from the EU as a whole, and the relatively positive response from Tony Blair, who made it clear that Britain believed Turkey's place was in Europe and would work to bring that about, did little to lighten the atmosphere.

The outcome at Luxembourg was a good deal better on the first issue (Cyprus) than on the second (Turkey). Having agreed to open negotiations with Cyprus in March 1998, the EU said that the objective was to benefit all communities and help to bring peace and reconciliation and to contribute positively to the search for a political solution to the Cyprus problem through the talks under the aegis of the United Nations which must continue. The European Council requested that the willingness of the government of Cyprus to include representatives of the Turkish Cypriot community in the accession-negotiating delegation be acted upon, and mandated the presidency (for the next six months the UK) and the Commission to undertake the necessary contacts to achieve this.

On Turkey a text was adopted which, while it recognized Turkey's eligibility for accession and made it clear that it would be judged on the basis of the same criteria as the other applicants, did nothing at all to advance its candidature. Moreover it linked progress to the resolution of the disputes with Greece in the Aegean over the continental shelf and air and sea boundaries, to Turkey's treatment of its minorities (a coded reference to the Kurds) and to support for the UN-led negotiations on a Cyprus settlement. The assumption was that this remarkably 'Greek' text had been smuggled in by the Luxembourg presidency, and no one had chosen to take issue with it.

The Turkish reaction was immediate and violently negative. Yilmaz publicly denounced the European Union as biased and hostile and said Turkey would freeze its relations with the Union, dealing only with the individual member states. He had no intention of accepting the invitation to the European Conference. The Turkish press took up the cry and there was some talk of withdrawing Turkey's EU application or of reneging on the provisions of the Customs Union Agreement, but none of that transpired. The only person who looked highly content was Denktash who, despite the supposed humiliation of his motherland, clearly enjoyed the opportunity to give full rein to his Euro-scepticism. He rubbished the offer to associate the Turkish Cypriots with the accession negotiations as implying their subordination to the Greek Cypriots and their acceptance of an illegal membership application.

Could this crisis in EU/Turkey relations have been avoided? Possibly, but more likely the unavoidable decision to open accession negotiations with Cyprus, with which the Turks had not yet begun to come to terms, and the difficulty of taking any concrete steps forward on Turkey's candidature, would have meant that, however bland the words the EU had chosen, there would still have been a row. The formulas employed simply rubbed salt in some very open wounds. As to Denktash the row was grist to his mill. He was only too well aware that progress on Turkey's EU candidature represented the greatest threat to his own domination of Turkey's Cyprus policy and to holding that policy to a hardline defence of the status quo. Anything that damaged Turkey's EU candidature was good news for him. And there was the added benefit that the row could help to cool the ardour to join the EU of many ordinary Turkish Cypriots and of the centre-left opposition parties in north Cyprus who were already beginning to scent a popular cause, on which Denktash was in an increasingly small minority among his people.

6

1998: Damage Limitation

For the first half of 1998 Britain held the EU presidency under the rotating arrangements then in force. My own role as the British Special Representative for Cyprus had had added to it the not very well defined job of EU Presidency Special Representative for Cyprus, which then continued for the second half of 1998 when the Austrians, who followed Britain in the presidency, asked me to carry on during their presidency. The prime minister, Tony Blair, also asked me to take on a temporary mission as his personal envoy to Turkey in an attempt to iron out some of the misunderstandings that had arisen between the EU and Turkey following the Luxembourg European Council in December 1997. None of these tasks looked likely to be easy; all were closely inter-linked and all were likely to affect the prospects for getting settlement negotiations under way.

In Cyprus itself the situation was complicated by two developments. The first was the latest in the regular quinquennial elections for the presidency in the south of the island, which was due to take place in February. The front runners were Clerides, who was standing for a second term, and George Iacovou, an independent, who had been George Vassiliou's foreign minister from 1988 to 1993 and who had the support of the Cypriot communist party (AKEL), which virtually assured him of a third of the votes even before campaigning began. Fortunately the Cyprus problem did not figure prominently in the campaign – as it had done in 1993 when Clerides had beaten Vassiliou by opposing the UN Set of Ideas – because there was so little happening and thus no obvious target at which to aim. But enough was said by both candidates about the determination of each, if elected, to proceed with the deployment of the S300 missiles to signal that that was not going to be one of the easiest of matters to deal with later in the year. In the end Clerides won, again by a whisker as he had done in 1993. One consequence of the presidential election was that it was not possible immediately to take up the sensitive issue of the offer to be made to the Turkish Cypriots of involvement in the EU accession negotiations due to begin at the end of March. The second development was that Denktash, as usual both mimicking and going one step further than Ankara, announced that he intended to have nothing further to do with anyone representing the EU, thus ruling out any contact with me for the whole of the year and also with the EU Commission.

EU/Turkey: picking up the pieces

The general view around the EU was that the Turks had over-reacted to the Luxembourg European Council but that they needed to be helped out of the hole into which they had thrown themselves. There was some awareness that the text of the conclusions of Luxembourg had been rather provocative, and a continuing feeling of guilt, everywhere except in Athens, that the EU had not been able to honour its commitment to provide financial aid under the 1995 Customs Union Agreement. All were only too well aware that there would be no progress in solving the Cyprus problem as long as Turkey was so deeply disenchanted with the international community.

The first priority, for Britain as the EU presidency in particular, was to see whether Turkey could be persuaded to change its position and attend the first summit meeting of the European Conference which was being planned for early March, before the accession negotiations began. So, having conferred with Hans van den Broek, the EU commissioner responsible for enlargement and for relations with Turkey, on 21 January, I set off the next day for Ankara. Getting to see the Turkish prime minister would not have been easy at the best of times but, armed with a message from Tony Blair and my new title as the prime minister's personal envoy for Turkey (the EU presidency part of that title being not too much emphasized for the moment), it was achieved after much bureaucratic struggle. Some flavour of the general atmosphere can be drawn from the ruling of Turkish protocol that, since I was travelling as the prime minister's personal representative, it would not be appropriate for me to see the foreign minister or anyone in the foreign ministry. One sometimes needed to remind oneself that one was visiting the capital of a NATO ally, representing the European country most favourable to Turkey's European aspirations, and was not going to Moscow at the height of the Cold War.

In the event the discussion with Yilmaz was calm and thoughtful. He was a great deal less taciturn than he had been in Downing Street in December. He explained with dignity why Turkey had been so angered by the Luxembourg conclusions. I had decided before the meeting that I would try to avoid getting from him a direct answer about attendance at the European Conference in London in March, since this was almost certain to be negative. Instead I set out the case for attending a meeting that would include all the other candidate countries, that would discuss a wide range of pan-European issues of common interest and at which Tony Blair personally very much hoped he would be present. I said we hoped he would think carefully about all this. I would return for his definitive answer in a few weeks. He agreed to reflect, without however giving even the slightest hint that his response might be positive. He continued to speak with great bitterness about the way Turkey's EU candidature was being handled. I said that much depended on Turkey itself. It was clear that, as of that moment, Turkey did not fulfil the Co-penhagen criteria and that there was therefore no early prospect of opening accession negotiations. But Turkey's friends in the EU, of whom Britain was among the closest, wanted to work in cooperation with Tur-key to help her meet the criteria. I added that my own personal experience of Britain's first two, unsuccessful, efforts to join the European Community was that the only people who were happy if the applicant reacted angrily were the people who did not want the applicant to join in the first place. What was needed was perseverance and determination. On Cyprus I concentrated on the desirability of Denktash responding posi-tively if we could get a worthwhile offer out of the Greek Cypriots of involvement in the accession negotiations, which we believed we would do, and on the case for resuming the UN-led process for a comprehensive settlement. Yilmaz lapsed into something close to his London taciturnity on a subject he clearly did not enjoy discussing.

When I returned to Ankara in mid-February, the answer about atten-dance at the European Conference was indeed negative, but it was a polite 'no' and not any longer an angry one. It was agreed that neither side would either criticize or extol Turkey's absence from the meeting, which would be treated as purely temporary. And that was how it was handled. Neither the Conference itself nor the opening of accession negotiations with Cyprus shortly afterwards led to any further deterioration of Tur-key's relationship with the EU. And some time later, when relations had much improved, Turkey slipped quietly into the meetings of the European Conference. In reality it had always been something of a forlorn hope trying to get Turkey to come to London in March. Not only were the wounds of Luxembourg too deep and too fresh to have healed, but the Turks in any case suspected that the European Conference was that alternative destination to which many Europeans who did not want Turkey in the Union were trying to direct them and which they were determined to reject. This was one of those tasks that EU presidencies have to take on, like it or not.

We were thus still left with the need to find a way to get Turkey and the EU working together again. The next opportunity for that was the regular six-monthly meeting of the EU/Turkey Association Council which was due to take place in May and which, if successful, could provide a basis for the Cardiff European Council in June to move on from Luxembourg. Together with the Commission we were beginning to think of ways in which the technical preparatory work to subsequent accession negotiations could be speeded up and intensified, thus giving Turkey an incentive to introduce the domestic reforms that would be required if she was to meet the Copenhagen criteria. And we were also thinking of ways of working around the roadblock over the customs union funds by concentrating on completely separate pre-accession aid funds which could be put to the same uses. Unfortunately, despite a major effort to put the May Association Council to good use, including a visit to Ankara by the foreign secretary Robin Cook as president of the Council, the Turks in the end declined to come to a Council meeting. Ismail Cem, at that stage a relatively new foreign minister, would have liked to have attended, but he was bludgeoned into submission by his senior officials, in front of the somewhat startled gaze of the visiting British team. As so often, the establishment in Ankara, that 'deep state' about which so much has been written, was determinedly looking at a half empty glass, not a half full one. It was not to be the last such occasion. So we had to do the best we could at the Cardiff European Council without the springboard of a successful Association Council, and in the face of a pretty negative Greek attitude, which remained committed to making life as difficult as possible for the Turkish candidature. A few small steps forwards were registered but it was not until 1999 that real progress on Turkey's relationship with the EU began to be made.

EU/Cyprus: a joint approach?

The other task handed to the British EU presidency at Luxembourg of working up arrangements for joint Greek Cypriot and Turkish Cypriot involvement in the accession negotiations due to start at the end of March was very nearly as poisoned a chalice as the one relating to the European Conference. The Greek Cypriots had made lots of positive noises about such involvement. But they had all so far been short on specificity and long on various 'red lines' that must not be crossed. From the Greek Cypriot point of view, while the desirability of Turkish Cypriot involvement was evident, the modalities were sure to touch on some of the issues most sensitive to them – the legitimacy, or rather lack of it, of the Turkish Cypriot state, their own right to aspire to EU membership whether or not the Turkish Cypriots went along, and the need to avoid Cyprus's application in any way being treated differently from that of the other applicants. Nevertheless they knew that the European Union had meant what it said at Luxembourg, and its members, especially those wary of migrating the Cyprus problem into the Union, would not be at all content if the offer they were being asked to make turned out to be couched in terms which the Turkish Cypriots would be bound to refuse. The Turkish Cypriots, on the other hand, were being offered an opportunity that their deeply Euro-sceptical leadership hardly recognized as being one at all and which involved, in their eyes, many heavy sacrifices in subordinating themselves to the Greek Cypriots and legitimizing their EU application.

As soon as the Greek Cypriot presidential elections were over I went to the island at the end of February and then returned there again a week later with van den Broek as part of a presidency/Commission duo. On neither occasion were the Greek Cypriots prepared to reveal their hand in detail, and there was little doubt they were having some difficulty in deciding how far to go. From the European side we concentrated on a number of key issues. Press leaks had suggested that the Greek Cypriots might opt for a system under which the Turkish Cypriots to be involved in the accession negotiations would be drawn from some non-governmental organization in the north such as the Turkish Cypriot Chamber of Commerce, or that the Greek Cypriots would seek some say in the choice to avoid having people who represented Denktash directly. We made it clear that neither of these approaches would be viable nor would be seen as the sort of non-prejudicial offer for which the Europeans were looking. Unpalatable though it might be to the Greek Cypriots, the choice of whom to appoint must be left to the Turkish Cypriots themselves, which of course meant that Denktash would have the final say. We also emphasized the need to demonstrate in the terms of the offer that the Turkish Cypriots were not simply being asked to join a Greek Cypriot bandwagon over whose direction they had no control, but that provision was being made for the eventualities that would certainly arise in the negotiations, when Greek Cypriot and Turkish Cypriot interests would not be identical and when special arrangements would need to be made for the north of the island, whether to take account of the huge gap in economic development between the north and the south or of the fears in the north that they would, immediately after accession, be flooded with Greek Cypriot investment and Greek Cypriot property owners and developers. Again these points produced more pensive looks than positive reactions. But they clearly registered.

As to the north, Denktash refused to have any contact with either myself or van den Broek, sheltering behind the supposed Turkish decision to that effect – by then looking a little skimpy, as I had twice seen the Turkish prime minister – and we were limited in our contacts with the Turkish Cypriots to opposition politicians and businessmen whose hopes were pinned on involvement in the EU accession negotiations but whose influence on decision taking in the north was at that stage close to zero. Van den Broek was able, however, in a bi-communal press conference to set out clearly the advantages of participation in the accession negotiations.

The next stage was to bring the Greek Cypriots to a decision point on the offer they would be ready to make and to ensure that Denktash responded to it. To try to avoid a predictably knee-jerk reaction to anything coming directly to him from the Greek Cypriots it was decided that any Greek Cypriot offer would be made to the EU presidency and, if the EU considered it was a fair and viable one, would be passed on by them to the Turkish Cypriots. Robin Cook invited Clerides and Denktash to London for separate talks on the issue. Clerides accepted the invitation but Denktash promptly declined, which meant that we would have to rely on communications with him through diplomatic channels. Clerides saw Blair on 11 March and Cook on 12 March and at the latter meeting produced the offer. This did indeed leave it entirely up to the Turkish Cypriots themselves to choose their representatives in the negotiating team, and it hinted that, where a common position could not be agreed between the two parts of the Cypriot negotiating team, the issue in question would be dealt with at a later stage in the negotiations. In our view and that of the Commission this was indeed a valid offer, which, though it was unlikely to be accepted as such by the Turkish Cypriots, provided them with some very clear opportunities for improvement if, for example, they were to respond with detailed questions on how the arrangements would actually work in practice. That was the view of the other EU members when they were consulted. In addition we had been offered by Clerides a very clear statement that agreeing to these arrangements in no sense prejudiced the position of either side in any settlement negotiations nor committed the Turkish Cypriots to accepting terms for EU member-ship that might emerge from the accession negotiations.

Perhaps of even greater value, Clerides authorized us to convey on his behalf to Denktash his readiness, in the event of Turkish Cypriots being nominated to the negotiating team and of agreement being reached on the modalities of the joint negotiating team, to discuss with the EU Commis-sion steps to make possible the resumption of preferential trade to the EU from the northern part of Cyprus and to facilitate the disbursement of EU funds there. This offer to contemplate finding a way round the European Court of Justice ruling that had brought direct preferential trade between the Turkish Cypriots and the EU to an end (always called, incorrectly, the 'embargo') and to find ways of committing EU aid to the north ad-dressed two of the most important grievances that Denktash raised against the EU. All this we conveyed to Denktash, who rejected it out of hand. He had in fact already done so in press statements even before the details of what the Greek Cypriots were prepared to offer were known – a classic case of preemptive diplomacy, but not one likely to convince European Union member states that he was trying very hard to reach common ground. A week later a Greek Cypriot delegation opened the negotiations for their accession to the European Union.

Even at the time it was evident that the Turkish Cypriots and their Turkish backers, who seemed to have no qualms about the line they were taking, were making an egregious error and missing an important oppor-tunity. The sighs of relief on the Greek Cypriot side that the offer was not taken up should have convinced them of that if nothing else did. Had the Turkish Cypriots taken up the offer, or at least explored it in detail, they would have greatly complicated the earlier stages of the accession nego-tiations, and there would have been a lot of pressure from the European side to clarify the details in ways that made it easier for the Turkish Cypriots to accept. In the longer run they would have increased their leverage over the terms of accession being negotiated, and they would have ensured that, if and when settlement negotiations did get under way, European pressure to reach agreement would have been deployed even-handedly on both sides. And if EU trade and aid had been resumed with the north that would have begun to narrow the massive prosperity gap between the two parts of the island and given both a stake in moving on to the full membership of a reunited island. All these advantages were sacrificed for what? For the ability to go on saying that the Greek Cypriot application was illegal and that the only basis on which the Turkish Cypriots would come to the table with the EU was if they were recognized as an independent state in their own right allowed to negotiate their own terms of accession. Neither of these were cards likely to take many tricks.

Holbrooke's throw

Richard Holbrooke had not played a particularly active role in the months following his appointment as President Clinton's Special Representative for Cyprus. He had stood well back from the Troutbeck and Glion talks, clearly believing that they would get nowhere. He had weighed in in EU capitals in support of getting a better deal for Turkey at the Luxembourg Summit. And he was inclined, following his experience in Bosnia and over the Imia crisis between Greece and Turkey in early 1996, to take a critical view of EU policy and to sympathize with Turkey's predicament. He had begun with some hopes of using an existing bi-communal business forum which brought together not only Greek and Turkish Cypriots but also some leading Turkish and Greek businessmen to build up momentum for a settlement and had put considerable effort into organizing meetings in Brussels in November 1997 (and later in Istanbul in December 1998). But the results of this Track 2 activity had been disappointing, in good measure because of the reluctance of some of the leading Turkish Cypriot businessmen to take any line that differed from that of Denktash and because experience showed that neither Turkish nor Greek businessmen had much influence on their respective governments' Cyprus policies. So he had been compelled to recognize that this route did not offer an alternative, nor even much of a supplement, to the more classical approach of negotiations between the two leaders.

It was to that classical approach that he now turned in May 1998 when he visited the island, accompanied by the State Department's energetic and able Special Cyprus Coordinator, Tom Miller, who was effectively his deputy. There was no evidence of elaborate preparation nor, not to my surprise, of any advance consultation with the UN or with any of the other players. The objective appeared to be to crack the main procedural stumbling blocks to a resumption of the settlement negotiations and to Turkish Cypriot involvement in the EU accession negotiations. It was to be a quick and short effort, with all substantive negotiation being left to a later stage. Holbrooke did manage to get Clerides and Denktash together and he put a major effort, including much high-pressure contact with Ankara and, to a lesser extent, with Athens, into getting them to agree, but he could not get them to agree to anything of substance. He seems even to have flirted with the concept of 'acknowledgement' by the Greek Cypriots of the Turkish Cypriots' separate status. But even that did not move Denktash. And although Holbrooke in his press conference before leaving the island took a carefully even-handed approach, within days of his return to the United States he made it clear publicly that the main obstacle to his making any progress had been Denktash, who, he said, had wanted the main fruits of the negotiation to be delivered to him in advance without ever sitting down at the negotiating table. 'The Turkish Cypriot side took a series of positions which amounted to making as preconditions for negotiations things which the negotiation was supposed to be about. Well that effectively freezes negotiations. You can't negotiate if the preconditions for a negotiation are the outcome itself.'

This episode really marked the end of Holbrooke's active personal involvement in the Cyprus problem, although he remained Presidential Special Representative for another year, during which time he was much more involved in the Kosovo crisis and also in the Congressional manoeuvring required to get confirmation of his appointment as the United States' UN ambassador. It also marked the end of attempts to kick-start the negotiation by getting Clerides and Denktash together to agree on the way ahead. From now on a more laborious and painstaking approach was adopted. I set out the case for negotiations on the core substantive issues without any preconditions about status in a speech I gave to the Turkish Cypriot Chamber of Commerce in July. Reaction from Denktash (who was still refusing to see me) was a good deal more muted than I had expected, which convinced me even more firmly that this was the way we would have to proceed. In the same speech I set out to dissipate some of the myths about EU membership that had been put about by Denktash and those Turkish Cypriots who were arguing that Cyprus must be kept out of the EU until Turkey itself was accepted and ready to join and by those Greek Cypriots who wanted to make the EU seem as unattractive as possible in the north. There was no incompatibility between continuation of the Treaty of Guarantee and joining the EU; nor would EU membership destroy the very close links between Turkey and north Cyprus even if the latter was in the EU and the former had not yet joined; nor would EU legislation simply be imposed on the north irrespective of the problems that might cause, the EU having a long tradition of finding imaginative solutions to such problems. Having cleared the speech in advance with van den Broek I felt on firm ground, and so indeed it was to prove in later years when the UN and the EU worked closely together to find just such imaginative solutions.

Denktash's muted reaction to this speech in no way, however, indicated that he was going to make the path towards negotiations without preconditions an easy one. At the end of August he launched a new initiative for a lasting solution in Cyprus, described wishfully as 'a final effort'. This initiative abandoned the hard-won Turkish Cypriot demand of the previous three decades for a federated Cyprus to replace the 1960 unitary, bi-communal state, and opted instead for a confederation, proposing:

1. A special relationship between Turkey and the 'TRNC' on the basis of agreements to be concluded.
2. A similar special relationship between Greece and the Greek Cypriot administration on the basis of symmetrical agreements to be concluded.
3. Establishment of a Cyprus Confederation between the 'TRNC' and the GCA (Greek Cypriot Administration).
4. The 1960 Guarantee System shall continue.
5. The Cyprus Confederation may, if parties agree, pursue a policy of accession to the EU, a special relationship will provide Turkey with the full rights and obligations of an EU member with regard to the Cyprus Confederation.

Quite apart from the fact that the new proposal could by no stretch of the imagination be fitted into the framework specified by the UN Security Council, it was clearly not going to be negotiable for a number of other reasons. It had more than a whiff of the partition policies of earlier years. Its basic objective was not so much the finer points of distinction between federations and confederations – the 1992 Set of Ideas had been named a federation but in reality it included a number of confederal concepts – but rather to achieve from the outset Denktash's basic demand that the TRNC as such be recognized as a sovereign and equal state. The only new point with some positive implications was the fifth one, which registered the first occasion when the Turkish Cypriots (and by implication the Turks) accepted the possibility that north Cyprus might be part of the EU before Turkey was. And while the initiative as such was dead on arrival, the Turks were later to regret allowing Denktash to nail his (and their) colours to the confederation mast, thus greatly complicating the conduct of the settlement negotiations when they eventually got under way.

The missiles diverted

By the autumn of 1998 the question of the S300 missiles was again becoming acute and it was clear that their deployment to the island could not be much longer fudged or delayed. For one thing the missiles themselves were ready for shipment and the Russians were agitating for payment; for another, Clerides had been re-elected in February on a platform of commitment to deployment, and his coalition partners, led by Vasos Lyssarides, had made it clear that they would only remain in the government if the missiles were deployed. The press was contributing to a noticeable increase in tension, with speculation in the Turkish press that action, even the use of force, might be taken to prevent their delivery from Russia. The pressure on Clerides from the US, the UK and the other Europeans to cancel or suspend deployment mounted steadily and began to have some effect. Clerides began to try out half-and-half approaches. Perhaps the missiles could be shipped to Cyprus but kept in hangars and not deployed. It was pointed out that this would not help much and would create a situation whereby any subsequent decision to deploy during a time of crisis would risk being seen by the Turks as a clear step towards actual hostilities. In addition to messages from the US president and the UK prime minister, Wolfgang Schüssel, the Austrian foreign minister, weighed in in his capacity as president of the EU Council. He explained very frankly that the EU and its member states would simply not understand it if Clerides proceeded with deployment when accession negotiations were under way and efforts were being made to achieve a Cyprus settlement before accession. The implications of this last message were very clear and they were not missed either in Nicosia or in Athens.

At this stage the Greek government reached a clear conclusion that they did not want to run the risk of a full-scale Greek–Turkish confrontation, which could well occur if deployment of the missiles went ahead. They began to discuss with the Greek Cypriots the possibility of diverting the missiles to Crete and possibly replacing them with shorter-range missiles already in the Greek inventory. This alternative plan rapidly took shape during December 1998. While the Turks continued to grumble a good deal, it became clear that the switch to Crete (which was considerably further from the Turkish mainland than Cyprus and put Turkish airbases out of range) and the fact that the missiles would no longer be under Greek Cypriot control, made a substantial difference and that diversion in this way would in fact mark the end of the crisis. There remained serious political problems for Clerides whose U-turn had provoked outrage in the press and the resignation of several ministers. Clerides let it be known at this stage that it was essential for him to be able to say that diversion of the missiles had been decided in order to give a new opportunity for negotiations for a settlement. In response to this appeal the US president and the British prime minister issued statements committing themselves to a 'major, sustained effort towards securing a just, comprehensive and lasting settlement in Cyprus' and to give 'complete and wholehearted backing to this effort'. In this way the scene was set for 1999. But everything remained to be done. And there was as yet no Turkish or Turkish Cypriot commitment to this objective.

7

1999: Getting the Show on the Road Again

With the diversion of the S300 missiles to Crete and a slow thaw beginning in the EU/Turkey relationship, the strength of some of the extraneous factors impeding a Cyprus settlement negotiation was beginning to abate. But the barometer was certainly not set fair. For one thing the mood in Cyprus itself remained distinctly sour. On the Greek Cypriot side there was considerable bitterness over the whole missile episode, seen as yet another occasion when Cyprus was manoeuvred around like a pawn by external forces over which it had no control. The possibility that acquiring the missiles could have been an expensive mistake, providing not increased security but instead more tension and risk, was hardly contemplated by anyone on any part of the political spectrum. On the other side of the island Denktash continued his boycott of any contact with the EU. So, when I visited the island in late January for an annual Heads of Mission conference with the British ambassadors from Ankara and Athens and the British high commissioner in Nicosia, I ran into a steady drizzle of Cypriot negativism. Arriving at Larnaca Airport I met by chance the Greek deputy foreign minister, Kranidiotis, on his way out. He warned me that Clerides was feeling bruised and that he himself had just been given an extremely rough ride by the Greek Cypriot press, an unusual occurrence for a Greek minister and one of Cypriot origin. This warning was soon borne out when a passing answer I gave the press about the possible relevance of the Swiss constitution to arrangements for a reunited Cyprus was blown up out of all proportion and led to Clerides refusing to see me, as had earlier been agreed. The same day Denktash declined to pay any attention to the fact that I no longer (with the end of the Austrian EU presidency and the advent of the German one) had any EU function, and also refused to see me. So any idea that carrying out the prime minister's and President Clinton's recent commitments to launch a new drive for a settlement – the same drive that Clerides had begged for when diverting the S300s – would be simple or easy was rapidly dissipated.

The question of how to proceed with these commitments had in fact already been discussed between the UK, the Americans and the UN. Miller, who by now was effectively in charge of day-to-day Cyprus policy in Washington, had come to London early in January, as had Dame Ann Hercus, the New Zealander who was running the UNFICYP operation on the island. We and the Americans were clear that we would have to give a lead in the next phase. It was evident that the Cypriots would not do so. There was no sign of help from the two motherlands, and the UN seemed bereft of ideas and unwilling to put in a real effort until they could see that the door was at least partly ajar. We were equally clear that failure to follow up on the US/UK commitments was a poor option in the medium and longer term. The Greek Cypriot feeling of alienation would increase, as would the risk of further destabilizing arms purchases. And the steady progress of Cyprus's EU accession negotiations brought closer a possible confrontation with Turkey over accession by a divided island. We also agreed that this time we should be aiming not simply at a Clerides/Denktash one-off meeting with an uncertain follow-up, but rather at a structured process that would involve the two sides, under UN aegis, becoming involved in serious negotiations on the core issues. Miller floated the idea of using the annual G8 Summit, due in June, as a launch pad for such a process and from then on the US and the UK, as two of the participants, began to work systematically to achieve that.

Three earthquakes: a transformation of Greek–Turkish relations

The first of the three 1999 earthquakes was not of the seismic variety, although the latter two were. Nor did any of them have much to do with Cyprus, although their indirect impact on the Cyprus problem was considerable.

The first earthquake occurred in February when Abdullah Ocalan, the fugitive leader of the Kurdish PKK terrorist movement was, following his capture in Kenya and return to Turkey, found to have been being sheltered in the Greek embassy in Nairobi and to have travelled on the passport of a Greek Cypriot journalist. This led, not unnaturally, to a major diplomatic row between Greece and Turkey and then to the resignation of Greek foreign minister Pangalos and a number of the other Greek ministers concerned and finally to Pangalos's replacement as foreign minister by George Papandreou, the son of Andreas Papandreou, Simitis's predecessor as prime minister. The policy implications of Papandreou's appointment were not immediately apparent. The turbulence caused in Greek–Turkish relations by the Ocalan affair took some time to subside. But by the spring, at least a change of style was becoming visible. In place of the exchanges of angry rhetoric by press communiqué, which had characterized relations between Greece and Turkey for a number of years, Papandreou and his Turkish opposite number, Ismail Cem, began to pick up the telephone to each other and to reduce the scratchiness in the relationship. Then, by the summer, they began to give thought to ways of talking about some of the less sensitive bilateral topics – tourism, trade, investment and culture. It gradually became clear that Papandreou had a different strategic view of Greece's relationship with Turkey from that of his predecessor and that this view was to some extent shared by Cem. For Papandreou, bad relations with Turkey damaged Greece, necessitating a high rate of defence spending and sacrificing many commercial and economic opportunities in Turkey's large and rapidly growing market. Moreover he saw that the alienation of Turkey from the EU was contrary to Greece's interest, since it was liable in the long run to destabilize Turkey and leave Greece with an erratic, unpredictable but still powerful neighbour.

At this point nature took a hand. In August a massive earthquake struck a heavily populated region of Turkey on the Sea of Marmara. There was considerable loss of life and huge material damage with which the Turkish government's emergency services were ill equipped to deal. Papandreou immediately helped to organize a high-profile Greek response in the form of emergency aid and relief teams, which in turn triggered a major outpouring of popular sentiment in both countries, contrasting sharply with the habitually chauvinistic tone of media comment about each other. In September a much smaller earthquake occurred on the outskirts of Athens, and Turkey reciprocated. The outcome, in political terms, of all this was to enable the two ministers and their respective governments to pursue a policy of rapprochement, towards which they had already been edging cautiously, with much more confidence and with less likelihood that it would be de-railed by a nationalist backlash on either or both sides as had so often occurred in the past. Not only were they able to negotiate a number of agreements and understandings on some of the less sensitive aspects of their mutual relations, but Greek policy towards Turkey in Brussels began to change. The provision of EU financial assistance for dealing with the consequences of the earthquake went ahead with no difficulty and it became clear that there would no longer be problems about Greece agreeing to the EU providing substantial sums of money to programmes designed to promote Turkey's EU candidature.

So, while the vexed issue of the EU's unimplemented financial commitment to Turkey at the time the Customs Union Agreement was concluded was never in fact resolved, having become inextricably linked in Greek domestic politics with the issue of possible Turkish claims to various uninhabited rocks and islets off the Aegean coast of Turkey, it gradually ceased to signify more than a formal grievance, as substantial EU financial commitments began to be made in the context of helping Turkey prepare for EU accession. Indeed Greece's whole attitude towards Turkey's candidature was transformed. From being the member state that had invariably thrown grit into any discussion of the subject and thus provided an excuse for other member states to shelter behind, Greece became one of the foremost protagonists within the EU of eventual Turkish membership.

None of this directly related to Cyprus but it did have important implications for the handling of the Cyprus problem. Few issues were as difficult to discuss in each of the capitals concerned as the inter-relationship between three crucial inter-locking issues – the Greek–Turkish relationship, the Cyprus problem and the EU/Turkey and EU/Cyprus accession prospects – but none was more important to understand. The word 'linkage' was taboo in each capital, although for entirely different reasons. In Ankara it was unacceptable because it implied that Turkish Cypriot vital interests and those of Turkey in Cyprus might be sacrificed on the altar of Turkey's EU candidature and of better relations with Greece; in Athens it implied that Greece was weakening in the national cause of supporting the Greek Cypriots and might be allowing Cyprus's EU candidature to become dependent on other factors; with the Greek Cypriots it implied that the Cyprus problem might be left unresolved while Greece and Turkey made up and Turkey moved towards the European Union; with the Turkish Cypriots it implied that they might lose control of Turkey's Cyprus policy and be sacrificed as a pawn in wider negotiations. Those sensitivities meant that the one thing everyone agreed about, as did the main external players, was that it made no sense at all to aim for a single, grand negotiation designed to find solutions to all three sets of issues at the same time – an approach known as 'one ball of wax', so called, it was said, by Henry Kissinger who had once flirted with the idea. But that negative consensus did not in any way dispose of the fact that the issues genuinely were inter-related and that they impacted on each other, either positively or negatively. So on the diplomatic circuit it was readily agreed not to use the word 'linkage', but also to recognize that these inter-relationships were real and needed to be understood and explored.

The immediate consequences of the Greek–Turkish rapprochement for the Cyprus problem were entirely positive but they were modest. The positive implications for the EU/Turkey relationship meant that that key part of any Cyprus equation began to look more promising and thus motivate the Turks to think a little more positively about Cyprus. But the effects should not be exaggerated and their limits were already visible. The Turks seemed no more willing than they had ever been to discuss Cyprus directly with the Greeks, and numerous attempts by Papandreou to get into a serious discussion of the core Cyprus issues with Cem were fended off. The Greeks on their side were soon brought up against the reality that too rapid progress on bilateral issues would put strain on their important relationship with the Greek Cypriots and give rise to criticism that Cyprus was being forgotten. And both Greeks and Turks were well aware that decisions important to both of them were likely to be taken at the meeting of the European Council in Helsinki in December 1999 and that the balance there between progress in the EU's relationships with Cyprus and with Turkey would raise sensitive issues and could easily go wrong, with damaging implications also for their bilateral rapprochement.

Laying the foundations for a negotiation: the G8 Summit

The tactical approach for which the US and Britain had opted, of starting with the G8 Summit scheduled for June in Bonn, proved to be the right one. The preparations of G8 Summits by the personal representatives of their heads of state and government (known as 'Sherpas') were much more discreet and therefore less exposed to frenzied lobbying by the parties and their motherlands than any negotiation of a resolution at the Security Council in New York could ever be. None of the G8 participants had an axe to grind over Cyprus, with the possible exception of Russia, which habitually took a straight Greek Cypriot brief for any UN discussions. But on this occasion, perhaps because their usual 'Cyprus' experts were less directly involved, there was not too much difficulty over reaching an agreed text. The objectives that the Americans and the British were pursuing required us to steer a narrow path between two approaches, neither of which would get anywhere at the negotiating table. The first of these, favoured by the Greeks and Greek Cypriots, would have involved explicitly reaffirming every Security Council pronouncement on the Cyprus problem, going back to the 1960s, and tying the secretary-general's hands in respect of the conduct of any future negotiations to the precise wording of these sacred texts. The alternative approach, favoured by the Turks and Turkish Cypriots, would have involved jettisoning everything which had emerged from the previous UN processes and negotiations and leaving Denktash free to pursue his own agenda of recognition of the TRNC and confederation. We also needed a text that was sufficiently firm and clear to propel the UN back into an active negotiating process and to give them a reasonable basis from which to begin. The text finally agreed by the heads of state and government in Bonn was as follows:

> The Cyprus Problem has gone unresolved for too long. Resolution of this problem would not only benefit all the people of Cyprus, but would also have a positive impact on peace and stability in the region.

> Both parties to the dispute have legitimate concerns that can and must be addressed. The members of the G8 are convinced that only comprehensive negotiations covering all relevant issues can do this.

> The members of the G8, therefore, urge the UN Secretary-General in accordance with relevant UN Security Council resolutions to invite the leaders of the two parties to negotiations in autumn 1999. They call upon the two leaders to give their full support to such a comprehensive negotiation, under the auspices of the UN Secretary-General.

> In accepting this invitation, the two parties/leaders should commit themselves to the following principles:

> - No preconditions;
> - All issues on the table;
> - Commitment in good faith to continue to negotiate until a settlement is reached;
> - Full consideration of relevant UN resolutions and treaties.

> The members of the G8 undertake to give their full and sustained backing to the negotiating process and hope that it will prove possible for its outcome to be reported to the meetings of Heads of State and Government at the OSCE Summit this November.

Laying the foundations for a negotiation: Security Council Resolution 1250

The G8 text achieved precisely the objectives that had been set for it. But in itself it was insufficient, since none of the parties had accepted it and the G8 had no decision-making authority. The need for this led us within ten days to the Security Council in New York where one of the bi-annual renewals of the mandate of the UN's peacekeeping force in Cyprus (UNFICYP) was due to take place before the end of June. The negotiations there were inevitably less straightforward than those in the G8. The Greek Cypriots in particular were deeply unhappy about the wording of the G8 text and its avoidance of the precise parameters of previous UN documents. And the Turks and Turkish Cypriots, who might have been expected to welcome the quite unusual degree of flexibility in the G8 text, instead, as usual, concentrated on the parts they did not like, in particular the reference to no preconditions and the time factor introduced for the first time of a report back to the Summit meeting of the Organization for Security and Cooperation in Europe which Turkey would be chairing in November in Istanbul. A further, New York, complication was the practice which had grown up over the years of mixing up in the same resolution elements relating to the UN secretary-general's Good Offices Mission to negotiate a comprehensive settlement and those more properly belonging to the renewal of the peacekeeping mission. Any such confusion on this occasion would inevitably lead to a loss of the flexibility in the G8 text and a complication in the secretary-general's task of thereafter getting the parties to the negotiating table. After a lengthy diplomatic tussle of a classical kind in New York, the G8 text, and in particular its four clear guidelines for the future negotiations, was preserved intact and relatively uncluttered in Security Council Resolution 1250. In parallel the preamble of the renewal of the peacekeeping mandate in Security Council Resolution 1251 was expanded to accommodate much of the subject matter from earlier Security Council resolutions. The text of Security Council Resolution 1250, which was adopted unanimously, was as follows:

The Security Council,

Reaffirming all its earlier resolutions on Cyprus, particularly resolution 1218 (1998) of 22 December 1998,

Reiterating its grave concern at the lack of progress towards an overall political settlement on Cyprus,

Appreciating the statement of the Heads of State and Government of Canada, France, Germany, Italy, Japan, the Russian Federation, the United Kingdom of Great Britain and Northern Ireland and the United States of America on 20 June 1999 (S/1999/711, annex) calling for comprehensive negotiations in the autumn of 1999 under the auspices of the Secretary-General,

1. Expresses its appreciation for the report of the Secretary-General of 22 June 1999 (S/1999/707) on his mission of Good Offices in Cyprus;
2. Stresses its full support for the Secretary-General's mission of Good Offices as decided by the Security Council and, in this context, for the efforts of the Secretary-General and his Special Representative;
3. Reiterates its endorsement of the initiative of the Secretary-General announced on 30 September 1998, within the framework of his mission of Good Offices, with the goal of reducing tensions and promoting progress towards a just and lasting settlement in Cyprus;
4. Notes that the discussions between the Secretary-General's Special Representative and the two sides are continuing, and urges both sides to participate constructively;
5. Expresses the view that both sides have legitimate concerns that should be addressed through comprehensive negotiations covering all relevant issues;
6. Requests the Secretary-General, in accordance with the relevant United Nations Security Council resolutions, to invite the leaders of the two sides to negotiations in the autumn of 1999;
7. Calls upon the two leaders, in this context, to give their full support to such a comprehensive negotiation, under the auspices of the Secretary-General, and to commit themselves to the following principles:
• No preconditions;
• All issues on the table;
• Commitment in good faith to continue to negotiate until a settlement is reached;
• Full consideration of relevant United Nations resolutions and treaties;
8. Requests the two sides on Cyprus, including military authorities on both sides, to work constructively with the Secretary-General and his Special Representative to create a positive climate on the island that will pave the way for negotiations in the autumn of 1999;

9. Also requests the Secretary-General to keep the Security Council informed of progress towards the implementation of this resolution and to submit a report to the Council by 1 December 1999;

10. Decides to remain actively seized of the matter.

This resolution remained from beginning to end the basis for the negotiations over the next three and a half years. The secretary-general and his special adviser reported from time to time orally to the Security Council and received from it, through carefully crafted declarations to the press, the support and encouragement that they needed to proceed with the negotiations. But at no stage did Kofi Annan report in writing to the Council until after the breakdown of the negotiations in March 2003, and there was therefore no requirement for a new resolution on the Good Offices Mission which might have superseded, or muddied the clarity of, Resolution 1250. Despite one or two fraught moments it also proved possible to keep the negotiations entirely separate from the unavoidable bi-annual negotiations on resolutions to prolong the mandate of UNFICYP.

Laying the foundations for a negotiation: changes in the network

As progress began laboriously to be made towards a resumption of negotiations, it became steadily clearer that the main UN negotiator could not be, as Cordovez was, based in Ecuador, and only infrequently visiting New York and the region. It was inevitably going to become a full-time job. Nor could it be done by a single diplomatic troubleshooter, without any back-up beyond one desk officer in the UN Secretariat. So, in the late spring of 1999, Annan asked Cordovez to step down and began what turned out to be a rather lengthy search for a replacement. His first choice was Ann Hercus who had been in charge of the UNFICYP operations on the island for more than a year and had proved herself energetic and competent in that post and, of course, had thereby acquired a good deal of knowledge of the subject matter and the main players. Her appointment caused no problems with Clerides and Denktash. But within a couple of weeks of taking over she resigned for personal, family reasons. Annan's next candidate was Jan Egeland, a Norwegian with considerable experience of international negotiation as part of the team that had worked on the Oslo Arab–Israel peace process and who had also participated in Holbrooke's Track 2 activities, trying to bring together Greek Cypriot and Turkish Cypriot businessmen. Whether because of this last involvement – Denktash was deeply irritated by Track 2 meetings, which he saw as a challenge to his own iron grip on the Turkish Cypriot negotiating position – or simply because Egeland was a European, albeit one from a country which was not a member of the European Union, Denktash vetoed the new appointment. In what was to prove a third time very lucky indeed, Annan chose Alvaro de Soto, a Peruvian diplomat and former close adviser to UN secretaries-general Pérez de Cuéllar and Boutros-Ghali and currently assistant secretary-general in the UN's Department of Political Affairs. This appointment caused no problem to the parties.

Although de Soto had only been very slightly involved with Cyprus in his previous UN Secretariat posts, he did, inevitably, know a good deal about a task that had been on the UN's plate for almost longer than any other. Moreover, as the main negotiator in the El Salvador peace process, he had acquired experience in multi-faceted and complexly multicultural settlement negotiations, which, for all the many differences between El Salvador and Cyprus, was to stand him in good stead during the next few years. Among his many qualities, imperturbability and precision were outstanding.

With the arrival of de Soto on the scene in the autumn of 1999 a number of aspects of the negotiating pattern changed for the better. Annan had told me at the time he appointed de Soto that he was aware of the need for the UN to cooperate as closely as possible with the US and the UK in the forthcoming negotiations, recognizing the weakness of the UN's earlier approach at Troutbeck and Glion, but he also asked most particularly that we respect the UN's independence and impartiality and that we accept at every stage that the UN was in the lead. I replied that, as far as the UK was concerned, I could give him an absolute commitment on these points; that was exactly how we saw any negotiation with a chance of success developing. He and de Soto could count on our full support and could be sure we would not pursue a national agenda or take solo initiatives.

As soon as de Soto had picked up the threads, he began to assemble a small but effective negotiating team, with an experienced and competent legal adviser, Didier Pfirter, on secondment from the Swiss foreign ministry, a young Australian, Robert Dann, as his jack of all trades, and experts on property issues and peacekeeping. Thus, as the negotiations wore on, de Soto had a competent in-house capacity to work on every aspect of the core issues, from map making to constitution drafting. If there was one gap, it was in EU expertise but that proved remediable thanks to the increasing cooperation with the EU Commission. It was also possible to come to a much clearer understanding of the respective roles on the one hand of the UN and on the other of the US, the UK and other European partners. Up till then every discussion with the UN had been bedevilled by UN requests for others, the US in particular, to do what was described as the 'heavy lifting' in Ankara, it being suggested that in the past this had been lacking and that the UN had been left high and dry. The US and UK response had been that in order to do heavy lifting, one had to have something to lift, and that required the UN to put together the main elements of a settlement which we and others could then try to get all concerned, including Turkey, to accept. Without these elements there would be no leverage. In any case, the clear public commitment of Clinton and Blair showed that our two governments did intend to put their backs into it.

In parallel with the changes in the UN team, there was a complete change also in the US team. Holbrooke's appointment as the United States' UN ambassador having finally received Senate confirmation, he bowed out. And Miller left to become US ambassador to Bosnia and Herzegovina in Sarajevo. In their places were appointed Ambassador Alfred Moses as the President's Special Representative and Ambassador Thomas Weston as Special Cyprus Coordinator. Moses had worked as a legal counsel in the White House in previous Democrat administrations and, more recently, had been ambassador to Romania. What he lacked in Cyprus expertise, he made up for in forcefulness and determination, and he worked effectively full time, although that was not his remit. Weston brought a wealth of diplomatic experience and in particular a knowledge of the European Union and how it worked, a commodity not always in ready supply in the State Department. With the installation of this team died any question of there being a separate US track to the negotiations. Although it took the regional players, particularly the Turks, a long time to grasp and to accept that point, it did immeasurably strengthen the UN's negotiating hand.

Also the role of the EU in any Cyprus settlement negotiations began to come into much sharper focus. There too there had been significant changes in personnel. Javier Solana had been appointed to the newly created post of High Representative for the Common Foreign and Security Policy, and, as a former secretary-general of NATO, he arrived with considerable knowledge of Greek–Turkish relations. At the EU Commission, following the resignation of the Santer Commission and the installation of Romano Prodi, Gunther Verheugen, formerly the German minister for Europe, took over responsibility for the enlargement negotiations. He was well aware from the outset that among the difficult political obstacles to the successful conclusion of those negotiations, the Cyprus problem, with all its inter-relationships with other problems, was going to be one of the trickiest to handle. It had always been difficult, and it remained so, to distinguish between, on the one hand, the European Union as a major diplomatic player in what was after all an issue with substantial foreign policy implications on its doorstep in the Eastern Mediterranean region, and, on the other, the European Union which both Cyprus, reunited or not, and Turkey were seeking to join and with which the whole paraphernalia of accession negotiations was either under way or in prospect. And yet it was important to distinguish these two roles. Back in 1996, the former was predominant but not particularly effective; as time passed the second role became the predominant one. At every stage it was essential to ensure that the two roles were played in harmony and did not cut across each other. Given the proclivity of international organizations, or even of different parts of the same international organization, to get at cross purposes and indulge in turf fighting, it was little short of the miraculous, and greatly to the credit of all concerned, that that did not occur over Cyprus.

The European Union's role as a diplomatic player was significant but not easy to articulate. This was not just because of the usual dichotomy between the as yet nascent Common Foreign and Security Policy and the policies of the principal member states, although that did play a relatively modest part. For member states such as France and Germany, their relationship with Turkey and their distinctly ambivalent attitude towards its possible accession to the EU were of infinitely greater importance than any Cyprus considerations; for them Cyprus was essentially a side-show and they were not prepared to allow the Cyprus tail to wag the EU/Turkey dog. For the UK, Cyprus itself mattered a good deal both for historical reasons and the continuing presence of the Sovereign Base Areas in the island; we did not have the same hang-ups about Turkish membership, indeed firmly supported it.

But beyond these differences of emphasis and interest between member states, there was a more pervasive problem. With Greece as a member state, the EU could not either be, or be seen to be, impartial and evenhanded on an issue that involved a fundamental conflict of interests between Greece and Turkey. So, hard as it tried to give the UN strong diplomatic support in the settlement negotiations, the effect was always less impressive than one would have hoped. The European Union's other role, as potential bride of all the main regional players in an economic and political union, moved from the extremely theoretical to the highly practical and operational as both sets of negotiations – those for EU accession and those for a Cyprus settlement – gradually came to a head. With Denktash interested only in using the EU as a surrogate for his sovereignty and status objectives and insisting therefore that any negotiation of Turkish Cypriot terms of accession could only be conducted separately with him as if the TRNC was an independent European state, it became clear that there was no classical way of handling the various problems posed for northern Cyprus by EU accession. And it also became clear that while some of these problems, such as the very considerable gap in terms of prosperity and economic development between the north and south of the island, could be handled through existing EU instruments and policies, the same could not be said for some of the issues at the heart of the settlement negotiations, where solutions could only be reconcilable with the *acquis communautaire* if considerable imagination and flexibility were displayed, involving possibly even some derogations, that is to say departures, from those sacred texts. For the EU to play this second role effectively, the very closest cooperation between the Commission and the UN would be required, and it was towards achieving this that de Soto and Verheugen and their staff, with my own pretty active encouragement, now began to set themselves.

Squaring the circle of settlement negotiations

With the G8 text, and its endorsement in Resolution 1250, the foundations for a settlement negotiation were well laid, but the consent of all the parties was still not achieved. The Greek government was supportive, and the Greek Cypriots were likely to agree, although they were sure to look at any terms of reference put forward by Annan with a beady eye, given their qualms about the amount of flexibility built in to the Security Council resolution. Denktash could be expected to be difficult, to try to advance his own recognition agenda and also to try to avoid the UN getting too expansive a mandate and playing too proactive a role in any negotiations that ensued. But in the last resort and despite his very strong influence over those who took decisions on Cyprus policy in Ankara, he was not a free agent. The decision would be taken in Ankara, and the new Turkish government of Bulent Ecevit was playing hard to catch, indeed did not very much want to be caught. This government, which had emerged from the general election at the beginning of the year, was somewhat less precarious than the ones that had preceded it and had a substantial majority in parliament. However, it was a coalition of three parties that had little in common and its sole raison d'être was to keep out the Islamic parties who had been briefly let into government by Ciller. Ecevit's party, the DSP, which had done unexpectedly well in the elections following the kudos derived from the capture of Ocalan, was a left-wing nationalist party, a combination not often found elsewhere in Europe, with a leader who believed the Cyprus problem had been settled by him in 1974 with the Turkish military operation, but with a foreign minister in Ismail Cem who was a liberal internationalist. The second biggest party, the MHP, was a new ultra-nationalist party which was certainly not going to allow itself to be out-flanked on the right over Cyprus. The third coalition party, Yilmaz's ANAP, had emerged much weakened from the elections, so its policy of giving absolute priority to EU membership was not strongly represented in the counsels of government. It was this somewhat unpromising combination, as far as Cyprus was concerned, that the US set about turning around.

The first move by the US was to invite Ecevit on an official visit to Washington, a rite of passage that meant as much, if not more, to an incoming Turkish prime minister as it did to his other European colleagues. While the talks in Washington in late September were by no means all about Cyprus, Clinton made it very clear that the US wanted settlement negotiations to begin, and, when he got a predictably negative reaction, that he was not prepared to take no for an answer. In the weeks following the visit to Washington, the US made much use of Clinton's possible attendance at the approaching OSCE Summit in Istanbul in November and the possibility, to which the Turks attached the greatest importance, of a bilateral visit to Turkey by Clinton immediately before it. The Americans let it be understood that both depended to a considerable extent on the Turks agreeing beforehand to terms of reference for UN-led Cyprus negotiations. The US president, it was said, would not want to be rejected again over Cyprus and it was surely not in Turkey's interest that any talks in November should be dominated by unresolved issues on Cyprus.

Gradually the pressure began to work and by the end of October there were signs of a many-sided negotiation on those terms of reference getting under way. The denouement, which could hardly have taken place under more confused circumstances, was reached just as the US president boarded his plane for the bilateral visit to Turkey and the subsequent OSCE Summit. Annan was on an official visit to Japan – in Tokyo and Kyoto – while de Soto was in New York. Moses was in Washington. Clerides and Kasoulides were in South Africa for the Commonwealth Heads of Government Meeting, divided between Durban and George (the weekend retreat of heads of government). The British prime minister and foreign secretary were also in South Africa for the same purpose and were in frequent touch there with the Greek Cypriots. Denktash was in Cyprus, but most of the contacts with him passed through the Turkish government. I was in London. All communication was by telephone over open lines; the difference in time zones of the various participants did not make life any easier. The outcome, announced late on 13 November, was a statement by Annan:

> I have spoken to President Clerides and he has agreed to start proximity talks in New York on 3 December in order to prepare the ground for meaningful negotiations leading to a comprehensive settlement of the Cyprus Problem. I have also spoken to Mr Denktash who has also agreed and I will welcome the parties to New York on 3 December.

This somewhat meagre result, following a bit of traditional scrapping between the UN, Denktash and Clerides over the way the two Cypriot leaders were referred to (under UN practice the two leaders were normally referred to as the leaders of their two communities, not as president or not president), became the basis for the talks that followed.

The Greek Cypriots had taken a good deal of persuading to accept this text, which was not at all what they would have chosen, and its reception in their domestic press was stormy. I was invited at short notice to Zurich, where Clerides and Kasoulides were stopping on their way from the Commonwealth Heads of Government Meeting in South Africa to the OSCE Summit in Istanbul, and found them decidedly nervous. I did my best to reassure them that, for all its inadequacies, the text was a lot better than nothing. None of the participants, Annan in particular, intended to allow the talks to focus exclusively on procedure, nor did they intend to let Denktash use it simply to advance his own agenda. The talks would be about the core issues for a settlement.

In reality Denktash and the Turks had gained a number of procedural points, none of which were of great value as time went on. They had refused to allow any mention of Resolution 1250 with its four guidelines and a proactive role for the secretary-general, but nothing they could do could prevent Annan operating on that basis, as he was bound to do. They had declined to permit face-to-face talks since Clerides would not agree to deal with Denktash as president of the TRNC and they had therefore insisted that the talks should be in a proximity format. In the event it was by no means clear that this was to their advantage, since Denktash was a forceful advocate of his own position and lost the opportunity to address anyone other than Annan and de Soto. The distinction between talks to 'prepare the ground' for a subsequent phase of 'meaningful negotiations' could have been more serious. It was part of Denktash's unvarying tactical approach to ensure that there was always at least one further decision-making process which he could veto between the present time and the moment when he (and the Turks) would have to say yes or no to the substance of a settlement. In practice the distinction proved impossible to sustain and ceased to be of any practical significance. But the least that could be said was that while the Turks had persuaded Denktash to come to the water, he and they were as yet showing no signs of wanting to drink it.

The other shoe drops: EU/Turkey

The Turkish general election and the subsequent formation of a coalition government with a large majority in the National Assembly might not have done much for the prospects of a Cyprus settlement, but it transformed the relationship with the EU. The new government was firmly committed to pursuing Turkey's EU application – Ecevit's DSP and Yilmaz's ANAP enthusiastically so, Bahceli's MHP much less so. Within days of Ecevit taking over as the head of the new government he had written formally to Chancellor Gerhard Schroeder in his capacity as president of the European Council asking the EU to take forward Turkey's application and making it clear that Turkey accepted that accession negotiations could not actually start until they had been deemed to have fulfilled the political dimensions of the Copenhagen criteria. This was an important clarification. Up till then successive Turkish governments had either maintained that they already met the Copenhagen criteria (which was evidently not the case) or that the criteria could be met during the no doubt lengthy accession negotiations (which the EU was never going to concede, having long before decided that they were a precondition for the major step of opening accession negotiations, which necessarily required the country being able to fulfil the basic political requirements for membership) or that they were just a discriminatory sham, an excuse to enable the EU to say no to Turkey. The Ecevit/Schroeder letter meant the two parties were at last on the same wavelength and at least implied that the new Turkish government was ready to introduce domestic legislation to bring Turkey into conformity with the Copenhagen criteria. The letter, arriving as it did just before the Cologne European Council, did not, however, immediately unlock the door; the Greek government, which had not yet completed the reassessment of its attitude towards Turkey's EU application which followed Papandreou's taking over as foreign minister, asked for more time to consider and this was agreed. But, as earthquake diplomacy kicked in and Greek–Turkish relations improved markedly, it became clear that important decisions about Turkey's EU application would be made at the Helsinki European Council in December and that Greece would not be the main obstacle to their being taken.

There did, however, remain one specifically Greek (or rather Greek and Greek Cypriot) problem in the run-up to Helsinki, which was made more acute by the progress being made in parallel to get Cyprus settlement negotiations under way again. This was the need, as the Greeks and Greek Cypriots saw it, to temper any EU support for Annan's efforts with a clear statement that a Cyprus political settlement was not an absolute precondition for Cyprus joining the EU. While the other member states had no intention of allowing Denktash and the Turks to frustrate Cyprus's EU application by filibustering the settlement talks, they equally did not want to give the Greek Cypriots carte blanche in their accession negotiations and had an extremely strong preference for a reunited rather than a divided Cyprus joining. The conundrum of how to capture these different priorities in a few short sentences preoccupied the member states right up to and at the Helsinki meeting, with much hyperactive Greek diplomacy and the peddling by them of a number of unacceptable formulae. In the end the formula agreed on 10 December was as follows:

> 9(a) The European Council welcomes the launch of the talks aiming at a comprehensive settlement of the Cyprus Problem on 3 December in New York and expresses its strong support for the UN Secretary-General's efforts to bring the process to a successful conclusion.

> (b) The European Council underlines that a political settlement will facilitate the accession of Cyprus to the European Union. If no settlement has been reached by the completion of the accession negotiations, the

Council's decision on accession will be made without the above being a precondition. In this the Council will take account of all relevant factors.

This masterpiece of constructive ambiguity was regarded by the Turks and Turkish Cypriots as giving the Greek Cypriots far too clear a commitment over accession, and indeed the initial Greek Cypriot reaction was one of euphoria, but for the Greek Cypriots the sting in the tail (the last sentence was always referred to as 'the Helsinki tail' in the frequent denunciations by the Greek Cypriot press) was all too obvious.

As to the handling of the Turkish application itself, this too gave rise to plenty of feverish intra-EU negotiation, not least because of the need to move away from the offending conclusions of the 1997 Luxembourg European Council without actually saying so. But no major issues of principle were at stake, because the position being set out, admittedly much more clearly and precisely than ever before, had been the EU's position all along. The crucial decision to open accession negotiations with Turkey was evidently still several years away. To be ungenerous to Turkey at this stage, when the Helsinki Council was opting for a big-bang enlargement, with ten candidates including Cyprus heading for accession in the first wave and with only Bulgaria and Romania left over for a later date, would have precipitated a major and unnecessary row with Turkey. So in the end the following text was agreed without too much controversy:

The European Council reaffirms the inclusive nature of the accession process, which now comprises 13 candidate states within a single framework. The candidate states are participating in the accession process on an equal footing. They must share the values and objectives of the European Union as set out in the Treaties. In this respect the European Council stresses the principle of peaceful settlement of disputes in accordance with the UN Charter and urges candidate states to make every effort to resolve any outstanding border disputes and other relating issues. Failing this they should within a reasonable time bring the dispute to the International Court of Justice. The European Council will review the situation relating to any outstanding disputes, in particular concerning the repercussions on the accession process and in order to promote their settlement through the ICJ, at the latest by the end of 2004. Moreover, the European Council recalls that compliance with the political criteria laid down at the Copenhagen European Council is a prerequisite for the opening of accession negotiations and that compliance with all the Copenhagen criteria is the basis for accession to the Union.

The European Council welcomes recent positive developments in Turkey as noted in the Commission's progress report, as well as its intention to continue its reforms towards complying with the Copenhagen criteria. Turkey is a candidate State destined to join the Union on the basis of the same criteria as applied to the other candidate States. Building on the existing European strategy, Turkey, like other candidate States, will benefit from a pre-accession strategy to stimulate and support its reforms. This will include enhanced political dialogue, with emphasis on progressing towards fulfilling the political criteria for accession with particular reference to the issue of human rights, as well as on the issues referred to in paragraphs 4 and 9(a). Turkey will also have the opportunity to participate in Community programmes and agencies and in meetings between candidate States and the Union in the context of the accession process. An accession partnership will be drawn up on the basis of previous European Council conclusions while containing priorities on which accession preparations must concentrate in the light of the political and economic criteria and the obligations of a Member State, combined with a national programme for the adoption of the *acquis*. Appropriate monitoring mechanisms will be established. With a view to intensifying the harmonisation of Turkey's legislation and practice with the *acquis*, the Commission is invited to prepare a process of analytical examination of the *acquis*. The European Council asks the Commission to present a single framework for coordinating all sources of EU financial assistance for pre-accession.

This was immediately transmitted to Ankara in the hope that Ecevit would come to Helsinki, along with the other leaders of the candidate countries, thus showing that it was no longer 12 + 1 but 13 candidates whose applications were being processed.

Experience should have warned that nothing could be taken for granted in Ankara, and the first reaction was indeed somewhere between hesitant and hostile. Particular exception was taken to the references to the Greek–Turkish disputes in the Aegean and to the UN negotiations for a Cyprus settlement, neither of which were in fact cast in the terms of conditions for making progress on Turkey's EU application. Rather than conducting a long-distance dialogue of the deaf, the European Council sent a mission composed of Solana and representatives of the presidency and the Commission overnight to Ankara, armed with an explanatory letter from the Finnish prime minister in his capacity as president of the European Council which read as follows:

Mr Prime Minister,

Today, the European Union has set out on a new course in its relations with the Republic of Turkey. I am very pleased to inform you officially of our unanimous decision to confer Turkey the status of candidate State, on the same footing as any other candidate.

When, in the European Council, we discussed the draft conclusions annexed to this letter, I said, without being challenged, that in §12 of the conclusions there was no new criteria added to those of Copenhagen and that the reference to §4 and 9a was not in relation to the criteria for accession but only to the political dialogue. The accession partnership will be drawn up on the basis of today's Council decisions.

In §4 the date of 2004 is not a deadline for the settlement of disputes through the ICJ but the date at which the European Council will review the situation relating to any outstanding dispute.

Regarding Cyprus, a political settlement remains the aim of the EU. Concerning the accession of Cyprus, all relevant factors will be taken into account when the Council takes the decision.

In the light of this, I invite you with the other candidate States to our working lunch in Helsinki tomorrow.

Paavo Lipponen

The mission and the message did the trick, and for once the Turks decided the glass was half full and not half empty. There was subsequently a considerable row with the Greeks when it transpired that Lipponen's explanatory letter had not been cleared with any of his colleagues in the European Council. But, although the letter somewhat weakened the force of the Council conclusions, it in no sense contradicted them. So the matter was smoothed over.

The New York side-show: the first round of proximity talks

The first round of proximity talks took place in New York from 2 to 14 December. For the most part they could well have been described as 'waiting for Helsinki'. Clerides and Denktash and their large entourages took turns to see Annan and to say not very much, and certainly nothing new, about their attitudes towards the core issues and (in Denktash's case) their own agenda. It was tacitly understood that the outcome of Helsinki would crucially affect the continuation of the Cyprus proximity talks.

Indeed Denktash managed to fire off a belligerent public salvo in the brief period when it looked as if the Turks were going to take issue with the Helsinki outcome, but, thereafter, when it became clear that they would treat it as acceptable and welcome, he was persuaded to fall into sullen silence. Clerides, after threatening to attend the candidate countries' session in Helsinki the day after the European Council meeting, which would have been remarkably provocative towards Denktash who, of course, was not invited, was persuaded not to go and to send his foreign minister instead. So, as the delegations left New York, there was, after more than a two-year gap, a show on the road, albeit a show that had not yet left the start line.

European Security and Defence Policy: a wild card

The European Council meeting in Helsinki took another set of decisions, ostensibly not directly concerned with either Turkey or Cyprus but in the event fraught with implications for them and with tricky complications arising from those other relationships. The members of the European Union decided that by the end of 2003 they would acquire the capability to put into the field a force of up to 60,000 men able to be deployed for peacekeeping and humanitarian interventions (the so-called 'Petersberg' tasks) should NATO as such not wish to be involved. The most immediate complications arose from the need for the European Union both to define the position in the European Security and Defence Policy (ESDP) of European countries not yet members but already applicants for membership and also to work out with NATO the precise EU/NATO inter-relationship of the new ESDP machinery they had decided to create. The first of these tasks necessarily involved defining Turkey's relationship with ESDP in the period of indefinite length while it was still not a member of the European Union. The second gave Turkey, as a member of NATO, a veto over EU/NATO arrangements (known as the 'Berlin-plus' arrangements) and in particular over giving the EU assured access to NATO machinery in the event of NATO not deciding to mount an operation and the EU deciding to do so. Beyond these complications with Turkey lurked some equally tricky ones with respect to Cyprus, a candidate for membership of the EU and, as such, another country whose relationship with ESDP needed to be clarified.

The Turks were unhappy about the ESDP decision, not because they were opposed to the policy – if they had been a member of the European Union they would almost certainly have supported it – but because it upset the delicate balance in their relationship with European security and defence developments which had been established some years earlier through their Associate Membership of the Western European Union (a body that was institutionally totally separate from the EU), which effectively gave them the status of member in all but name. The Helsinki decisions implied the demise of the Western European Union and its replacement by the European Union's new Security and Defence Policy, and the Turks knew, although they were unwilling to admit it, that they could not simply become a member of the European Union in all but name. So they were determined to use their veto in NATO to get an ad hoc set of arrangements governing their relationship with and participation in ESDP of an extremely elaborate and advanced kind. In the course of the long and tortuous negotiations over this, which lasted three years (and were only finally settled at the time of the Copenhagen European Council in December 2002), the Turks not only tried the patience of their European partners extremely hard, but they managed, probably inadvertently, to turn a problem between the EU and Turkey into a problem also between Greece and Turkey, with the Greeks taking strong exception to some of the elaborate consultative and cooperative procedures designed to meet Turkish requirements.

If the Turks were unhappy about ESDP in general, they were even more unhappy about the thought of Cyprus (divided) becoming a member of it, as it would if and when it joined the European Union. In the event of a Cyprus settlement preceding EU membership there was probably not much of a problem, since Turkish Cyprus would be in the European Union with a degree of control over Cypriot foreign and security policy, and in any case the reunited Cyprus was to be demilitarized of local Cypriot forces, leaving Cyprus in a position analogous to that of Iceland in NATO. But could one rely on things turning out that way? Obviously not. And if they did not, the prospect of a militarily ambitious southern Cyprus participating in ESDP was one that disturbed the Turks deeply. These concerns were complicated by the Greek Cypriots themselves (and to some extent the Greeks too) at every turn treating ESDP as if it involved a commitment to the territorial defence of its members (which it did not, most of them being members of NATO which already provided that guarantee, and 'Petersberg' tasks having nothing to do with the defence of EU member states), and also by the Greek Cypriots ignoring the urging of EU members to make any declarations of practical and operational support for ESDP solely in the hypothesis of a demilitarized Cyprus, that is to say one following a settlement and admission to the EU of a reunited island. The Turkish solution to all this, that Cyprus, even as an EU member, should simply be excluded from ESDP, was not negotiable, given the nature of the European Union's institutional structures and Greek and Greek Cypriot views. The idea that a country which was going to be in the European Union (Cyprus) should be excluded from ESDP, while a country that was not necessarily even going to be a member (Turkey) should be given a privileged position within ESDP, did not make a lot of political sense.

The one thing that all concerned with this imbroglio were agreed about was that there was nothing to be gained and much to be lost by allowing these ESDP complications and their resolution to be linked in any formal way with the various other negotiations going on – Cyprus's accession to the EU, the UN's efforts to get a Cyprus settlement, Turkey's relationship to the EU. And so, kept apart they were, from beginning to end, although the inter-relationships between them undoubtedly weighed on the minds of all the participants, usually in a negative and unhelpful way.

8

2000: Proximity, Equality, Walk-Out

The first round of proximity talks took place at the end of 1999, but as has been recorded in the previous chapter, barely got to grips with the subject matter, all eyes being turned on Helsinki and on the Turkish government's reaction to what happened there. The next round of proximity talks took place in Geneva from 30 January to 8 February. There was then a long gap, necessitated by presidential elections in the north of Cyprus and by Clerides's need for surgery. The next round, broken in two to allow Denktash to celebrate the anniversary of the 1974 hostilities, again took place in Geneva from 4 to 12 July and from 23 July to 4 August. There was another round in New York from 10 to 26 September. And the last round of the year, and, as it turned out, the last round at all, of proximity talks took place in Geneva from 31 October to 10 November.

The proximity format of these talks, on which the Turks and Turkish Cypriots had insisted and from which they refused to budge, was extremely cumbersome. Kofi Annan, who was present for part of each round but not for their entirety, or de Soto saw Clerides and Denktash and their negotiating teams on most days for separate working sessions. The UN declined at this stage to pass on to the one what the other was saying, which at least hampered the normal Cypriot practice of concentrating on vigorous, intemperate critiques of the position of the other side and avoiding to the greatest extent possible any development of its own negotiating position. In order in part to counter this tendency Annan had requested the sides to respect a news blackout on what was being said at the talks. Both sides honoured this request more in the breach than the observance, and an assiduous reading of the more extreme positions reflected in each other's press provided plenty of raw material for traditional jousting.

In between the formal sessions de Soto fitted in as many private meetings with the two leaders as he could manage, with the aim of getting a better understanding of their bottom-line positions. In addition both Greece and Turkey were represented by delegations, led respectively by Alecos Sandhis and Korkmaz Haktanir who during the course of 2000 became their countries' ambassadors to London but continued their roles as representatives to the Cyprus negotiations. These two delegations naturally spent much time in conclave with the Greek and Turkish Cypriots. Beyond that there was what could be called the penumbra of the talks: the Cypriot party political leaders on each side, the Greek Cypriots meeting almost daily as the National Council, the Turkish Cypriots less systematically organized and more clearly discriminated between those who supported Denktash and those who did not. The US and UK delegations who met with de Soto on a daily basis compared notes and concerted the contacts they were having with the other players: a number of other special representatives, including increasingly often some officials from the EU Commission, and the press, frustrated by the lack of news and of progress and ever ready to give credence and currency to any rumour that either side or the Cypriot politicians accompanying them might choose to plant on them. There was much socializing but, and this was both striking and sad, I am not aware of one single contact, however discreet or innocent, across the Greek–Turkish, Greek Cypriot–Turkish Cypriot divide. I did manage to bring the Turkish Cypriots and Turks into fairly systematic contact with the Commission in the person of Leopold Maurer, the Austrian who was leading the Cyprus accession negotiations at the official level. But an attempt to get the Cyprus foreign minister, Kasoulides, who was not part of the official negotiating team, together with Haktanir, who was not either, foundered on the latter's unwillingness even to sit down at a lunch-table with an official representative of a country that Turkey did not recognize.

The early rounds of proximity talks

The December 1999, the January–February and the first half of July 2000 sessions of proximity talks fitted into a similar pattern: the UN listened, questioned and prompted, but did not put forward any suggestions, let alone any proposals. They did their best to cover the four main core issues – governance, security, territorial adjustment and property – as fully as possible, with varying success, and to avoid the flow of the talks being side-tracked on to other less tangible and less manageable subjects such as status and sovereignty. Not altogether surprisingly, given that the press reporting reflected, on the Greek Cypriot side, the view that nothing had changed, that no real negotiation was going on and that Denktash was operating outside the scope of Security Council resolutions, and on the Turkish Cypriot side an impression of adamantine determination to defend Denktash's confederation proposals of 1998 and to re-establish as preconditions for any real negotiation his basic requirements on status and sovereignty, neither side was prepared to reveal many of its cards during these early rounds. These preliminaries were necessary, as they always are at the beginning of any long and complex negotiation, if only to enable each side to empty their pockets of their carefully constructed opening positions, but they were not very fruitful.

Clerides was not particularly forthcoming during this period. He did not see anything useful coming out of such a laborious process, and continued himself to favour face-to-face talks designed to enable the main substantive trade-offs to be identified and deals on them to be struck. He was being criticized at home and in the National Council for having agreed to talks on such a flexible and imprecise basis. He was worried lest the UN should give ground to Denktash on some aspect of the status and sovereignty issues that would call in question his government's title to represent the Republic of Cyprus as constituted in 1960 and its right to join the European Union. Nevertheless, despite those rather negative constraints, he set out an approach that indicated a willingness to negotiate with reasonable flexibility on all aspects of the core issues. On territory he made it clear that there would have to be a substantial adjustment to the benefit of the Greek Cypriots (as Boutros-Ghali had proposed in 1992 when he had tabled a map which would have reduced the Turkish Cypriot controlled zone from the current 37 per cent of the island to 28.2 per cent). But he was careful not to make any specific territorial claims, thus leaving the details for negotiation at a later stage and thus also avoiding staking out a position from which he would find it difficult to resile if he crossed one of the other side's red lines. And he began to hint that his attitude on the return of property would be materially affected by the scale of the territorial adjustment.

On security issues he plugged his own, by now fairly old, proposals for the total demilitarization of the new Cyprus, i.e. the removal of all Turkish and Greek troops as well as the disbanding of all Greek Cypriot and Turkish Cypriot ones. But he indicated that if those proposals were not negotiable with Turkey, he would be prepared to contemplate not only the continuation of the 1960 Treaty of Guarantee with its unilateral right of intervention in the last resort for each of the guarantor powers (Greece, Turkey and the UK) but also some modest (numbers not speci-fied) continuing Turkish troop presence on the island. In that context he placed great emphasis on an international troop presence, on which he had shifted away from his early flirtation with the idea of a NATO force (the Kosovo war in 1999 having made NATO a dirty word in Cyprus, and in particular with the communist party (AKEL), whose support for any settlement was essential) or even an EU one – neither of which were even remotely negotiable with Turkey – back towards a reshaped UN force, which, coincidentally, was likely to be less objectionable to Turkey. As to governance, it was clear that, without actually saying so, he could live with the approach in the 1992 Set of Ideas: a federal government with a relatively limited range of powers and no residual powers, everything else remaining with the two zones, Greek Cypriot and Turkish Cypriot, over which the two communities would exercise full autonomy. He was unwilling to go too far into sensitive details such as a rotating presidency and the extent of the right of veto of one community over the other until he got into actual negotiation with Denktash. Clerides's views on prop-erty were not spelled out in detail, being to some extent linked to territory, but in no circumstances would he accept an outcome such as that Denktash was putting forward under which all claims would be settled by compensation and no Greek Cypriot would have a right to return to the north.

Denktash was, if anything, even less forthcoming, the even less being because he did not even hint at any possible flexibility beyond his stated position. As usual with Denktash what you saw was what you got. He said flatly that he was not prepared to talk about a specific territorial adjustment until the very end of the negotiation, a position it would have been easier to sympathize with if one had been sure that he would ever admit that that criterion had been met (he did not in fact do so by the time the negotiations broke down). Meanwhile he was prepared to talk about criteria for determining such an adjustment, but, when tabled, these turned out to be fully capable of producing a zero adjustment. On secu-rity he simply said that Turkey would have to be satisfied, and it was not for him to talk about the specifics. His views on governance were set out extensively but exclusively on the basis of a confederation. And when he tabled the worked-out version of his thinking on this it basically amounted to two separate states linked by little more than a permanent diplomatic conference in which each side had a veto on any decision of substance or procedure. He insisted that all property claims must be settled by compensation and that no Greek Cypriots (or Turkish Cypriots for that matter) should have the right of return. When it was pointed out that, during the 1992 negotiations he had been prepared to contemplate a limited right of return, known in the jargon as the 'fishing net' approach, he simply said that that was then and this was now.

Denktash also focused heavily on other issues: status and sovereignty and the EU. He insisted that whatever the outcome of the negotiations, this must include the recognition of the sovereignty of the TRNC, suggesting disingenuously that it might be only for half an hour before the signature of the agreement (thus effectively at that point extinguishing the claim of the Greek Cypriots to represent the Republic of Cyprus) and that sovereignty belonged to the two founding states of the new Cyprus, being partially allocated by them to whatever unified institutions they established. On the European Union he appeared to be reneging even on his proposals of 1998, because he no longer spoke of the possibility of the north of Cyprus entering with the south and ahead of Turkey but rather of what was described as the 'synchronization' of the accession of Turkey and of the north of Cyprus, although it has to be admitted that the practical implications of that Greek-rooted word were often left a little obscure.

The least that could be said of these early exchanges was that they revealed two mutually incompatible positions on many points, including some that had appeared close to agreement or provisionally settled in 1992. And they demonstrated rather clearly that the two parties were not likely, spontaneously, to develop positions that were compatible or at least negotiable. By mid-July, therefore, it was obvious that the UN would have to begin to reveal some thinking of its own if the talks were to move forward.

A presidential election

The proximity talks were suspended after the February round to allow for the quinquennial presidential elections in the north, due at the end of April. Denktash stood for what was effectively a sixth five-year term as president (the first two occasions pre-dated the unilateral declaration of independence of the TRNC). His principal opponent, as at the previous election in 1995, was Dervish Eroglu, the leader of the largest party in the Assembly (the UBP) and prime minister. Denktash won 43.7 per cent of the votes in the first round (slightly better in fact than in 1995 when he had only won 40.4 per cent in the first round, followed by 62.5 per cent in the second), and on this occasion there was no second round, as Eroglu withdrew under strong pressure from the Turkish government. Denktash was therefore elected unopposed. As in previous presidential elections the votes of the centre-left parties, which were generally more favourable to a settlement than either Denktash or Eroglu, were split, as both party leaders, Mustafa Akinci (TKP) and Mehmet Ali Talat (CTP), stood in the first round and were eliminated; moreover one of the centre-left doveish parties (TKP) was still cohabiting uneasily with Eroglu's hawkish UBP in a coalition government.

The outcome of the election thus gave no indication of the rise in dissatisfaction with Denktash's leadership, provoked by the prolonged economic crisis in the north which began with Turkey's own economic woes and the IMF bail-out in 2001, peaked with his conduct of the settlement talks in 2002 and was reflected in the mass demonstrations at the end of that year. If there was a fault-line at all visible at this stage, it was in attitudes towards accession to the European Union. Opinion polls showed overwhelming support among Turkish Cypriots for EU accession, accompanied, quite reasonably, by the view that this needed to be preceded by a settlement of the Cyprus problem. Denktash's vigorously Euro-sceptical views were thus out of line with the majority of his compatriots (and with those of most mainland Turks too) but with settlement talks at an early stage and the end of Cyprus's EU accession negotiations not yet in sight, these differences remained masked, and Denktash was able to keep anger focused on the EU for ever accepting an application from a divided Cyprus, let alone agreeing that a divided island could one day join, as it had done at Helsinki.

The UN speaks up

The view that it was time for the UN to break its silence in the negotiations and to try to nudge things forward was shared in equal measure by the UN negotiators, including the secretary-general, by the US and the UK. Our daily tripartite meetings with de Soto had shown that no real progress was being made. None of us had picked up any signals that either party or their motherlands were contemplating initiatives that might move things along. As to the content of any UN initiative, there was no serious disagreement about that either. It was desirable to set out a framework for the future and to avoid recognizing the distinction, beloved by Denktash who was ever on the look out for an opportunity to filibuster, between preparation and negotiation proper. That framework was as follows: an effort should be made to set aside for the moment the argument over federation v. confederation, given that the idea of a limited number of centrally exercised powers, with the rest exercised by the two zones or states, was more or less common ground and, for this purpose, the terms 'common state' and 'component states' were coined. Some satisfaction should be given to each side on points of great significance for them: political equality and non-domination for the Turkish Cypriots; for the Greek Cypriots indissolubility of the common state, an international force with a UN mandate, a property settlement based on an appropriate combination of restitution, exchange and compensation. Some issues were fudged for the meantime. The link between the territorial adjustment and the property settlement was hinted at. The only issue that gave any difficulty was that of property. Denktash was, even by his own standards, remarkably tough on this subject, saying that he would reject any solution based on any element of return to the north by Greek Cypriots; everything had to be done by compensation. But we concluded that a document that went down that road, or appeared to contemplate doing so, would be both unnegotiable with the Greek Cypriots and indefensible because it would be a legitimization of ethnic cleansing and would fly in the face of the jurisprudence emerging from the European Court of Human Rights. So on 12 July de Soto set out what he called his 'Preliminary Thoughts' to each of the parties and asked them to respond when they returned later in the month:

1. As we are about to break until 24 July, I would like to share with you some preliminary thoughts on the way ahead. It is difficult to draw a balance sheet of a process which has not yet entered the negotiating phase as such, and that is not my purpose today. Nor has the time come for submitting proposals, let alone comprehensive proposals. I am intentionally refraining from covering the entire spectrum at this time. One step at a time. I first wish to obtain reactions to these preliminary thoughts, which contain a mixture of procedure, assumptions, emerging trends, and pending issues.

2. I am not asking for approval or concurrence with what I am about to say. My purpose is to elicit your comments, not now, but when you return from the break.

3. General points:

- The aim is a comprehensive settlement covering all issues on the table, encompassing all legal instruments and other agreements involving non-Cypriot actors.
- The settlement should be self-executing and provide for appropriate mechanisms for verification of compliance.
- The settlement should leave nothing to be negotiated subsequently.
- The settlement should include binding timetables of implementation.
- Labels are to be avoided, at least for the present, so as to concentrate on the underlying concepts.
- Nothing is agreed until everything is agreed.

4. General aims:
- Political equality for Greek Cypriots and Turkish Cypriots.
- Maximum security and institutional protection for Greek Cypriots and Turkish Cypriots to ensure that neither can dominate the other.
- Equitable solutions for the exercise of property rights, for the right of return, and on territory.

5. Among the broad features of a potential settlement that are emerging, I see the following:
- A common state consisting of an indissoluble partnership of politically equal, largely self-governing component states, sharing in a single international legal personality. Each component state shall have its own constitution, government, powers and distinct citizenship. The comprehensive settlement would enshrine the basic legal framework of the common state.
- A common Cypriot nationality and government with specified powers.
- Effective participation of Greek Cypriots and Turkish Cypriots in the common government.
- Free movement throughout the island.
- An international force to be deployed under a Security Council mandate; dissolution of Greek Cypriot and Turkish Cypriot forces; prohibition of arms supplies; substantial reduction of non-Cypriot forces to equal levels. Security arrangements will have to recognise the crucial role of the Treaty of Guarantee and the Treaty of Alliance.
- The need to honour property rights. My sense is that this will require an appropriate combination of restitution, exchange and compensation. The exact make-up will be closely linked to the extent of territorial adjustment.
- The extent of territorial adjustment will require considerable further reflection. There also seems to be a correlation between territorial

adjustment and the degree of integration of, or separateness between, Greek Cypriots and Turkish Cypriots in general.

- An additional factor in this equation is the powers and structures of the component states and the common state respectively.

These linkages confirm the view, which I am sure we all share, that we must advance on all issues simultaneously.

Finally, let me state my assumption that a comprehensive settlement shall commit Cyprus to EU membership while taking into account legitimate concerns in this regard.

I have attempted to share with you my impression of the state of play. The resulting snapshot is unavoidably blurry. More cannot be expected in the short time available to me because of the early break. It is obvious that considerable work remains to be done on all issues, but we must take the long view. I look forward to your comments on 24 July so as to build on what we have so far.

The responses when the leaders and their delegations returned to Geneva later in July were not particularly encouraging, but nor were they worryingly negative. Each side pocketed without recognition or thanks the elements that suited them and continued to press the points that did not. On one issue, however, there did appear to have been some progress – the setting aside of the form of governance for the new Cyprus, federal or confederal, to be decided only at a much later stage in the negotiations. While Denktash continued to push his confederal option and to draft every piece of paper produced by the Turkish Cypriot side rigorously and explicitly within that framework, neither side objected to the use by the UN of the two placebos of 'common state' and 'component state' to identify the central and the autonomous functions of the new Cyprus, and argument about the options was allowed to lapse. This was not too surprising. The Turks had never been greatly enamoured of the confederal concept, which they knew was unnegotiable, a bit of a red herring and which placed Denktash firmly outside not only Security Council resolutions but also the High-Level Agreements that he had himself signed with Makarios and Kyprianou in 1977 and 1979 when acceptance of a federation (to replace the 1960 unitary, bi-communal state) had been a major concession by the Greek Cypriots. In a private conversation with the Turkish foreign minister in London earlier in the year, Cem had asked me whether there was any chance of agreeing to a confederation. I said none whatsoever. The fact that it was Denktash's own proposal and that he was pushing it in a form that would be quite unworkable meant that it would never be accepted by the other side. But that did not mean that there could not be elements of a confederal nature (as well as some of a federal nature) in any constitution for a new Cyprus, as in fact had been the case in Boutros-Ghali's 1992 Set of Ideas. Cem had looked pensive and said no more.

Equality

One set of issues that were certainly not put to one side by de Soto's 12 July 'Preliminary Thoughts' was Denktash's obsessive preoccupation with status and sovereignty. He continued to harp on these at every meeting he had with Annan and de Soto (and indeed with the rest of us), virtually to the exclusion of everything else. This began to worry de Soto, who was concerned that it might bring the whole negotiation to a halt. And it propelled Moses, the US Special Representative, into an attempt to cobble together some formula that could be agreed by both sides and free up the possibility of getting to grips with the core issues. I was less worried by Denktash's antics and a good deal more concerned that the cure might prove worse than the disease. I pointed out that Denktash was in fact in the process of destroying the 'no preconditions' precept of Security Council Resolution 1250 and, if we were to attempt to broker some agreement on status and sovereignty, we would be conniving in that. Once this precept was destroyed, there would be no end to Denktash's preconditions and no end either to the negotiations. Nevertheless Moses struggled on through a series of lengthy meetings with Denktash and Haktanir. He was given a very dusty answer by Clerides when he broached the subject with him, and I noted myself that Clerides was deeply unsettled by these signs that the Americans wanted to draw him into a negotiation on ground on to which he was unwilling to venture. Towards the end of the session, in early August, Moses concluded that there was no chance of getting Clerides and Denktash to agree on a formula; Denktash invariably asked for too much, and Clerides was unhappy about doing anything at all.

When we took stock at the end of the session, I suggested we had broadly two choices. We could struggle on as things were, with Denktash concentrating heavily on status and sovereignty and reluctant to engage on anything else. Or we could try to park at least the trickiest parts of these issues for the duration of the negotiations. To do that we would need to stop trying to get the two sides actually to agree to any formula, since that was clearly not going to fly; rather we should contemplate a unilateral but formal statement by the secretary-general which would not be binding on either party. But for that statement to have a positive rather than a negative effect it would need to be extremely carefully drafted, and it would, above all, need to avoid offering Denktash anything up front but rather be based on what would be obtainable by him in the context of his acceptance of a comprehensive agreement. De Soto and Moses agreed with this analysis and opted firmly for the second alternative. De Soto said he would now work up a formula and clear it with the secretary-general for his use with Clerides and Denktash on the opening day of the next session of negotiations in New York on 12 September. He was adamant that there must be no pre-negotiation of the formula with either side if we were to avoid it being torn to pieces by the two of them. This was agreed. De Soto was as good as his word and produced an extremely carefully crafted form of words with which neither Moses nor I had any problems. And we passed to the UN the undertaking of our two governments to back Annan if he decided to go ahead on this basis. The text that Annan read out to Clerides and Denktash on 12 September was short and went as follows:

> The Greek Cypriot and Turkish Cypriot parties have been participating, since December 1999, in proximity talks to prepare the ground for meaningful negotiations leading to a comprehensive settlement. I believe the time has now come to move ahead.

> In the course of these talks I have ascertained that the parties share a common desire to bring about, through negotiations in which each represents its side – and no-one else – as the political equal of the other, a comprehensive settlement enshrining a new partnership on which to build a better future in peace, security and prosperity on a united island.

> In this spirit, and with the purpose of expediting negotiations in good faith and without preconditions on all issues before them, I have concluded that the equal status of the parties must and should be recognised explicitly in the comprehensive settlement which will embody the detailed negotiations required to translate this concept into clear and practical provisions.

Although brief, this formula contained some important elements. In its first paragraph it clearly indicated the secretary-general's intention to finesse the distinction between talks and negotiations and to do so without seeking explicit agreement and thereby giving either side a veto. In the second it stated more clearly than ever before that, *within the negotiations* each side only represented itself and was politically equal with the other; but it did not, as Denktash would have liked, say that those principles applied also *outside the negotiations*. It did, however, refer to 'a new partnership', which were sacred words in the Denktash lexicon and represented about the limit of what an intensely concerned Clerides could contemplate. Finally, in the third paragraph, it made clear Annan's view that the equal status of the parties would need to be recognized explicitly in any comprehensive settlement, and that that settlement would need to embody the results of detailed negotiations that would have to translate equal status into clear and practical provisions at some point in the future. The statement was silent on the issue of sovereignty.

It had been clear from the outset that this statement would send out considerable shock waves, and indeed it did. It had also been clear that the Greek Cypriots would not much like it, even though it did not in fact cross any of their red lines on recognition or sovereignty. But the iron law of Cyprus negotiations was that any move that might help or please your opponent must necessarily be to your detriment, and this statement certainly qualified under that criterion. What really upset the Greek Cypriots, however, was that the statement had been prepared and delivered without their having the slightest inkling of it and thus without their having any opportunity to influence it. Clerides's immediate reaction was sulphurous and he retired to the Waldorf Astoria where he remained holed up for the next three days refusing to attend any further meetings with Annan and receiving much bad advice from most of the members of the National Council, with the notable exception of his immediate predecessor as president, George Vassiliou, to the effect that he should either seek the withdrawal of Annan's statement or himself withdraw from the negotiations. Meanwhile on the other side Denktash was not helping by putting out public interpretations of Annan's statement that went far beyond what was justified by the text. This provoked a firm rebuke from the secretary-general's press spokesman on 13 September to the effect that the statement was Annan's own, that he was therefore the only source of interpretation of it, and that interpretations of it by others did not have any validity. Denktash's reaction to Annan's statement was, by his standards, reasonably positive but disobliging, putting the emphasis on its insufficiency rather than its merits. The Turkish reaction was a good deal more positive.

The brunt of persuading Clerides that the situation was less bad than he thought or feared fell on Papandreou, who, along with other EU foreign ministers, was by now in New York for the annual ministerial session of the UN General Assembly. He rose to the challenge without hesitation, despite being subjected to a pretty vitriolic press campaign from the Greek and Greek Cypriot press who were egging each other on to heights of hyperbolic excess. Other EU foreign ministers played their part too, pointing out to Clerides that they saw nothing untoward in Annan's statement and that a decision to leave the talks would be very badly received by the EU. But more than mere persuasion was needed. In the end the device of getting the UN to deny on the record some of the wilder interpretations being put on the statement did the trick. On 14 September de Soto issued a statement which was quickly called 'the Three Noes' and which read as follows:

> Earlier today Mr Alvaro de Soto, the Secretary-General's Special Adviser on Cyprus, was asked three questions by a correspondent, in connection with the statement that the Secretary-General read to Mr Clerides and Mr Denktash when he met them on 12 September 2000:
>
> 1.'Does the Secretary-General's statement imply recognition of the 'TRNC'?
> 2. Does the Secretary-General's statement imply a step in the direction of the recognition of the 'TRNC'?
> 3. Does the Secretary-General's statement imply 'derecognition' of the Republic of Cyprus?
>
> To each question Mr de Soto replied 'no'.

Denktash grumbled a bit and said that much of the value of Annan's original statement had been removed, a judgement that said more about his real agenda than about his ability as a trained lawyer to construe the text. Clerides returned to the daily meetings with Annan, which continued until 26 September. And, although the Greek Cypriot National Assembly unanimously adopted a resolution in October denouncing Annan's statement, Clerides never conveyed this to the UN (although Denktash tried to interpret it as a formal rejection). And when Annan repeated the 12 September statement word for word as part of a much longer one that he made to the two sides at the November session in Geneva, Clerides did not turn a hair or utter a word of dissent.

Had this piece of brinkmanship by the UN been worthwhile? I would say it was. It set out very clearly for the first time some points that were of great significance to the Turks and Turkish Cypriots and which they had every right to have clarified. For those in Ankara who needed a signal that their interests were not going to be overlooked or brushed aside, this was exactly that. But for those there who refused to contemplate any outcome that was not totally consistent with all their demands, it was also a signal that a serious negotiation was now under way which would require difficult decisions and compromises. On the Greek Cypriot side, for all the ferocity of the storm while it blew, there were no lasting negative consequences. And the Greek government had shown that it was a good as its word in its commitment to supporting the secretary-general's effort to get a settlement.

The UN's next step

Annan had left his interlocutors in no doubt during the latest New York round of talks in September that he wanted the following round in Geneva in November to get to grips with the core issues and that he saw a role for himself in helping that process along. Indeed his 12 September statement, which had been the focus of much of the activity in New York, had clearly stated the need to move on. While the EU accession negotiations with Cyprus had not yet reached a critical stage, the Greek Cypriots and the Commission were by now ticking off the various technical problems and there was little, if any, doubt that the crucial decisions on enlargement in general would be taken within the next two years. Indeed Cyprus was always in the first or second place among the ten accession countries in satisfying the EU that it met or would meet the various demands made of it – 'closing chapters' in EU parlance. Given the past record for procrastination by the Cypriot parties, that was no excessive amount of time to bring the settlement negotiations to a head, rather the contrary. A whole year had been by now devoted to clearing the approach route. This same message was conveyed in New York by ministers and officials from the US, and from the UK and other EU countries, and it was conveyed as much to the Turks and the Greeks as to the two Cypriot parties.

The Greek Cypriots (and the Greeks) were on the whole responsive to this message. They wanted to move on to a serious negotiation on the core issues, and their main preoccupation, which became an obsession during the weeks between the New York and Geneva sessions, was whether the UN would take a further step to handle Denktash's status and sovereignty concerns. Denktash wanted nothing less, and spoke at length about the inadequacy of the 12 September statement. But it was made very clear to him that that statement was not going to be extended or amplified, and that, if he pressed for changes in it, not only would he not get any, but the statement itself would then be contested by the other side and become worthless. This point seemed to have registered at least with the Turks. In other respects their position remained totally obscure. In what was to become an all too familiar pattern when an important stage in the negotiations was about to be reached, Ankara was gripped by policy paralysis. Some understood full well that if progress was ever to be made towards a settlement, the secretary-general would have to give a lead and explore the possibilities for compromise, and they were considerably encouraged by the 12 September statement which had met a number of points of great importance to Turkey.

But others were fearful of any initiative by Annan, convinced (correctly) that it would not embrace Denktash's completely unnegotiable positions, and would compel them to examine compromises that would be difficult to accept. This second school was also deeply attached to a highly restrictive view of the UN secretary-general's scope for independent thought and action; they argued that in a Good Offices Mission, such as this one undoubtedly was, the secretary-general had no right to advance suggestions or ideas of his own without first getting the explicit authority and agreement of the parties to the dispute. This highly academic, and effectively rather absurd, concept, which would have given Denktash (and Clerides for that matter) a veto over anything Annan said, had no serious basis in law or in practice. It clearly made sense for the secretary-general to feel his way forward carefully and try to ensure that any ideas he floated did not arouse fundamental objections from the parties. But giving the parties a veto on what he said would largely remove the point of having the secretary-general involved in the first place. This was not how previous secretaries-general (Pérez de Cuéllar and Boutros-Ghali) had handled the Cyprus problem, nor was it how they had worked in any number of other disputes in which they had been constructively engaged. Nor was it a view that had been expressed by the Security Council in its handling of the Cyprus problem; rather the opposite had been the case, with the Security Council urging the secretary-general to be active and imaginative. All this was explained to any Turk or Turkish Cypriot who was ready to hear, but it did not affect Denktash's own attitude. So Ankara's views at this point remained largely obscure, limited to rather general and vague concerns that the UN should not try to push Denktash too far and that they should not make any formal proposals.

It was against this background that de Soto consulted Moses and me in mid-October. On some points we were clear. The 12 September state-ment must be left as it was, unamended and unembellished. It had contained all that it was necessary to say on status at this stage, and it was the absolute maximum weight that the Greek Cypriot bridge would bear until substantive progress was made on the core issues. We were agreed too that the distinction between preparation and negotiation must be bypassed. There was no disagreement also that it would be premature at this stage for the secretary-general to come forward with formal proposals or a complete plan or blueprint. This pointed towards some fleshing out of de Soto's 'ideas' put forward in July, aimed at moving the talks into a substantive negotiating phase. There were some differences of emphasis over the degree of urgency and the degree of specificity to be aimed at. Moses, who was only too conscious of the impending US presidential election, the ending of President Clinton's mandate, whatever the out-come, and of the possibility of the traditional hiatus in US foreign policy that follows the arrival of a new incumbent in the White House, favoured pressing ahead as far and as fast as possible in November. I was slightly more cautious, and de Soto considerably more so. As usual we left the tactical judgements and decisions to Annan and de Soto.

In parallel with this meeting I visited Brussels and talked things through with both Enlargement Commissioner Verheugen and EU Foreign Policy High Representative Solana and their teams, making sure that they were fully in the picture about the way the UN was planning to proceed. About the EU/Cyprus accession negotiations there was not a great deal to be said except to urge the Commission to begin thinking actively about the implications for the terms of accession of a reunited Cyprus if a settlement of the sort beginning to be discernible in the UN's thinking were to come about. This Verheugen readily agreed to do. And he also agreed to keep in check attempts by Greek Cypriot hardliners to use the *acquis communautaire* to rule out certain types of solution in the settlement talks which would certainly be needed if there was to be an agreement. He was by now fully aware of the rather odd anomaly that was taking shape by which a number of specific EU matters would need to be settled in the talks on the Cyprus problem and that therefore these would need to be discussed in detail in advance between him and de Soto, so as to enable him to keep the EU member states on board in due course.

The main active subject in Brussels, however, was, yet again, EU/Turkey. The EU's commitment to Turkey at the Helsinki European

Council to enter into an Accession Partnership, which would provide a framework and funds to prepare for Turkish membership, was coming to fruition, with the Commission due to make formal proposals to the Council early in November and the Council to reach agreement with Turkey by the end of the year. The Accession Partnership document would need to make some reference to Cyprus, since the Helsinki European Council conclusions, on which it was based, did so. But it was essential to avoid any formal linkage between progress on EU/Turkey and progress in the UN settlement process and to stick to the clarification contained in the Finnish prime minister's (as president of the EU's Council) letter to Ecevit that all the EU was asking in respect of Cyprus was that it should be part of an 'enhanced political dialogue' over mutual support for Annan's efforts.

There was a further complication: the timing of the Commission's Accession Partnership proposals, in juxtaposition with Annan's next session with Clerides and Denktash in Geneva. This was awkward and all too likely in any case to arouse suspicion in Ankara that the two issues were being deliberately linked. But neither the Commission's proposals nor Annan's next session could be delayed without conveying precisely that impression. So we had to live with it. What made things far worse was that the Greek Social Affairs Commissioner, Anna Diamantopoulou, provoked a major and extremely well-publicized row in the Commission over the wording of the proposed Accession Partnership, trying to bounce through an explicit linkage with Cyprus. By the time this was all sorted out in the Council and the Accession Partnership agreed with Turkey in early 2001 in terms precisely consistent with the Helsinki conclusions, the damage had been done. In the view of many in Ankara there had been a whiff of blackmail in the air and that greatly helped the rejectionists.

The session of proximity talks in Geneva from 31 October to 10 November was not an easy one. The after-shocks of the 12 September statement were still being felt by the Greek Cypriots, and Clerides in particular was in a highly nervous, febrile mood. It was well known that when Annan arrived towards the end of the session he would have important things to say on the future of the negotiations. The day before Annan's arrival, Moses and I were separately summoned. I had never seen Clerides in such a state, his people clearly horrified by what he was saying and threatening to do. He told me that if Annan went further than he had done in September on status and sovereignty, he would leave the talks, return to Cyprus and hold a referendum on his decision to walk out.

While I was certainly not in a position to say what Annan would or would not say the next day, I told him that I thought his fears exaggerated. I could not believe that walking out of the talks would be well received in EU capitals. This provoked a familiar Clerides diatribe to the effect that if he had to choose between accepting a bad settlement and losing the chance to join the EU he would have no hesitation in rejecting the former and reconciling himself to the latter. Overnight I arranged for a calming message from Robin Cook. In the event Annan's statement did not (and had never been intended to) touch the neuralgic point. And another storm blew over, with Clerides leaving Geneva and making it clear that he was prepared to work within the framework put forward by Annan, even though it contained word for word (in paragraphs 4 and 9) the 12 September statement that had caused so much trouble two months earlier.

Annan's identical statement to Clerides and Denktash on 8 November was a good deal longer and contained rather more detail than de Soto's 'Preliminary Thoughts' of 12 July, but in substance it did not depart significantly from the earlier presentation. Once again, and this was made clear in a brief press statement by the secretary-general, what was being put forward were not proposals, nor any formal document (it was explicitly stated that what Annan had said was only being handed over in writing to ensure that they had an accurate record of his oral remarks), that decisions would be taken by the two sides and not the UN, that he was not seeking Clerides's and Denktash's agreement but wanted them to reflect on what he had said and respond to de Soto, who would be visiting the region for that purpose, and finally that he would look forward to continuing the dialogue in January 2001. The text of what Annan said was as follows:

> 1. I am very glad to join you and wish to thank you for accepting my invitation to continue and intensify efforts to achieve a comprehensive settlement. I was gratified that, in New York, we saw the first signs of the real engagement and I understand that this has continued here in Geneva. I realize, of course, that there is a long way to go.
>
> 2. Since we are now seriously engaged in the substance, I wish to make a number of observations. Further to my statement of 12 September, I want to give you my thoughts, first about procedure, and then about some substantive aspects of a possible comprehensive settlement, in the hope of facilitating negotiations. However, I wish to make clear that, as with Mr de Soto's 'Preliminary Thoughts' of 12 July, and the subsequent ideas we have offered, I am not at this stage putting forward a proposal, nor am I

covering all the ground. I do not intend to make these remarks public, but I will leave you with notes of what I say just for your record.

3. On *procedure*, the first thing I wish to do is to confirm that, as concerns the United Nations, these negotiations are being conducted pursuant to Security Council Resolution 1250, which sets out four guidelines:

- No preconditions;
- All issues on the table;
- Commitment in good faith to continue to negotiate until a settlement is reached; and
- Full consideration of relevant United Nations resolutions and treaties.

These four guidelines cannot be invoked selectively; they all apply.

4. In these negotiations, each party represents its side – and no one else – as the political equal of the other, and nothing is agreed until everything is agreed.

5. The aim is a comprehensive settlement covering all issues, encompassing all legal instruments and other agreements needed to achieve and implement it, including any agreements involving non-Cypriot actors. In other words, it should be self-implementing. To this end, it should provide for appropriate mechanisms for verification of compliance and binding timetables of implementation. It should leave nothing to be negotiated subsequently. The settlement should include the test of a 'basic law' and texts on security arrangements, territorial adjustments and the property regime, as well as the initial body of 'common state' legislation.

6. The comprehensive settlement should be submitted for approval in separate referenda so as to ensure the democratic endorsement, legitimisation, and ratification of the comprehensive settlement by each community. Unless otherwise specified in the comprehensive settlement, subsequent changes to it could only occur by the same method.

7. Since no useful purpose would be served by myself or Mr de Soto conveying proposals from the parties back and forth, we are working towards a single negotiating text as the basis for negotiations. For this process to succeed it is essential that you provide specific comments on ideas put forward by the UN. I would ask you to give us indications of what you feel might not be fair or viable in the ideas we put to you, and why. This would be more helpful to the process than substitute proposals, position papers or suggested amendments. Without your specific comments, and those of the other side, we cannot take them on board in revising our

submissions, and your participation in shaping the negotiating text will be hampered. I ask you to engage with us fully in this way so as to enable us to advance on all issues simultaneously.

8. On *substance*, as you know, we have intentionally avoided labels in these talks so as to concentrate on the underlying issues. I would like to give you a general outline of elements I believe should be a part of a comprehensive settlement. Again, I am not seeking your agreement on them at this time. Rather, I wish to indicate what I believe the parties ought reasonably to accept as a fair and viable compromise. I will now describe the elements – which, I emphasize, are not an exhaustive list.

9. The comprehensive settlement should enshrine a new partnership on which to build a better future in peace, security and prosperity on a united island. The equal status of the parties in a united Cyprus must and should be recognized explicitly in the comprehensive settlement, which will embody the results of the detailed negotiations required to translate this concept into clear and practical provisions.

10. Cyprus should have a single international legal personality. Whatever is eventually agreed regarding the status of the two 'component states', there should be one sovereign, indissoluble 'common' state. I mean that neither side could separate from the 'common state' that emerges from these negotiations, nor try to unite all or part of the island with Greece or Turkey. Nor should either side be able to dominate the 'common state' or the other 'component state'. There should be a single citizenship. Human rights and fundamental freedoms should be guaranteed.

11. The 'common state' should have what we are calling, for now, a 'common government', with a 'basic law' prescribing powers exercised by legislative, executive, and judicial branches. The 'common government' should be able to function efficiently in the modern world. This includes being able to take decisions in international bodies of which the 'common state' is a member. In the operation of the 'common government', the political equality of Greek Cypriots and Turkish Cypriots should be respected. Political equality, whilst not requiring numerical equality, must involve effective participation of Greek Cypriots and Turkish Cypriots in the 'common government', and protection of their fundamental interests.

12. There should be what we have called, for now, two 'component states' – Greek Cypriot and Turkish Cypriot – each with its own 'basic law'. The 'component states' should be largely self-governing, it being understood that they must not contravene the 'basic law' of the 'common state'. They

would have power over all matters other than the essential competencies and functions that will be listed in the comprehensive settlement as being the responsibility of the 'common state'. Neither 'component state' would be able to interfere in the governance of the other. It might be possible for the 'component states' to confer additional internal citizenship rights on persons who possess Cypriot citizenship.

13. I take it that a comprehensive settlement would commit Cyprus to EU membership. At the same time, I would hope that the EU would be prepared to address special and legitimate concerns in regard to accession. In this context, it is clearly important that the provisions of the comprehensive settlement should not represent an obstacle to such membership nor need to be renegotiated when the terms of accession are established.

14. Concerning property, we must recognize that there are considerations of international law to which we must give weight. The solution must withstand legal challenge. The legal rights which people have to their property must be respected. At the same time, I believe that a solution should carefully regulate the exercise of these rights so as to safeguard the character of the 'component states'. Meeting these principles will require an appropriate combination of reinstatement, exchange and compensation. For a period of time to be established by agreement, there may be limits on the number of Greek Cypriots establishing residence in the north and Turkish Cypriots establishing residence in the south. It is worth mentioning in this context that the criteria, form and nature of regulation of property rights will also have a bearing on the extent of territorial adjustment, and vice-versa.

15. I find it hard to imagine a comprehensive settlement without a return to Greek Cypriot administration of an appreciable amount of territory. In my view, in negotiating the adjustment, a balance must be struck between a maximum return of Greek Cypriots to areas being returned to Greek Cypriot administration, and a minimum of dislocation of Turkish Cypriots. The focus should be on the number of persons affected more than the amount of territory involved. Clearly, the moment is approaching where discussions should proceed on the basis of detailed geographic data.

16. I am confident that arrangements can be made which effectively address the security concerns of each side. It is clear that one side's security must not be assured at the expense of the security of the other, and I think that both parties would be willing to come to an arrangement acceptable to all. Such an arrangement should include the continuation of the security regime established in 1960, as supplemented to reflect the

comprehensive settlement; the dissolution of Greek Cypriot and Turkish Cypriot forces; a prohibition legally binding on both exporters and importers of arms supplies; agreed equal levels of Greek and Turkish troops; a United Nations mandated force and police unit that function throughout the island; and a political mechanism which can assist in resolving security issues.

17. I am making these observations on the main issues before us after nearly a year of listening and testing ideas. My purpose is to make a further step in the direction of developing an overall picture of a comprehensive approach to a settlement. Please reflect on what I have said. I hope you will use my observations as the course to follow in the talks ahead.

18. I think it is necessary to schedule further talks early in 2001. Accordingly, I invite you to continue the proximity talks in Geneva from late January 2001. In the meantime, I am asking Mr de Soto to travel to the region and the island late this month or early next month.

19. In the time between now and the next session, I would also ask you to reflect on one final point. A strong impression that I have formed during the proximity talks is this: it is not only the sad events of the past that are the tragedy of modern Cyprus; it is also the absence of a solution. The absence of a solution prevents all Cypriots from sharing fully – and equally – in the fruits of prosperity, security and progress. A united and independent Cyprus, in which Greek Cypriots and Turkish Cypriots are equal and protected and free, as citizens of Europe, is the promise of the future. I hope that you will seize what is perhaps the best chance yet for a Cyprus settlement, in order to bequeath that promise to succeeding generations.

20. In closing, let me say again that I do not intend to make these remarks public, and I trust that you will also keep them to yourselves.

Of the very few new elements which were introduced since July, two are worth mentioning. The first was a purely procedural suggestion (paragraph 7) that from now on the negotiations should be based on a single negotiating text to which each side should react by agreeing, disagreeing or amending, and that this process should replace the practice of each side tabling extensive drafts of their own approach to core issues. This seemingly harmless surfacing of a diplomatic technique used in countless international negotiations caused massive offence on the Turkish side, who described it as a UN diktat (which it was not) and who clearly saw it as a way for the UN to play a more central role in the negotiations (which it certainly was). In any case, if they did not like it, all they had to do was to say politely to de Soto when he visited the region that they were not yet ready to move to that stage, in which case the idea would have been set aside for the time being. With the benefit of hindsight it would have been better not to have included this novel thought in Annan's presentation in Geneva but to have explored it informally in de Soto's subsequent contacts. It was yet another example, which one ignored at one's risk, of the extent to which Denktash and his close advisers, and the Turkish officials who specialized in Cypriot affairs, were cut off from the development of international negotiating practices and techniques and also of how ready they were to interpret any innovation as a secret weapon being deployed against them. The second novel thought in Annan's presentation was a brief passage on EU accession (paragraph 13) where he suggested for the first time that any provisions in a settlement should not represent an obstacle to EU membership nor require to be renegotiated when the reunited Cyprus's terms of accession were established. This idea provoked less outrage than the other (and none at all from the EU itself, to which it was directed). But it is interesting to note that the Turks managed to construe this paragraph as meaning that the EU had a veto over the terms of a Cyprus settlement when in fact the meaning and thrust of the paragraph was exactly the opposite: that the Greek Cypriots should not expect to be able to unpick any settlement later in the European Court of Justice.

Annan's presentation was given, deliberately, on the last day of the November session in Geneva, with the object of avoiding knee-jerk reactions from either side. This was in fact achieved. Clerides was relieved at the absence of any new material on status or sovereignty and let it be known soon afterwards that he would be content to move forward on the basis proposed. Denktash's reaction was typically curmudgeonly, but, since that characterized the whole range of his negotiating technique, it was never easy to be sure whether there was any significance in it or not. But de Soto was sufficiently worried to have canvassed with the US and the UK the possibility of immediately sending a written report to the Security Council containing Annan's statement and thus putting Denktash and the Turks on the spot. We both counselled against this, not because there was the slightest doubt that the Security Council would back Annan, but because past experience had shown that lining up the Security Council against Denktash did not work and that a written report of the kind envisaged tended to be interpreted – as it had been in the case of the Set of Ideas in 1992 – as marking a definitive breakdown in the efforts to achieve a settlement. Denktash did, however, ominously as it turned out, say that he could not accept the invitation to a further round of proximity talks in January 2001 without having first consulted the Turkish government.

Denktash walks out

It took some time for those outside the Turkish governmental machine to understand just how fundamentally Denktash and the accompanying Turkish delegation to the Geneva talks had misunderstood (the charitable interpretation) or misrepresented (probably closer to the truth) Annan's 8 November statement. One consequence of the statement having been issued on the last day of the talks was that there was no opportunity for the two sides to go over the ground with the UN and at least reduce some of their concerns. But gradually, as the UN and others of us closely concerned came to be exposed to Turkish versions of what they believed had been put forward, we realized just how wide of the mark their analysis was. For one thing the rather large number of points that were helpful from their point of view – the reiteration of the 12 September statement, the firm endorsement of the 1960 Treaties of Guarantee and Alliance, the need for any settlement to be endorsed by referendums on both sides, the avoidance of domination of the 'common state' by either side, the flat statement that the 'component' states, which would each have its own constitution, would have power over all matters other than those explicitly granted to the 'common' state – were simply ignored or taken for granted. The dilution of the Treaties of Guarantee and Alliance was asserted, although there was no evidence for it, the provisions on property were alleged to ensure an absolute right of return for all Greek Cypriot refugees, although that was not what was provided for, and the territorial adjustment, although no details of the scale envisaged had been provided by the UN, was exaggerated.

This was the background against which Denktash went to Ankara late in November to discuss the next steps with the Turkish government. Following a meeting, which included the president, the prime minister, the coalition party leaders and the chief of the general staff, Denktash emerged and described the proximity talks as 'a waste of time as long as our parameters are not accepted. They are being run on the basis that the Greek Cypriots are the sole legitimate government on the island.' He said he would not attend further UN proximity talks unless the existence of the TRNC was recognized. 'The truth is the co-existence of two states, two peoples, two sovereignties and two democracies. ... There is no point in attending talks until the existence of our state is accepted.' He did say, however, that he would reconsider his position if 'a new basis' for the talks was created. Later the same day, as if to slam firmly shut even the tiny crack that Turkish foreign ministry officials were trying to hold open, Ecevit said publicly that he supported Denktash's decision (sic) not to attend the meetings. In this way a whole string of Turkish Cypriot and Turkish preconditions to negotiations were reinstated in contradiction to Resolution 1250. Annan, who had been given no advance warning of what was in the offing, was told he had been wasting his time, and all pressure to show flexibility was lifted from the Greek Cypriots.

Why did the Turks opt for quite such a kamikaze approach to their Cyprus diplomacy? Without a detailed knowledge of the inner workings of the Turkish establishment and bureaucracy it is not possible to say with any certainty. Neither Denktash nor Ecevit had ever really been committed to a negotiation in good faith for a settlement that would necessarily involve some elements of compromise over their publicly stated positions; they had been pushed into it by international pressure, particularly from the US and the EU. They could now see that the negotiating train was beginning to move down a track towards a destination at which they did not wish to arrive – and here the misrepresentation of what Annan said may have played an important role. They could also see that the UN's role was becoming more prominent and that their capacity to filibuster endlessly was going to be limited. They may well have exaggerated the likely effect of taking off their shoe and beating the rostrum. One thing was clear: once Denktash and Ecevit had spoken publicly as they did, there was no diplomatic wiggle room left, at least in the short term. The process was blocked and a way would have to be found in Ankara to unblock it.

9

2001: Trench Warfare

One of the eventualities to which little thought had been given by the UN and its supporters, the US and the UK and the other main European Union countries, was that Denktash, with full Turkish support, would simply walk out of the negotiations and refuse to return. We had bargained for an endless filibuster or even for some dramatic breaks but not for an attempt to destroy the whole basis on which the negotiations had begun a year earlier. This approach had seemed rather unlikely, if only because the main victims in terms of diplomatic damage were the Turkish Cypriots and the Turks themselves. And yet this was the situation we now faced. This became quite clear after a visit to Cyprus, Turkey and Greece, which I made in early January 2001. While Denktash attempted to equate his action with that of Clerides when he had absented himself from the talks in New York in September 2000, there was in fact no similarity at all. Clerides had resumed his participation after a very short (three-day) break and basically on the terms laid down by the UN, with a little bit of diplomatic finessing with the 'Three Noes', and he had subsequently ceased to contest the matter that had caused the problem in the first place. Denktash was thoroughly enjoying the breakup he had precipitated, went daily to the press with his aggressive rhetoric about the proximity talks having been a waste of time, and had publicly set terms (the usual status/sovereignty mantra) for his return which he knew to be unnegotiable. He showed no inclination whatsoever to discuss constructively ways of resuming the settlement process, nor was he to do so at any time during 2001 up until his own decision in November to take the initiative. He thus ruled himself out as a participant in any procedure designed to pick up the pieces.

Working with Turkey

When de Soto sat down with Moses and myself in New York on 18–19 January we had no difficulty in agreeing on the way ahead, even if we had no illusions that it would be easy or quick. There was no inclination to take no for an answer. The arguments for pressing on, in particular the approach of the conclusion of the EU enlargement negotiations, remained convincing. Nor was there any inclination to discuss Denktash's preconditions. They had been set out so starkly and in such maximalist terms as to rule out any possibility that the Greek Cypriots would respond positively; and, since they had just given some ground on status issues by effectively swallowing Annan's 12 September statement, there was no convincing reason why they should be asked to do more at this stage. We were also agreed that Annan's statement of 8 November must not be allowed to wither on the bough or to become the sacrificial price for getting Denktash back to the table. Not only were the Turks scandalously misrepresenting it, but, in the view of all of us, it represented the only viable approach to a negotiated solution that stood any chance of being agreed. So, if one sacrificed it or allowed large chunks of it to be lopped off, one might end up with a resumed process, but a process without negotiable content.

Since we were aiming to get the Turks and Denktash back to the negotiating table without making any concessions of substance, we agreed to a division of labour. De Soto would lead on all matters relating to Annan's 8 November statement. He would try to demystify it, and explain why it contained much material of use to the Turks and Turkish Cypriots which could be developed through negotiation into a settlement that would respect both their vital interests. He would avoid any accusation of outright misrepresentation and would not move aggressively into the task of getting Denktash back to the table, thus hopefully avoiding damaging his impartiality should the US and the UK succeed in bringing that about. The US and the UK would meanwhile use all means possible to bring home to the Turks that Denktash's walk-out was damaging them to an increasing extent as time passed. I had begun this effort when I visited Ankara in early January and sustained it when I returned there in May. The US was uncomfortably placed since we were in the last day of Clinton's presidency, and Moses, who was a political appointee, was unlikely to continue. No commitments could therefore be entered into with regard to the incoming Bush administration's policy. But Weston, who was to take over the lead in Washington when the decision was taken (not on Cyprus grounds, but out of a general desire to cut back the number of special representatives) not to replace Moses, made it clear that contacts with the transition team indicated the likelihood of US policy on Cyprus being unchanged.

This was a crucial dimension since not only was the US by far and away the most influential player in Ankara, but the Turks, like many others, had nurtured all sorts of illusions that the new Republican administration would be more friendly to them, in general and on Cyprus issues in particular, than the outgoing Democrat administration had been. Until that illusion had been dissipated we would get no change of policy in Ankara. Weston was in fact as good as his word: US policy on this issue did not change by an iota; and the new administration's firm view that Denktash needed to return to the table without preconditions was made known by the incoming secretary of state, Colin Powell, when Turkish foreign minister Cem visited Washington in March. In addition to these efforts we agreed that other EU governments should be encouraged to bring home the same messages to the Turkish government and to underline, without making any direct linkage, that Turkey's present Cyprus policy would inevitably over time conflict with their aspirations to join the EU. This was indeed done with some effect, all the more so since the European Union's willingness during this period to move ahead with the Accession Partnership with Turkey, without making any unacceptable linkage with the Cyprus problem, demonstrated that Turkish fears in the autumn of 2000 had been exaggerated.

In truth it was not difficult to marshal the arguments in Ankara that showed that the walk-out was damaging Turkey's interests. For one thing it was propelling into the European Union a divided Cyprus. It was inconceivable that if the 'relevant factors' referred to in the Helsinki European Council conclusions included a Denktash who refused to negotiate further, the EU would punish the Greek Cypriots and refuse to admit a divided island. Moreover a prolonged vacuum in the negotiating process would inevitably lead to further Greek Cypriot pressure to purchase sophisticated weapons, with tiresome implications for Turkey's security interests in the region. Turkey's long-term European aspirations were simply not consistent with a Cyprus policy of refusing to negotiate except on Denktash's terms, nor indeed was the further development of a Greek–Turkish rapprochement on which Papandreou and Cem had lavished so much effort. And should the business world conclude that Turkey's EU aspirations were unlikely to get anywhere and that there would be more tension in future in the Eastern Mediterranean, this would over time have damaging implications for Turkey's already fragile economy and for inward investment. Nor was there a lack of positive points to make. A Cyprus settlement would facilitate Turkey's EU application, would mean fewer Turkish troops tied down and less Turkish money spent, and would mean a Turkish Cypriot presence in EU decision taking. All these, and more, were points made to Cem and his officials when I visited Ankara in the first half of 2001. The Americans were making the same points.

The Turkish response was less discouraging than we had feared. For one thing they rapidly stopped their misrepresentations of Annan's 8 November statement, realizing that many of the allegations about it simply did not fit what was said in the statement. Rather more positively they did not contest the long list of negative consequences for Turkey that were only too likely to flow from a prolonged hiatus in the negotiating process. And they understood, even if they did not like, the analysis that if Denktash was offered substantive concessions to return to the negotiating table, then no doubt there would be further walk-outs in the future designed to achieve the same ends. I was struck during my first visit to Ankara by the clear recognition by Mumtaz Soysal, Denktash's hardline Turkish constitutional adviser, that the walk-out had been a tactical error. But, if logic got them so far, it did not immediately bring about a change of policy. Denktash himself was not helping them in that respect; he and they were all too aware that most of the negative consequences impacted on Turkey and not on Turkish Cyprus. If, like Denktash, you did not want Turkey to join the EU in the first place there was no great discomfort. Nor were these arguments getting through directly to two critical constituencies, the prime minister, Ecevit, and the Turkish general staff with whom, by this time, no direct contact with outsiders was permitted. So while we could feel that we were winning the argument, there was as yet no evidence that this was getting us anywhere.

Meanwhile, in the short term at least, there was not much to be done with the Greek Cypriots and Greeks, who were tactically sitting in clover. Cyprus's EU accession negotiations were making rapid progress, unimpeded by any doubts over their eventual accession. Indeed, thanks to Turkish policy, the view became more and more prevalent in the European Union during 2001 that accession by a divided island was virtually a foregone conclusion; and by the autumn it was proving quite difficult to persuade the Commission and some of the more nervous EU member states that it was not yet time to begin drafting the consequential legal provisions based on that assumption. As always a prolonged period of contacts by the main players with the Turks led to periodic outbreaks of nervousness among the Greek Cypriots that they would be expected to pay the price for getting Denktash back into the negotiations. And assurances to the contrary, however firm and clear, never quite dissipated these endemic fears.

A US/Turkish scenario

From the late spring of 2001 onwards the US became locked into a process with the Turkish Ministry of Foreign Affairs aimed at defining in precise terms the way in which Denktash should be brought back into the negotiations. This was no simple task, particularly since the Turks on this occasion, unprecedentedly, decided to proceed without consulting Denktash and in strict confidentiality. Given the opacity of the decision-making process in Ankara, it was never very easy to be sure who knew about what and who was on board, as the approach took precise shape. But assurances were given that Ecevit had given his blessing to what was being done and agreed that the negotiations needed to be resumed. Neither the UN nor the UK played a direct role in the elaboration or negotiation of the scenario but each was kept informed at every stage by Weston, the US Special Coordinator.

The main elements of the scenario as finally agreed in June were as follows:

(i) The UN would contact Denktash and invite him to meet Annan in New York in late July to discuss the way forward with the UN Good Offices Mission (and thereby give Denktash a fig leaf for the resumption of the talks).

(ii) After the Annan/Denktash meeting de Soto would go to the island to give new impetus to the UN process through discussions on substance.

(iii) It would be agreed in advance of (i) and (ii) that all this would lead to substantive talks without preconditions on all issues with the secretary-general in September 2001 at the latest.

(iv) The UN would not make the 8 November statement a specific point of reference in future talks or in public statements so long as Denktash did the same. Any assertion that the 8 November statement was 'off the table' or had been repudiated by the UN would be unacceptable. In subsequent talks the UN would continue discussion with the parties on the specific issues that must be agreed as part of a comprehensive settlement. The parties would also be able to relate their views on the status question.

(v) It was understood that this scenario for restarting the UN process would not reopen the question of whether the ground had been prepared. The secretary-general's 12 September statement on equal status and equality already did that. Reopening this issue would only call into question the continued solidity of the 12 September statement.

(vi) The UN would start the process at (i) once Turkey could assure them that Denktash had agreed to this scenario for moving ahead.

This extremely satisfactory agreement, which safeguarded all the points to which the UN, the US and the UK had attached importance when they had worked out their tactics in January, was confirmed by the Turks to the US as being acceptable to them. They undertook to put it to Denktash (which was understood to be a polite way of saying that they would put the whole Turkish government's weight behind it and get Denktash to agree to it). In due course they gave the Americans the green light, who passed that on to the UN, it being understood by all concerned (Turkey, US, UN) that the sequence was a single whole to which all were committed in its entirety from the outset, not an à la carte menu. But it was also understood by all concerned that no reference must be made, in particular publicly or to Denktash, to the existence of a scenario of this sort; it must simply be played out.

Preparation for resumption of the negotiations

The UN had not been idle during this long hiatus in the negotiations, during which they had been unable to play an active diplomatic role. Rather they had put in hand detailed work on the main elements of a comprehensive settlement so that they would be well prepared to move the negotiations on to issues of substance whenever a resumption was agreed. On territorial issues they had begun the detailed cartographical analysis required to achieve a substantial return of territory to the Greek Cypriots, which would at the same time accommodate the maximum possible return of Greek Cypriot refugees, while displacing the minimum possible number of Turkish Cypriots. It was already clear to them that they could improve on the 1992 Boutros-Ghali map in both respects. They also identified quite a large number of different territorial options that would provide some degree of flexibility if and when negotiations got under way, although in no case did they stray very far away from the basic Boutros-Ghali proportions (which had been endorsed in 1992 by the Security Council) of a Turkish Cypriot zone of 28-plus per cent and a

Greek Cypriot zone of 72-minus per cent. They also began to relate each option to the scale of limited settlement (including returns) by Greek Cypriots in the Turkish Cypriot component state as it would emerge from any settlement.

On governance they began looking for ways of avoiding Denktash's requirement for a veto on every decision, whether substantive or procedural, but at the same time of ensuring that the Turkish Cypriots could not just be brushed aside, as they had in effect been in 1963. This led them towards arrangements for a collective decision-making executive body with a rotating, but effectively powerless, presidency, rather close to the Swiss model. For essential tie-breaking purposes they were looking towards a major role for the Supreme Court, on which some non-Cypriot judges would supplement the equal numbers of Greek and Turkish Cypriots.

As to the division of responsibilities between the common and component states, they worked on a very restricted list of powers for the common state, with many of those central responsibilities actually being exercised in Brussels once the new Cyprus joined the European Union, and thus on a very extensive list of responsibilities for the component states, who would also have residual responsibility for any matters not allocated to the common state.

For security issues they envisaged the continuation of the 1960 Treaties of Guarantee and Alliance, not only not diluted in any way but actually extended in that they would now specifically include the guaranteeing of the territorial limits and constitutional order of the component states (which had not existed in 1960). They foresaw the maintenance on the island of a substantial, but much reduced, number of Turkish and Greek troops (numbers not yet identified and, ideally, to be agreed mutually in advance by Turkey and Greece), demobilization of all Greek Cypriot and Turkish Cypriot armed forces, a legally enforceable arms embargo, and a UN-mandated military presence, on which some consultation with the US and the UK had already taken place.

They had also done a great deal of detailed work on the methods for achieving property compensation (the greater part of any property settlement) and restitution (the smaller, strictly limited and quite considerably delayed part of any property settlement). All this work, which was built on the foundations of Annan's 8 November statement, was to come to good use in due course.

In addition a good deal of thought had been given to the issues of continuity, status and sovereignty, which were obviously going to be among the most sensitive to be settled as part of any comprehensive agreement. I had been pressing the UN since the July 2000 session of proximity talks in Geneva to open up the issue of continuity with the two sides. I suggested that there could be more common ground on this than met the eye and that it could lead on to a less confrontational approach to status issues. The fact was that the Greek Cypriots, while they rejected any recognition of the TRNC as such, fully realized that there would need to be some degree of legitimization of all the decisions and legal acts taken by the Turkish Cypriots between 1963 and the date of the entry into force of any settlement. The Turkish Cypriots needed that legitimization, which they could not hope to gain outside a settlement. Moreover, while the Greek Cypriots would never contemplate any suggestion that the new Cyprus should be a successor state of the 1960 Republic, they were prepared to see the 1960 constitution abrogated and replaced by a new one and for the new state of affairs to be unrecognizable from the old. They too had an important stake in continuity. At first the UN had been reluctant to raise the issue of continuity as being too sensitive, but they gradually warmed to the idea. They had not, however, got anywhere with it by the time the talks were broken off in November. Now, in the hiatus that followed, they developed the concept that came to be known as the 'virgin birth' of the new Cyprus, by which a politically new, but legally not new, Cyprus, with elements of continuity with what had passed on both sides of the island since 1963, would come into being the day after approval by the referendums on the two sides, which would in any case be needed to approve any comprehensive agreement.

There remained the vexed question of sovereignty, to which Denktash and the Turks attached fundamental importance, but which they wanted to resolve in a number of different ways. None of these ways had any chance of being accepted by the Greek Cypriots, who had made it very clear that any solution that explicitly located sovereignty with the component states – for example a phrase like the common state's sovereignty 'emanating from the component states' – would not be acceptable. The Greek Cypriots in their turn wanted sovereignty to be the sole perquisite of the common state with no reference at all to the component states having any attributes of sovereignty. The obvious solution was simply to avoid any reference to sovereignty at all, but this was easier said than done in technical and legal terms and was anyway said to be unacceptable to either side. It was agreed that this was too sensitive an issue to be allowed at an early stage of drafting to drift to one or other side of the argument, since whichever side got their way would never later concede the point and whichever did not might well break up the negotiations over it. It would thus have to be held back to a late stage. I suggested to de Soto that part of a solution might lie in calling the 'component' states 'constituent' states – a precedent for which existed in the not very happy example of the Yugoslav federal constitution – or in allowing some reference to the existence of two 'peoples' rather than 'communities', an idea which the Greek Cypriots greatly disliked because of its connotations of self-determination but which might just possibly prove acceptable in a document that banned any possibility of secession, thus making impossible any act of self-determination other than through an irreversible affirmative vote in the referendum endorsing the settlement. He tucked those two ideas away for future reference.

On the basis of all this work, much of which had been carried out in close consultation with the US and the UK, de Soto felt able in July – when it was expected that the negotiating process would resume in September – to share the first draft of an overall view of the various elements that would make up a comprehensive settlement. He clearly hoped to be able to begin familiarizing the parties with it once negotiations resumed, as we all assumed they would. The US and the UK both said they were comfortable with it. The document read as follows:

1. The comprehensive settlement would comprise a short document to which would be attached annexes with the detailed specific legal instruments covering all matters that have to be resolved.

2. The short document, which might be entitled 'JOINT DECLARATION OF AGREEMENT ON A COMPREHENSIVE SETTLEMENT OF THE CYPRUS PROBLEM', could be signed by the two leaders, the three guarantors, and the SG/SASG as witness. Its language would, inter alia,

- signify the leaders' and guarantors' agreement to the comprehensive settlement contained in the document and the annexes thereto;
- outline the general framework of the agreement and the basic principles on which it is based [this would include language on the range of core issues, on virgin birth, on indissolubility, on non-domination, etc];

- state that the new partnership contained in the comprehensive settlement supersedes that reached in 1960 (in particular, the 1960 constitution), without prejudice to the continuation of the 1960 treaties, which it would be clearly stated remain in force [as supplemented by the protocol on security arrangements];
- state that the comprehensive settlement would come into force and be binding only once approved in separate referenda by Greek Cypriots and Turkish Cypriots, conducted in a manner to be outlined in one of the annexes;
- state that, once it came into effect, the comprehensive settlement would be binding on all parties to the agreement and having the force of the law operating in the 'common state' and the 'component states';
- state that, should the comprehensive settlement fail to gain the approval of either side by referendum, it would remain null and void and of no legal affect; and
- list the annexes to the joint declaration of agreement.

3. The annexes to the joint declaration of agreement on a comprehensive settlement could contain the following legal instruments/texts:

I. Protocol on security arrangements.
II. 'Basic law' of the 'common state'.
Appendix to Annex II: Property of the 'common state'.
III. Delineation of territory of the 'component states'.
IV. Treatment of property affected by events since 1960.
V. Dispositions relating to EU accession.
VI. List of international treaties to remain in force for the 'common state' of Cyprus.
VII. 'Common state' legislation to be in force upon entry into force of a comprehensive settlement.
VIII. 'Basic laws' of the 'component states'.
IX. Conduct of referenda to approve the comprehensive settlement (including EU accession).
X. Implementation arrangements.
XI. Establishment of historical clarification commission.

4. It would be ideal to achieve a watershed of broad agreement covering the issues in annexes I–IV by the end of the first half of 2002 so as to make possible full participation of the Turkish Cypriot side in the negotiations over Cyprus's EU membership as early as possible. Whether this watershed is achievable, and how it might be informally marked, will depend upon developments.

It was in fact the first outline of the structure of the proposals that Annan was to put to the parties in November 2002.

Failure and success

When the time arrived for the US/Turkey scenario to be played out, the auguries were not entirely promising. Increasingly extensive leaks about some kind of US understanding with Turkey began to appear in the press, provoking understandable restiveness in Denktash and also among the Greek Cypriots. Since the nature of the understanding could not be commented on and its very existence had to be denied, this left free rein to the press on both sides of the island and in Ankara, which was not renowned for the accuracy and restraint of its reporting. Nevertheless the first stages went ahead as planned. The Turks gave the US the green light, having allegedly squared Denktash, and the Americans asked the UN to act. The meeting between Annan and Denktash took place in Zurich during August, and not in New York, purely for reasons of convenience. In addition de Soto and I were able to persuade Verheugen to interrupt his holiday and also to see Denktash (in Salzburg) with a view to assuring him that the European Union would not allow the rigidities of the *acquis communautaire* to cut across or to undermine provisions in a Cyprus settlement.

Neither meeting was particularly promising. Denktash certainly did not give the impression that he was someone on his way back to the negotiating table but he did not say he was not. Thereafter de Soto began planning his follow-up contacts, and Annan issued invitations to Clerides and Denktash to resume negotiations in New York on 12 September. At this point Denktash, having apparently squared Ecevit, declined the invitation. No explanation was ever given by the Turks, who simply went into an elaborate state of denial about the very existence of a scenario and their own role in making it work. Of only one thing can one be certain and that is that the talks would not have happened in New York on 12 September as planned, even if Denktash had accepted, because the Al Qa'eda attacks on the World Trade Center and the Pentagon took place the day before and travel into and out of New York was interrupted for several days as was the conduct of any UN business other than that relating to the attacks. Those who had put so much effort into restarting the negotiations were now left, like Sisyphus in the fable, watching the stone rolling back down to the bottom of the hill yet again.

In the event, although this was in no way evident at the time, the situation was less hopeless than it seemed. It appears likely that Denktash's rejection of Annan's invitation was more a tactical manoeuvre designed to remind those in Ankara who believed they could negotiate about Cyprus behind his back that he could always outfox them and to reassert his own primacy in the determination of Turkey's Cyprus policy. There were some indications also that the Turkish general staff were surprised and dismayed that the negotiations had not been resumed, as planned, having concluded that the degree of isolation arising from Denktash's refusal to negotiate was harmful to Turkey's interests. Be that as it may, early in November Denktash wrote, completely out of the blue, to Clerides proposing that the two of them should start face-to-face negotiations on the island without any preconditions. This fairly astonishing volte-face in fact went further than the US/Turkish scenario, which had envisaged nothing more ambitious than a resumption of the proximity talks broken off in November 2000, and it quite simply jettisoned a series of Denktash preconditions that had been said many times to be unnegotiable.

Denktash's letter reached Clerides in New York where he had gone for the resumed session of the United Nations General Assembly, postponed after the attacks on the World Trade Center. I saw Clerides in his suite at the Waldorf Astoria as he was considering his response and he showed me the draft reply that had been submitted to him. This, while stopping short of rejection, was full of legalistic quibbles, only too likely to set off a lengthy and possibly fruitless exchange of correspondence. I said I thought something shorter, more political and more positive was called for. The only really tricky point was the involvement of the UN in the proposed negotiations, which Denktash had passed over in silence but which needed to be secured. Assuming that Clerides was prepared to contemplate negotiations in Cyprus and not, as before, in Geneva or New York, which he said he was, there was everything to be said for concluding these preliminaries rapidly and positively. Clerides said he agreed with all that, and was as good as his word, replying very positively. The UN point, although it caused a bit of haggling, with much warning by Denktash that de Soto should not get above his station and must remain 'a fly on the wall' simply taking the note, was also settled satisfactorily, with UN participation in all meetings being agreed and the negotiations to take place on UN ground, in the buffer zone at the former Nicosia international airport.

The switch of the negotiations to Cyprus was an interesting example of how quite trivial procedural points can come to assume an exaggerated importance and then, quite suddenly, disappear. It had been an article of faith for several years – with the UN, with those who supported its efforts and with the Greek Cypriots – that any negotiations must take place off the island. The considerations were that the ubiquity of the Cyprus press and the proximity of the politicians on both sides, together with unhappy experiences with previous rounds of negotiation on the island, meant that this option, which Denktash favoured as a matter of personal convenience, must be resisted at all costs. In the event none of these considerations proved to be very solid. The Cyprus press was ubiquitous whether one was in Geneva or Nicosia; the involvement of politicians was inevitable and necessary; the arguments for allowing two, by now rather elderly, gentlemen to meet and negotiate close to where they lived and without extensive air travel were compelling. In the end no one regretted the decision.

Following the completion of the exchanges of correspondence between the two leaders and the UN, which set January 2002 for the opening of the face-to-face negotiations, and following Clerides's return to the island, there was a further and quite unexpected burst of bonhomie and optimism. Clerides invited Denktash to dine with him at his home in the south of Nicosia, and Denktash then reciprocated in the north. The two leaders thus broke any number of taboos of protocol and status, on which massive quantities of ink had been spilled over the previous three decades and more. Both spoke in a generally upbeat way to the press, Denktash going so far (unwisely as it turned out) as to predict the conclusion of a settlement by June – but there was also a distant roll of thunder in what he said about his need to have heart surgery in the second half of the year. Meanwhile the UN set in hand a crash programme (with generous assistance from the US government) to refurbish some of its pretty dilapidated property at Nicosia Airport so that an adequate conference centre, with air conditioning, could be available for the talks. It all sounded too good to be true, and of course it was; but it was certainly an improvement on everything that had passed hitherto.

10

2002: Countdown to Copenhagen

The face-to-face talks duly began in Cyprus in mid-January and proceeded intensively until the end of September with a break in August. There were two and sometimes three meetings a week, although they became more desultory as the deadlock intensified. In addition to these meetings of the leaders accompanied by their negotiating teams, de Soto pushed hard and with some success for informal meetings attended only by himself, Clerides and Denktash, with no advisers present. He also arranged a number of seminar-type meetings in which he and his UN team went over particularly tricky or complex issues, such as the 'virgin birth' of the new Cyprus or the property issue, with each of the Greek Cypriot and Turkish Cypriot negotiating teams. From the very start Denktash reminded de Soto constantly that he was there only as a 'fly on the wall' – a description used by de Soto in the pre-Christmas bargaining over the format of the talks but which he came to regret. Denktash would not allow the UN to try to capture on paper any emerging areas of common ground, particularly at their informal tête-à-tête meetings, but of course he could not stop the UN gradually building up a more detailed and comprehensive picture of the positions of the two sides and identifying where there was potential overlap between them.

The talks took place in a hastily refurbished line of Nissen huts on the former civil airport at Nicosia. A large, air-conditioned conference room and a suite of offices for the UN team was constructed out of this somewhat unpromising material. Nicosia Airport had been left stranded, like a beached whale, in the UN-controlled buffer zone between the two cease-fire lines when the fighting stopped in 1974. Since then it had remained in a kind of time warp. On the runway stood the rusting carcases of several civilian aeroplanes that had suffered collateral damage in the fighting. The control tower was vandalized and pock-marked with bullet holes. Most of the land within the old airport perimeter had reverted to scruffy scrub, some of which had been cleared to make a golf course, and which harboured rather more bird life than was usual in Cyprus. A few houses, used as quarters by the UN, were dotted around, including the large ugly villa used by the head of the UN peacekeeping force and known to the cognoscenti as 'Lenin's tomb'. The airport, which is on a plateau a bit above the broad plain in which Nicosia is situated, has stunning views. To the north are the Kyrenia Hills and to the south the Troodos Mountains, both easily visible on clear days, which is most days in Cyprus. It had three other inestimable advantages. It was easy of access for both sides, each leader having to go for no more than a ten-minute drive to get there; it was neutral ground; and access to it was controlled by blue-bereted UN soldiers, so there was no question of demonstrators being able to get there.

The Turkish government had spoken with great insistence to both us and the Americans before the face-to-face talks began, asking us not to shadow the negotiations closely as we had done the proximity talks in New York and Geneva. Denktash, they said, needed space to breathe and to develop his thinking if he was to negotiate with flexibility. We both agreed to this request, while expressing lively anticipation of the day when Denktash began to show flexibility. In fact the situation was quite different from New York and Geneva. There we had had little or no Cyprus expertise in residence to cover the negotiations in concert with the UN. In Cyprus we each had an ambassador and fully staffed missions with plenty of expertise on the Cyprus problem. So we worked to a quite different pattern. On the island the UN briefed our missions after every session. We had secure conference telephone calls between de Soto, Weston and myself on average about once or twice a week. And we set out on a Baedeker tour for our tripartite meetings, of which we held 12 in 2002 – two in Paris, two in London, one each in Rome, Vienna, Nicosia and Copenhagen, three in New York and one at Vevey in a delightful hotel high above Lake Geneva between Lausanne and Montreux. Weston and I visited the region frequently and Cyprus even more frequently, but our visits were not connected with particular negotiating sessions as they had been during the proximity talks. Only once did we all meet in Cyprus, our triple presence tending to get the press over excited. This three-layered system of coordination worked admirably and caused less stress to everyone than our previous practice, and it ensured that neither side nor their supporters ever managed to slip even a cigarette paper between our positions. Indeed both the Greek and Turkish Cypriots, inveterate practitioners of playing third parties off against each other, paid us the great compliment of stopping even trying to do so. Once, when I asked Denktash what he had said on a particular point to the Americans, he said, crossly, that he was not going to waste his time telling me, because we already knew the answer.

The early months

The early stages of the face-to-face talks showed some promise. It was not that there were any breakthroughs. There were not. But the atmosphere was reasonably relaxed, the core issues began to be seriously addressed, and there was at least something that could come to life as a real negotiation at short notice if the will was there to make it happen. The contrast with the previous, fallow year, with actual face-to-face talks coupled with the inexorable progress towards the EU's decision-making summit at Copenhagen, seemed to inject a sense of momentum.

Clerides in particular seemed to take on a new lease of life. While he remained sceptical that Denktash was negotiating in good faith, he shook off the grumpy pessimism that had characterized him through the proximity talks and began to hint at, and sometimes to set out reasonably clearly, the sort of concessions he might make as part of an otherwise satisfactory package. He had clearly been impressed by the major effort the international community had made to bring Denktash back to the table without any concessions. And, like the rest of us, he hoped that Turkey's consideration of its European policy would lead it to value more highly a settlement in Cyprus. He accepted the advice that we and the Americans gave him that he should set out up front a conciliatory negotiating position on security issues. We pointed out that, since the Turkish military were unquestionably going to have a major influence on the outcome, it made no real sense to hold back on concessions he was ready to make on security until the end. Better to indicate at an early stage that Turkey's security concerns could and would be met in a comprehensive settlement.

This advice he followed – indeed it matched his own instinctive feeling which had begun to surface during the proximity talks – and after the first few meetings, Denktash and the Turks had no excuse if they did not understand that the structure of a strengthened and open-ended Treaty of Guarantee, a continued Turkish troop presence on the island and a removal of all the existing Greek Cypriot troops and their weapons was potentially on offer. On governance also he hinted that he would not be too demanding over his list of powers for the central authority, which was longer than that which Denktash and even the UN had in mind, and would be prepared to see it whittled away a certain amount. He allowed de Soto to develop the thinking that would subsequently emerge as the virgin birth approach to the new Cyprus. He stated flatly that he was prepared to see the 1960 constitution of the Republic of Cyprus abrogated and not merely amended or adapted, as he and Alecos Markides had originally proposed. He continued to say that his attitude on Greek Cypriot returns to property in the north would be crucially affected by the scale of the territorial adjustment and that he could show flexibility on one if he got satisfaction on the other. And when the vexed issue of the mainland Turks in the north, the 'settlers', could no longer be avoided, he was astute enough to say that if Denktash's first figure of 35,000 could be validated (which of course it could not be as it was a gross understatement) that would cause him no problems. This was a brave, if tactically astute, move by Clerides since it put the Turkish Cypriots thereafter on the back foot as they refused to produce a list of names and argued for much higher figures.

The position of Denktash was quite different. Predictably he began to construct a new version of his preconditions over status, equality and sovereignty. This time it was called 'agreeing on a vision of the new Cyprus'. Once this vision was agreed, he said (and this was a line much favoured also by Cem), then everything else would fall into place. The vision naturally involved recognizing the realities on the island, i.e. two states, making it clear that sovereignty belonged to those states and was granted to the new Cyprus by them and ensuring that political equality required Turkish Cypriot agreement to each and every decision, even procedural ones. But at least at this stage of the negotiations he did not push his point of view to the extent of refusing to discuss the other core issues. He flatly declined, however, to contemplate any discussion of the details of a territorial adjustment until that elusive and ill-defined moment, the final stage; and he continued to insist that the property issue must be dealt with in its entirety by compensation, with no returns by Greek Cypriots to the north. Nevertheless in those early exchanges there were at least some glimmers of hope that progress could be made. However, as Annan's subsequent report on the negotiation put it, 'regrettably, the glimmers seldom lasted beyond the meeting, subsequent meetings often reverting to debates about history or visions' (S/2003/398 of 1 April 2003).

This systematic extinction of glimmers of light began before long to have a negative impact on the talks process. An example gives a picture of what was occurring. After a useful discussion on 23 January of a variety of options for what was destined in due course to be Article 1 of the new constitution of Cyprus and which included the names to be used instead of the current placebos of 'common state' and 'component state', de Soto sent to the two leaders a piece of paper setting out seven possible alternatives as follows:

Possibilities for Article 1 of the Constitution

Option 1. The United Cypriot Republic
The United Cypriot Republic is an independent and sovereign State with a single international legal personality and a common state government and consists of two component states, namely the Greek Cypriot State and the Turkish Cypriot State.

Option 2. The Union of Cyprus
The Union of Cyprus is an independent and sovereign State with a single international legal personality and a central government and consists of two component states, namely the Greek Cypriot State and the Turkish Cypriot State.

Option 3. The State of Cyprus
The State of Cyprus is an independent and sovereign State with a single international legal personality and a common government and consists of two component states, namely the Greek Cypriot State and the Turkish Cypriot State.

Option 4. The State/Union of Cyprus
The State/Union of Cyprus is an independent and sovereign State with a single international legal personality and a federal government and consists of two constituent states, namely the Greek Cypriot State and the Turkish Cypriot State.

Option 5. The United State of Cyprus
The United State of Cyprus is an independent and sovereign State with a single international legal personality and a common state government and consists of two component states/republics, namely the Greek Cypriot Republic and the Turkish Cypriot Republic.

Option 6. The Federal Partnership of Cyprus
The Federal Partnership of Cyprus is an independent and sovereign State with a single international personality and a federal government and con-

sists of two partner states, namely the Greek Cypriot State and the Turkish Cypriot State.

Option 7. The Federation of Cyprus/Cypriot Federation
The Federation of Cyprus/Cypriot Federation is an independent and sovereign State with a single international legal personality and a federal government and consists of two constituent partner states, namely the Greek Cypriot State and the Turkish Cypriot State.

The next day Clerides replied in writing, accepting with some qualifications four of the alternatives (Nos. 1, 3, 4 and 7) and, at the subsequent meeting, accepted a fifth (No. 5) which had been the only one Denktash had accepted the day before. Denktash then rejected all seven. It was difficult to understand what was going on on the Turkish Cypriot and Turkish side of the fence. It was rapidly becoming clear that the decision by Denktash and the Turks back in the autumn of 2001 to initiate face-to-face talks, and thus to execute a complete procedural U-turn, had not been accompanied or followed up by any definition of a series of negotiable positions on the core issues. Denktash himself seemed to be navigating without a compass. He was not allowed to walk out of the talks, as he had done in November 2000 and as he would probably have liked to do again, but he had been given no clear idea of where the Turkish red lines were and what his ultimate destination was intended to be. In these circumstances he reverted to playing for time in a filibuster which it was increasingly difficult to sustain as the months went by. The backing and filling to which he resorted, and which became part of a pattern, was less easy to explain. Was it simply the result of advice he received from his hardline Turkish (but not Turkish government) adviser, Soysal? Or was he actually being pulled back by the Turkish government itself? And, if so, why? The probable answer was that it was a mixture of all these elements but, at least during the course of the negotiations, no explanation was vouchsafed.

The effect of this on Clerides was thoroughly negative. He began to regret that he had shown so much flexibility at an early stage of the face-to-face negotiations and to worry that this risked exposing him to his domestic critics. He told de Soto that he was no longer prepared to come to tête-à-tête meetings, since Denktash invariably clawed back at later plenary meetings any movement he had demonstrated at the private ones. There was then a substantial hiatus in such private meetings, which was only overcome by the persuasion of the UN, the US, the UK and, even-

tually, of the Greek government too, all of whom pointed out that filibustering at the plenary meetings was much easier than at the private
ones and that it was important to keep up the pressure which Denktash
clearly felt at the private meetings. Meanwhile the plenary sessions began
to deteriorate into exchanges of lengthy papers recycling the respective
positions taken up by the two sides in the proximity talks two years
before, and into polemical exchanges, both spoken and written, in which
the forensic skills of Markides came to the fore but not to any very useful
purpose. In parallel with this deterioration of the atmosphere within the
negotiations, the public perception of what was going on remained completely negative and cynical. Denktash, who had never been much
troubled by Annan's request to maintain a press blackout, defended at
great length in the media his fundamental views on status and sovereignty. On the Greek Cypriot side the desire not to reveal publicly any
flexibility being shown in the negotiations themselves was reflected in a
presentation that depicted the negotiations as totally stuck because of
Denktash's obduracy, which was part of the story but not the whole of it.
So by April the negotiations had bogged down and were badly in need of
a shot in the arm.

The secretary-general lends a hand

As the pace of the negotiations slowed and the prospect dwindled of the
two parties making substantial progress, the need for some external
impetus to get things moving forwards became more urgent. Already the
end-June target date for completion of a comprehensive settlement, so
surprisingly put forward by Denktash before Christmas, was losing
credibility, and he himself was daily subverting it in his press comments.
It was, however, evidently too soon for the UN to be putting on the table
a proposal for a comprehensive settlement, and to table proposals on one
or another of the core issues was certain to arouse objections all round. So
the UN and its supporters were not spoiled for procedural choices. Annan
could, as was the normal practice, invite the two leaders to meet him in
New York or in some European capital where his hectic travel schedule
might take him in the late spring of 2002, or he could himself visit the
island, which no secretary-general since Waldheim had done. The latter
approach had a number of advantages. It avoided the possibility of a long
haggle with the leaders about whether a visit to New York was desirable
and, if so, when it should be; it sent a much stronger public message that
the negotiations were for real; and it provided Annan with an opportunity

to deploy his undoubted presentational skills in reviving what was fast becoming a moribund public image of the negotiations. For all these reasons the US and the UK strongly favoured a visit to the island and so too, more hesitantly, did the UN itself, once they had overcome their qualms about committing the secretary-general to a meeting which was highly unlikely to result in a breakthrough. Annan decided to visit the island from 14 to 16 May and so briefed the Security Council. Faced with the unlikelihood of any breakthrough on a core issue, the UN set as its objective getting a green light from the two leaders for de Soto to begin codifying the outcome of the face-to-face talks, which was of course diplomatic speak for beginning to create the building blocks of a comprehensive settlement.

Annan duly came and went, but there was not much to show for the visit. The personal atmosphere at the talks remained calm and friendly. Annan himself demonstrated yet again his skill at managing the most awkward interlocutors and avoided the temptation to lock horns with Denktash, which had proved his predecessor Boutros-Ghali's undoing. But he did not succeed in getting a green light for de Soto to codify the negotiations (although de Soto in fact began tentatively to do so within weeks). And when, in his farewell statement, Annan expressed the hope that, even now, the end-June target date might be met, Denktash, in a statement that was as gratuitous as it was counter-productive, contradicted him.

Nevertheless, within a matter of days, it looked as if the visit might indeed register a change of gear because by the end of May the two sides were tantalizingly close to agreement on the outline for handling security issues. The open-ended and undiluted continuance of the Treaties of Guarantee and Alliance and their adaptation to the circumstances of a bizonal island, which in particular strengthened the terms of the Treaty of Guarantee by extending the guarantee to the territorial integrity and constitutional order of the two component states as well as of Cyprus as a whole (as had been the case in 1960), was agreed. So too was the demobilization of all Cypriot armed forces, the removal from the island of their weaponry, and the need for a legally binding arms embargo. And the need for a UN-mandated international military presence, to operate island-wide and not just along the Green Line, to underpin but not to enforce the terms of an agreement, was also settled. De Soto had got both sides to agree that he put all this down on paper and there remained a minimal number of square bracketed points to be negotiated. In addition the troop levels of the residual Greek and Turkish military presence in the south and the north of the island remained to be negotiated, but it had always been envisaged that this figure should be left to be determined at the end of the whole process, preferably by direct negotiation between the Greeks and the Turks.

At this point Denktash performed one of his infuriating two-steps. Having cooperated in discussion of the text, he drew back and said that Turkey was unhappy about the provisions for a UN-mandated international military presence. They needed more time and would want a weaker text, as they were said to be concerned that the UN mandate could lead to aggressive implementation in the teeth of opposition by Turkey. Clerides then withdrew his provisional agreement to the whole document. It was made clear by both sides that further discussion of this issue in the short term would be fruitless. Clerides's willingness to agree the security chapter, albeit provisionally, had been something of a gamble. It had contained major concessions on his part to the Turkish and Turkish Cypriot point of view, and allowing security to be settled and banked before any of the other core issues had been settled was likely to be sharply criticized by his rejectionist opponents once it became known, which it inevitably would.

Why the Turks (because on this occasion it seems clear that it was their doing) passed up this opportunity to nail down an agreement strongly favourable to them remains a mystery. When I took the matter up with Ziyal soon afterwards he replied, somewhat feebly, that the Turks wanted to have some concessions in hand for the final stage of the negotiations. Certainly the alleged Turkish problems with de Soto's security text were never raised in the ensuing months of the negotiations, nor was a word said from the Turkish side when the same text emerged in the successive iterations of the Annan Plan. I am inclined to suspect that the problem arose in the somewhat defective coordination between the Turkish foreign ministry and the military. Be that as it may, the consequence of this setback was that the end-June target date no longer had any meaning at all. A wider consequence was that it put an end to steps to negotiate issue by issue, banking the points provisionally agreed as one went along, the normal way most successful negotiations proceed.

Britain's role in the negotiations

As one of the UN's main backers in the effort to get a comprehensive settlement of the Cyprus problem, Britain needed to be active but not too

prominent in the process. We needed to be in touch with all the participants, oiling the wheels where we could, exercising discreet pressure here
and there and helping two multilateral organizations, the UN and the EU,
not very accustomed to working together, to cooperate effectively. But we
also needed to avoid appearing to take the process over, partly because it
was only going to succeed if the UN remained centre stage and in charge
and partly because Britain's historical inheritance in the Eastern Mediterranean of suspicion and residual hostility made it unlikely that any
activity that was clearly labelled as British would succeed.

But we could move things forward discreetly, and we did. Peter Hain,
the minister for Europe at the Foreign and Commonwealth Office, visited
Cyprus in April 2002 for talks with Clerides and Denktash. He decided to
try to give the public diplomacy surrounding the negotiations a bit of a
push by means of a speech to a bi-communal audience at the Ledra Palace
Hotel on the Green Line. Such occasions were not unprecedented but
they were unusual, press conferences at the Ledra Palace being more
common, as Denktash normally banned Turkish Cypriots from attending
any event where they might meet Greek Cypriots. The turn-out was
excellent even if the Turkish Cypriot parties that supported Denktash,
and his own entourage, were noticeable by their absence. On the Greek
Cypriot side, unusually, the foreign minister, Kasoulides, attended. As so
often, it was striking how warm the personal relationships between
Turkish and Greek Cypriots were. Both in the opening paragraph of the
speech and in the peroration Hain referred to 'the peoples of Cyprus/of
this island'. In the code-dominated vocabulary of speeches about Cyprus
this reference came high on the Richter scale, it being obligatory in the
south to refer to the Turkish Cypriots as a 'community' (although the
Greek Cypriots did not hesitate to talk about themselves as 'the Cypriot
people' when outside the island). Anyway the reference to 'peoples' did
not pass unnoticed by either side. There was great satisfaction in the
north where the habits of verbal denigration never failed to draw blood
and to win adherents to Denktash's demands for full recognition. In the
south there was the usual media furore designed to get the erring visitor
to recant and recognize the error of his ways. But Hain stood his ground
and told the House of Commons that he would not fancy telling his
Welsh constituents that they were not a people. In reality the Greek
Cypriot concern that the use of the word 'people' opened the door to self-
determination, which was but one step away from secession, was over-

blown. But it did show the astonishing sensitivity to such semantic questions.

A few weeks later Cem, the Turkish foreign minister, took advantage of a NATO ministerial meeting to lobby his colleagues on behalf of Denktash's 'vision first' approach and to try, by handing over a non-paper, to persuade them of the virtues of the Turkish vision. The UN, who were not in any case present at a NATO meeting, were not well placed to explain the essential unreality and unnegotiability of the Turkish approach; as facilitators of the negotiation they had to be extremely careful to avoid crossing swords openly with either side. Britain and the US, both of whom had been lobbied, could more easily do so and did. Jack Straw's reply to the non-paper pointed out: 'The overall impression we have from your paper is that its proposals are more like a permanent negotiating diplomatic conference between two independent states likely to spend much of its time in, or approaching, deadlock, than the functioning institutions of a state which would have assumed the rights and responsibilities of UN and EU membership and would need to be able to speak with one voice in the counsels of those bodies and fully to implement its obligations within them.' Such straight talking was crucially important for the UN negotiations.

My own worries about the way the negotiations were going, or rather not going, had begun to focus on the fact that no one in Turkey outside the small group of officials in the foreign ministry who dealt with Cyprus seemed to have the slightest idea of how far the possible solutions were moving towards meeting basic Turkish interests and concerns. So, having consulted de Soto and our own ambassador in Ankara, Peter Westmacott, I decided that, on my next visit to Ankara, I would speak out about the shape of the solutions emerging. My interview with Mehmet Ali Birand of CNN Turk on 6 June caused plenty of waves. I pointed out that the new Cyprus would have a new flag, a new national anthem, a new name (it would not be called the Republic of Cyprus). It would in fact be the new partnership, for which the Turks and Turkish Cypriots had been calling. It would have a new constitution and it would be made up of two constituent states in which Greek Cypriots and Turkish Cypriots would be masters in their own houses for a whole range of policies. The effect of this interview in Turkey was entirely beneficial. It contributed to what developed later in the year into a thoroughly healthy national debate about the pros and cons of Turkey's Cyprus policy instead of the tacit acceptance of the conventional wisdom that had prevailed up to then. In the south of Cyprus the effect was pandemonium. There were demands for me to be banned from the island or for the British government to be asked to sack me. A heavily sedated and cynical public opinion had suddenly realized that something quite far-reaching might be about to happen. Luckily I had pre-positioned transcripts of the interview in Athens, Ankara and Nicosia, so the wilder claims of the commentators, for example that I had called for the recognition of two states in Cyprus, could easily be refuted. Gradually the storm blew itself out. When I next saw Clerides at the end of August I thought I had better apologize for all the trouble my interview had caused him. Forget it, he said; it is all in a day's work.

One further modest British contribution was made. De Soto's travelling between the three regional capitals was greatly complicated by the fact that it took the better part of a day to get from Nicosia, where he was based, via Athens and Istanbul to Ankara, where he was certainly going to need to go frequently in the final stages of the negotiations, and the better part of a day to get back again. So a visit to Ankara took three days (flying directly from the RAF base at Akrotiri to Ankara took about 1½ hours). This absurdly long detour was necessitated by the fact that there were no scheduled flights between Cyprus and Turkey, except for those from the north of the island which, for political reasons, de Soto could not use. So he appealed to a number of European countries for help in hiring a private aircraft (the US had budgetary problems which prevented them doing so) and this was forthcoming, with the British contribution the largest. The aircraft was much in use in October, November and January and enabled de Soto to leave Nicosia by UNFICYP helicopter to Akrotiri, to fly from Akrotiri to Ankara for lengthy talks and to return the same way, all in a working day.

The European Union: the parallel track

From the beginning of 2002 there was no longer any serious questioning of whether the critical decisions on the European Union's enlargement would be taken at the end of the year and the terms of accession for the ten applicant countries in the first wave, including Cyprus, would be definitively settled at the December meeting of the European Council in Copenhagen. The European Union, having dithered and temporized and become bogged down in detail over many years, had now changed gear and was lumbering towards the finishing line. What still remained in doubt was whether the Cyprus that would be admitted would be a divided one or a reunited one, and whether some important step in the handling of Turkey's EU candidature would be taken at the same time. These two issues were of the greatest importance to the Cyprus settlement negotiations. As time went by, it became increasingly unrealistic to hope that the settlement negotiations would be wound up successfully in good time for the outcome to be taken on board in an orderly fashion at Copenhagen. A more likely scenario was of decisions on both tracks being broadly simultaneous, a prospect that bristled with problems both technical and political.

The two 2002 European Union presidencies were held by Spain during the first half of the year and by Denmark in the second half. Neither country had very strong links with or major interests in either Cyprus or Turkey, indeed neither at the outset even had diplomatic missions in Nicosia, although both remedied that. Perhaps helped by this detachment, both performed their presidency role to perfection. I worked very closely throughout with the Spanish minister for Europe, Ramon de Miguel, and with the permanent-under-secretary equivalent at the Danish foreign ministry, Friis Arne Petersen. The Spaniards had the easier hand to play. They had to set the stage for negotiations that would only come to a head after the end of their presidency. On Cyprus they needed to re-emphasize the European Union's strong preference for admitting a re-united island over a divided one, without detracting an iota from the position established at Helsinki that a political settlement was not a pre-condition for accession. Of even greater importance, they needed to repeat and endorse at heads of government level a position earlier agreed at the end of 2001 at foreign-minister level that the European Union would 'accommodate' any UN settlement when admitting a reunited island, while reiterating two firm but relatively uncontentious European Union conditions that had been set out by the presidency of the Commission, Romano Prodi, when he visited Nicosia in the autumn of 2001, that a reunited Cyprus must be able to speak with a single voice at the EU and to implement its EU obligations. On Turkey they needed to signal that important decisions on Turkey's candidature could (not would) be taken at Copenhagen but that much depended on how Turkey handled matters in the meanwhile. The Seville European Council in June 2002 set out these points admirably, and the fact that it did so with Greek concurrence was particularly important. The text read as follows:

> In respect of the accession of Cyprus, the Helsinki conclusions are the basis of the European Union's position. The European Union's preference is

still for the accession of a reunited island. The European Council fully supports the efforts of the Secretary-General of the United Nations and calls upon the leaders of the Greek Cypriot and Turkish Cypriot communities to intensify and expedite their talks in order to seize this unique window of opportunity for a comprehensive settlement, consistent with the relevant UN Security Council resolutions, it is to be hoped before the conclusion of the negotiations. The European Union would accommodate the terms of such a comprehensive settlement in the Treaty of Accession in line with the principles on which the European Union is founded: as a Member State, Cyprus will have to speak with a single voice and ensure proper application of European Union law. The European Union would make a substantial financial contribution in support of the development of the northern part of a reunited island.

The European Council welcomes the reforms recently adopted in Turkey. It encourages and fully supports the efforts made by Turkey to fulfil the priorities defined in its Accession partnership. The implementation of the required political and economic reforms will bring forward Turkey's prospects of accession in accordance with the same principles and criteria as are applied to the other candidate countries. New decisions could be taken in Copenhagen on the next stage of Turkey's candidature in the light of developments in the situation between the Seville and Copenhagen European Councils, on the basis of the regular report to be submitted by the Commission in October 2002 and in accordance with the Helsinki and Laeken conclusions.

The story of the Danish presidency belongs to a later part of this chapter.

Over the years the Commission had done everything they could to prepare for the eventuality of the admission to the EU of a reunited island. They had tried to improve knowledge and understanding of the European Union in the north through their delegate in Nicosia. They had attempted to find ways to build up their own technical data on the economy and legislation of the north so that a necessarily crash programme to examine the compatibility of this with the *acquis communautaire* would not need to start from scratch. They had sought ways of preparing projects in the north for European Union funding should a settlement make this possible and had earmarked substantial funds for that object. But at every step they had been thwarted by Denktash and by the government of the TRNC.

The foreign minister of the TRNC, Tahsin Ertugruloglu, seemed to have little better to do than frustrate every attempt by the Commission delegate in Nicosia to work in the north; petty harassment was the order of the day. He could not, however, prevent the Turkish Cypriot Chamber of Commerce cooperating closely with the Commission over the provision of factual material about the EU, nor could he prevent the member states (of whom he was rather more respectful than of the Commission) running seminars in the north with expert speakers who could respond to the steadily increasing appetite there for information about the European Union and all its works. But every attempt to prepare the legislative ground for accession and to get EU money flowing towards the north was shipwrecked on the issue of status and recognition. This reached its highest absurdity when Denktash's sidekick, Olgun, told the Commission that he would only cooperate if they wrote to him officially as 'the undersecretary to the president of the TRNC', a title that he knew perfectly well not one of the representatives of the EU member states in Nicosia would be prepared to give him. It was very clear from this campaign by the Turkish Cypriot authorities that they regarded the prospect of membership of the European Union as a serious challenge to their grip on Turkish Cypriot politics and to the hard line on a settlement they were pursuing in the negotiations, just as Denktash regarded the prospect of Turkey's eventual membership of the European Union as a threat to his own grip on Turkey's Cyprus policy.

The endorsement by the Seville European Council of the commitment to 'accommodate' a UN settlement in the terms of accession for a reunited Cyprus gave the Commission and its officials a more solid basis from which to intensify the contacts they had already begun to develop with the UN negotiating team. It had been clear from the outset that any negotiable settlement would need to offer the Turkish Cypriots reassurance that their component state would not be flooded with Greek Cypriots buying up property and businesses once the normal provisions of European Union law applied to the whole island, as they would do when a reunited island was admitted. There were other tricky issues such as the European Security and Defence Policy and those that would arise with respect to the access by Turks to the Turkish Cypriot component state once it was part of the European Union and had to apply the Schengen provisions of the *acquis*. Now it became urgent to define the necessary transitional arrangements or derogations that would need to be included in any comprehensive set of proposals the UN might put to the two sides later in the year. All this had to be done with the greatest discretion given the tendency of many Greek Cypriots to believe that application of the *acquis communautaire* to the north unamended would deliver to them outcomes that they could not get the Turkish Cypriots to accept at the UN negotiating table. Verheugen gave this work his full support, despite the fact that he was precluded from clearing his lines in advance with member states; he and his officials therefore had to make a judgement cold on what they thought the EU market would bear.

On one issue alone the Turkish Cypriot authorities' attitude to the European Union was less than totally negative, namely the decision-making processes to be applied in a new Cyprus to establish positions on European Union business. For some time a group of ethnically Turkish Belgian academics had been pressing on Denktash and on the Turkish government the attractions of the internal machinery for coordinating EU policy, which the Belgian government had set up some years before when Belgium had become a highly devolved federal state. This machinery covered not only issues for which the central government was responsible but also those for which the component state governments in a federation were responsible and issues where responsibility was shared between the central and the component state governments. All this surfaced in the UN negotiations in late June 2002 with the tabling by the Turkish Cypriots of a paper entitled 'Some characteristics of the Belgian state that may apply to the new partnership state of Cyprus'. This was the single most convincing and influential paper the Turkish Cypriots tabled throughout the negotiations. It is hard to believe that Denktash and Soysal fully understood the implications of it. But the UN certainly did and much of it found its way into their proposals.

Another Turkish earthquake

Quite soon after the face-to-face talks got under way, and once the bloom had worn off them, it became apparent that Clerides and Denktash were not going to be able to conclude a comprehensive settlement unaided. Later it also became evident that an incremental approach, with the parties, assisted by the UN, reaching tentative and provisional agreement on this or that issue and banking it while they moved on to other issues, was also not going to be possible. So, gradually, the option that had from the outset seemed the most likely one – for the UN secretary-general himself to table a draft comprehensive settlement – became the only viable one to hand. But it had been agreed between the UN, the US and the UK that no hint of that should be allowed to surface and no planning should be undertaken until after the end-June target date for completion had been overrun. That it was likely to be overrun had been obvious for many weeks but it made no sense to throw away even the modest amount of leverage afforded by the target date before one had to. At a tripartite meeting in Paris on 5 July thought was given to a timetable that would have involved Annan bringing the leaders to New York early in October, presenting them with his proposals and then beginning an open-ended negotiating process with them, probably outside but close to New York. This timetable, while already quite a tight one in view of the European Union's enlargement timetable, offered some scope for consultation recesses and dramatic interruptions of the kind to be anticipated in any Cyprus negotiation.

Within days of that meeting, however, the Turkish coalition government began to collapse and this put paid to any such a carefully calibrated countdown. The Turkish government had been in difficulties ever since the winter, when a well-publicized row between the president and the prime minister at a National Security Council meeting had sent the financial markets into a tailspin from which they had not recovered and which the government was ill equipped to handle. By the beginning of July the financial crisis, the government's inability to master it, the effects of a massive forced devaluation of the lira, the looming consequences in terms of inflation and unemployment, the failing health of the reclusive prime minister, Ecevit, and the tensions between the three coalition parties, all of whom were shown by the opinion polls to have almost no popular support, brought things to breaking point. The government then proceeded to collapse in slow motion over a period of weeks. The foreign minister, Cem, resigned not only from his office but from Ecevit's DSP and went off to found a new party, defections of members of parliament from the governing coalition parties became a daily occurrence and the pressure to call an early election mounted. By the time the dust settled at the end of August, there was only an interim, caretaker government, still led in title, but no more, by an ailing Ecevit and with a new foreign minister, Sükrü Sina Gürel. A large package of EU-compliant legislation had been passed at Yilmaz's behest in a last-ditch attempt to rescue his party's fortunes, and a general election had been called for the first week of November. The opinion polls were predicting (quite accurately in the event) that because of Turkey's 10 per cent threshold for being represented in parliament, none of the three coalition parties nor the main opposition party (Ciller's DYP) would be represented in the new parliament. The only parties that would be represented on these predictions would be Erdogan's Islamic AK party, which had risen from the ashes of earlier, banned Islamic parties, and the CHP (Atatürk's and Inönü's old party) which had been out of the previous parliament, having fallen short of the 10 per cent threshold.

None of these dramatic political events was even remotely caused by developments in Cyprus but they did have a considerable impact on them. By the time of the next tripartite meeting in Vienna on 27 July it was already becoming clear that the previous scenario was unrealistic, and when we met in Paris on 7 September a number of points had come into sharper focus. Nothing positive could be expected from the interim government whose prime minister believed he had settled the Cyprus problem in 1974 and whose foreign minister (who had previously been the minister for Cyprus, not directly involved in the negotiations for a settlement but more concerned with disbursing the $200 million dollars or so which Turkey had to spend every year – not counting military costs – to prop up the TRNC) was generally reckoned to be even harder line than Denktash. So if Annan made his proposals before the Turkish election they could well be rejected out of hand. It would in any case be extremely unwise to throw a complex settlement plan, which concerned a national issue for Turkey, into the mêlée of a general election campaign. So a month was lost which could ill be spared. Another consequence of the recent events was that Yilmaz's EU legislative package had placed Turkey in a better position than before to hope for a positive result at Copenhagen. Of this hope the interim government wasted no time at all in reminding its EU partners. Gürel's visits to EU capitals in September were designed to push that case, but they also provided an excellent opportunity to remind him forcefully that EU governments were expecting Turkey to help get a Cyprus settlement by the end of the year – a message that fell on deaf ears.

The run-up to the proposals

Annan invited Clerides and Denktash to meet him in Paris on 6 September. The week before I spent some days in Cyprus and over the weekend was able to see the leaders in relaxed conditions, outside their offices. My objective was to bring home to each of them that time was running out to reach a solution during the time frame before Copenhagen when international interest and pressure were creating the best circumstances for achieving the necessary compromises. The subliminal themes – which had to remain subliminal, because it was not my job to predict precisely

what the UN would do and when – were that the face-to-face talks process had now gone as far as it could, that the UN had a shrewd idea of
where each side's genuine red lines were, and that the time was fast
approaching when the UN would need to draw all the threads together
and provide the basis for a negotiated settlement. I found Clerides, as
usual at his best out on the sea in his beloved boat and swimming off Cape
Greco, the south-eastern tip of the island, very calm and determined to
see the process through to the end and to demonstrate the flexibility
needed to get a deal if that was reciprocated by the other side. He believed he would be able to negotiate effectively up to December; after that
it would be more problematic (a presidential election was due in the south
in February 2003 and candidacies would be declared, at the latest round
about Christmas). This was in sharp contrast to earlier dire warnings that,
come the autumn, his hands would be increasingly tied by electoral
politics. He was watching the electoral campaign in Turkey with interest
and some hope, but remained to be convinced that the outcome would
bring much change.

Denktash the next day was just as hospitable, in the pool at his house
by Snake Island, looking over the sea towards Turkey, and afterwards at
lunch on the terrace. He seemed rather subdued, preoccupied by the
gathering signs that his political supporters in Ankara were doing badly in
the election campaign and that he was likely shortly to find himself dealing with a completely new and unpredictable government formed by a
party that all his secular and Atatürkist instincts inclined him to dislike.
We went over familiar ground at lunch, much of it to do with the core
issues and mercifully little with the 'vision' set of preconditions; unusually he took copious notes throughout.

In Paris on 6 September Annan did not mince his words, to Denktash
in particular. He referred to a 'profound sense of disappointment' that
more progress had not been made since they had last met in May. He
explained why neither of the two simple overall approaches, recognition
of the TRNC or absorption of the TRNC into the existing Republic of
Cyprus would work, and urged Denktash to see the virtues of an approach that did not mention the word 'sovereignty' at all, but focused
instead on the exercise of powers at different levels of authority – by the
EU, by the common state and by the component states – with no hierarchy between them. He set out the prize to be achieved in the shape of an
entirely new Cyprus in terms almost identical to my CNN Turk interview. He pressed hard for full engagement on the core issues, explaining

why Denktash's refusal to discuss a territorial adjustment was blocking consideration of tight numerical controls on Greek Cypriots returning to their property in the north, which Clerides was willing to contemplate. He went over the ground on governance, pointing out why giving the Turkish Cypriots a veto over every decision, whether procedural or substantive, was not necessarily the best way of protecting their interests. He argued that Clerides's recent hint that he could accept a rotating, non-executive presidency marked a real breakthrough, and warned Denktash against his practice of publicly misrepresenting Clerides's position in unjustifiably negative terms. And he warned that if the pre-Copenhagen opportunity for a settlement was not taken the Greek Cypriots' position would strengthen: 'The most leverage you will ever have is right now.'

Clerides got off more lightly, but he too was warned that time was getting short, that while his relative flexibility up to now had been very welcome more would be required ('If Mr Denktash does engage seriously, down the road, in a genuine negotiation, you will be pressed to be flexible on other points as well'), and a clear indication was given that a UN comprehensive proposal was in the offing ('We are preparing avenues so that, should the moment be right to make a move, we will be ready to do so'). The responses were, as usual, sharply contrasted. Clerides replied in broadly positive generalities; Denktash treated Annan to a lengthy, para-noid disquisition on how unfair everyone – the Security Council, the European Union – had been to the Turkish Cypriots and how all these injustices must first be corrected if there was to be a settlement. He repeated his 'vision' for a new Cyprus, but did at least refer to my CNN Turk interview as 'a bold, yet half-way attempt' to meet Turkish Cypriot needs and interests. He simply declined to grapple with any of the core issues. The only concrete outcome to the meeting was an agreement to meet in New York on 3–4 October.

With the two leaders back on the island, de Soto launched a major effort to push the negotiations ahead on the core issues, and in particular to get some sort of dialogue going on the territorial adjustment and on the – linked – constraints on the right of Greek Cypriots to own property in the north, many of whom would be returnees. He only had limited suc-cess in this because of Denktash's continuing refusal to discuss territory and his insistence that, before he could do so, he must be assured that the Turkish Cypriots would exercise sovereignty over that part of the island allocated in an agreement to the Turkish Cypriot component state. Meanwhile a small, informal group composed of Markides, Soysal and

Pfirter, de Soto's deputy and legal adviser, had begun to identify a framework within which there could be a systematic discussion of the international obligations the new Cyprus would assume from those entered into by the Republic of Cyprus and the TRNC, of the validity of acts taken by each prior to the entry into force of a comprehensive agreement and also of the mostly uncontentious but very substantial body of legislation that would be required by the new common state. This framework, which might have been called a 'sovereignty umbrella' if the sovereignty word had not been so sensitive as to be unmentionable, had actually found its way on to paper by 26 September and so was available for the New York meeting on 3–4 October.

Meanwhile that rumble of distant thunder, first heard from Denktash in December 2001 when the face-to-face talks were initiated, to the effect that he might need heart surgery in the second half of 2002, was rapidly materializing into an imminent storm of unpredictable dimensions and duration. First it was announced that he would be having a check-up in New York after the talks in October, then that he would definitely be going in for surgery on 5 October immediately the talks had concluded. Even if the timetable ahead had been less tight and even if Cyprus had not been a place whose every inhabitant was a conspiracy theorist, a good deal more would have been read into these announcements than met the eye. As it was, the speculation that Denktash was playing a hospital card as part of a continuing filibuster was almost universal, and not merely among his adversaries in the south of the island. That Denktash needed heart surgery was not in doubt; he had had several heart problems over the preceding years. That he had not lost the considerable amount of weight his doctors said was necessary before an operation was also not in doubt. The motivation of the timing of the operation can only remain an unsolved mystery until, if ever, more is known about the medical background. What is clear is that nothing was done at any stage, either at the time of the operation or in the weeks following, when complications set in, to mitigate the effect of his absence from the negotiating table.

When Annan met Clerides and Denktash in New York on 3–4 October the departure of Denktash from the negotiating scene, at least for some weeks, was already a given fact, but not one that was taken too dramatically in the light of the continuing shadow cast by the Turkish elections over that period and by the need, increasingly less well concealed, for the UN to work intensively on the preparation of its package of proposals. Annan therefore concentrated on getting agreement on the setting up of a number of working groups that could carry forward the absolutely essential technical work during the month of October. He aimed for three, one dealing with the international obligations of the new Cyprus, one with the legislation for the common state and one to go over the technical aspects of a territorial adjustment and of property compensation and restitution. On 3 October the two leaders agreed to all three. The next day Denktash withdrew his agreement to the third working group but not to the other two. This latest two-step by Denktash was even more open and more damaging to Turkey than the previous ones, since the obvious assumption, possibly but not certainly correct, was that Turkey had told him overnight to draw back on the key issues of territory and property. The loss of the third working group was at the time not taken too tragically since no one at that stage knew or even suspected that Denktash would simply fail to nominate his representatives to the other two groups for over two months, thus ensuring that they could neither meet nor do any work for the rest of the year. That blatant act of bad faith had serious implications for the final stages of the negotiation, when the failure of the two groups to have completed their heavy work schedule was given by Denktash as a reason why any referendum on Annan's proposals in the spring of 2003 would be premature.

With Denktash in hospital in New York, and unable, as a result of medical complications, to return to Cyprus until the very end of November, the process of twice or three times weekly face-to-face meetings came to an end. In its place de Soto undertook an intensive process of consultation, with the Turkish and Greek governments, with the European Commission and with the UN's main backers, the US and the UK. The latter consultations (with the US and the UK) have since been grossly exaggerated to the extent of suggesting that the Annan Plan was virtually written by one or other or both of the governments. It was not. Naturally much of the thinking in the Annan Plan had evolved over many years of negotiation, going back to Boutros-Ghali's Set of Ideas and beyond, and much of what was in the plan had emerged from the intensive process of coordination that the US, the UK and the UN had practised ever since the latest effort to get a comprehensive settlement really got under way at the end of 1999. But in the last hectic month before the first version of the plan (Annan I) was put forward the consultation with the US and the UK was about policy issues and choices, not about texts, which the UN kept to themselves and, quite rightly, did not share. In some cases the advice given was not followed. For example the US and the UK favoured sticking to Annan's original preference for not mentioning the word 'sovereignty' at all, but the UN at a late stage diverted to an approach that clearly gave sovereignty to the new Cyprus but equally clearly said that the component states exercise their own extensive powers 'sovereignly'. In other cases the advice was accepted. For example, the idea of putting four asterisks in place of the numbers of residual Turkish and Greek troops to remain on the island, thus effectively creating a bracket between 1,000 and 9,999, was one the UN accepted. One specific piece of consultation related to the UK alone. We were asked if we could, as a guarantor power, agree to the amendments to the Treaty of Guarantee extending its scope to cover the territorial limits and constitutional order of the two component states. We said we could.

Consultation with the European Commission also proceeded smoothly. This was confined to the policy areas where the Plan created potential overlap or incompatibility with the strict wording of the *acquis communautaire*. With Greece and most particularly with Turkey, the process was more wide ranging. The Greeks were thoroughly supportive and made it clear that they were prepared to enter into bilateral negotiations with Turkey at any convenient time to establish the exact size of their residual troop presence in Cyprus. They favoured as low a number as possible but did not specify one, and they left the impression that this was unlikely to be a sticking point. De Soto paid several visits to Ankara during October for talks with Ziyal and his foreign ministry team (at which, however, the military were never represented). These talks were long, difficult and substantive. The Turks engaged on the substance of all the core issues, without sheltering behind the preconditions of which Denktash was so fond and indeed giving the impression that they found the 'virgin birth' approach to a new Cyprus interesting and potentially acceptable. They were also fully aware by now that they were in the last stages of the preparation of a comprehensive set of proposals by the UN and they took no exception to that. They were extremely nervous about discussing territory and would not get far into that issue. On governance they insisted on the need to avoid any scope for Greek Cypriot dominance of the institutions, and showed a preference for a Swiss-style executive council with collective responsibility over a non-executive rotating presidency with a prime minister chosen by a majority in the legislature. Their reserve on security issues was confirmed as being tactical and concerns about how UNFICYP II, as it was called, would operate and would relate to the residual Turkish troop presence in the island did not appear to be insurmountable. On property they continued strongly to prefer a scheme based on compensation alone but seemed to understand that the complexities of the UN ideas were designed to come up with a result that was not too different from that in practice.

When I visited the island from 24 to 26 October (the only occasion on which Weston, de Soto and I were there together), I found myself in the middle of one of those mini-crises in which the Greek Cypriots special-ized. While intellectually they accepted that the UN needed to consult intensively with the Turks, they found the actual process particularly nerve wracking. During this period of waiting for the UN to make pro-posals, when they were themselves seeing relatively little of de Soto and his team, having made all their points ad nauseam already, they watched de Soto's frequent comings and goings to Ankara with rising panic. Were they perhaps being stitched up? Would they be confronted with unac-ceptable proposals cooked up between the UN and the Turks?

At this point they came by (a polite way of saying they had purloined) a document that was either an early draft of the UN's proposals or part of such a draft. It contained ideas that upset them. A long and hysterical letter was sent off to de Soto threatening all kinds of dire consequences if any of these ideas surfaced as proposals. Weston and I did our best to calm them down with some success. When I taxed Clerides with having purloined the UN's documents, he gave me a guilty smile, like a child caught with his hand in the toffee jar. Nothing more came of the matter. But, as we had feared from the outset, the Greek Cypriots made so much of a fuss that eventually it got to the ears of the Turks who were naturally quite convinced that they had yet again been outwitted by the wily Greek Cypriots and some of whom purported to believe that the UN team had shared the draft with the Greek Cypriots and not with them. In fact the UN made no changes at all to their proposals as a result of this rumpus, but because the document the Greek Cypriots had acquired had been a very early draft there were plenty of discrepancies with the final version of the proposals which the Greek Cypriots no doubt congratulated them-selves as being a result of their efforts.

While all this was going on in the south, in the north nothing was going on at all. Denktash was in New York, sometimes in hospital, some-times recuperating in his hotel, sometimes back in hospital when complications set in. Olgun was with him throughout, but communica-tion with Olgun was sporadic and limited mainly to medical bulletins. Soysal had retreated to Ankara. There was literally no member of the negotiating team with whom one could speak. The TRNC government had no responsibility for the Cyprus problem, thanks to the intense rivalry between Denktash and Prime Minister Eroglu, which meant that the latter was totally frozen out of the negotiations. The intention might not have been that the Turks alone should speak for themselves and the Turkish Cypriots during this vital period but that was the effect. Meanwhile I saw all the Turkish Cypriot party leaders (including the rejectionist ones in the government) and was able to note the rising tide in the north of dissatisfaction with Denktash's policy. Above all, the imminence of the European Union's decision at Copenhagen on the admission of Cyprus, with the all too likely outcome that the Greek Cypriots would be admitted, Turkey's candidature would be advanced and the Turkish Cypriots would be left in a kind of limbo, was having a powerful effect and convincing more and more Turkish Cypriots that their leaders were in the process of missing an extremely important bus. The Turkish Cypriot Chamber of Commerce, under the leadership of the younger generation of businessmen, mounted an increasingly effective campaign to put pressure on Denktash.

The Annan Plan

Annan sent his proposals to Clerides and Denktash, and to the governments of the three guarantor powers (Greece, Turkey and the UK) on 11 November. Just over a week before, the predicted electoral landslide had taken place in Turkey, returning the AK centre-right Islamic party to power with a large overall majority in the single-chamber parliament. The only other party with substantial representation was the CHP, a centre-left party which had not been in the previous legislature. Ecevit's DSP, Yilmaz's ANAP, Bahceli's MHP and Ciller's DYP, together with Cem's new party, all failed to get 10 per cent of the vote and thus to get into the parliament. So, from the day of the election, there was no real doubt that Turkey was going to have its first single-party government for many years, and the processes for its formation were immediately put in hand with what was, by Turkish precedents, lightning speed. The political situation was not, however, quite so clearcut as it looked, since the effective leader of the AK party, Recep Tayyip Erdogan, was still barred from taking office as a result of a conviction for religious incitement, and the new prime minister, Abdullah Gül, was clearly only an interim appointment, intended to hold office for the few weeks or possibly months it would take to remove the impediments to Erdogan taking that post. But, from the outset, both within Turkey and outside it, Erdogan was treated as the leader of Turkey even though he as yet held no official position. The clear outcome of the Turkish election and the speed with which the new government was being formed removed the last obstacle to Annan making his proposals, the Copenhagen clock by now being only one month to midnight.

The structure of Annan's proposals was complex, but ingenious, designed to make the most of the similarly complex but extremely tight timetable for European Union enlargement. The overall package, which ran to more than 130 pages and which included a constitution for the new common state of Cyprus (but not for the component states, the drafting of whose constitutions were left to the two sides themselves, so long as they were not incompatible with the overall settlement), and numerous annexes dealing with security, property, the territorial adjustment and EU issues, as well as other more technical matters, was a single, integrated whole. But it was so subdivided that not all the subject matter had to be settled and accepted straightaway. The two leaders and the guarantor powers were asked to sign a two-page 'Comprehensive Settlement' document before Copenhagen, which also bound them to accept an attached seven-page 'Foundation Agreement' containing most of the key, politically sensitive provisions of the settlement and in addition a fair number of the most important parts of the constitution and other annexes. The negotiations would then continue after Copenhagen, to fill in all the gaps and matters left over, with an absolute cut-off for the negotiations of 28 February 2003, the UN secretary-general having a casting vote if there were any deadlocks. The month of March would be left for referendum campaigns in both south and north, the referendums taking place on 30 March. The whole set of agreements would, if both referendum results were positive, enter into force the next day. This structure was, among other things, designed to enable the European Union to take the political decision to admit the new reunited Cyprus at Copenhagen and the new reunited Cyprus to sign the Treaty of Accession to the EU in Athens in mid-April. But the structure, complicated further by Denktash's failure to nominate his representatives to the technical working groups agreed on 4 October, also provided for a two-month catch-up period to remedy that.

The Annan Plan sought to navigate through the shoals of status, sovereignty and continuity with some ingenious legal drafting. The agreement would 'establish a new state of affairs in Cyprus' (not a new state); it would be called simply Cyprus or, as a long title, the State of

Cyprus; it would be a single, sovereign state with a single international legal personality, composed of two states, the common state exercising the powers allocated to it in the constitution 'sovereignly' and the component states exercising 'sovereignly' all other powers not allocated to the common state, with no hierarchy between them. Continuity would be provided by legitimizing all acts, whether legislative, executive or judicial, prior to the entry into force of the comprehensive settlement so long as they did not contradict the provisions of that settlement and by listing all the international agreements and laws binding on the new Cyprus (these including much material derived both from the Republic of Cyprus and from the TRNC). The two nightmares of secession and domination were dealt with explicitly, the new state of affairs being proclaimed indissoluble, with secession prohibited, and domination of any institution by one side being also declared to be unconstitutional.

The plan allocated to the common state responsibility for foreign affairs, relations with the European Union, central-bank functions, common-state finances (but the common state had responsibility for virtually no policies involving substantial public expenditure), economic and trade policy, aviation and navigation policy and some more technical matters including meteorology, weights and measures and intellectual property. The executive would follow something like the Swiss model with an executive council consisting of Greek Cypriots (4) and Turkish Cypriots (2) chosen by each side on its own. No decision could be taken without the agreement of at least one member of each side. There would be a president and vice-president chosen by the Council from among its members, the offices rotating every six months and never providing less than a 2:1 rotation (although this provision was overridden for the first 36 months of existence of the new state of affairs during which the two presidents in office at the time of its entry into force – Clerides and Denktash – would act as co-presidents). There would be two houses of parliament, the upper one being split 50:50 between Greek Cypriots and Turkish Cypriots elected by the legislatures of the component states, the lower house being elected by popular mandate with no side having fewer than 25 per cent of the seats (the Turkish Cypriot population share being roughly 18 per cent). Both houses would have to approve any legislation, and there were provisions ensuring that the Turkish Cypriot nightmare of one of their representatives being suborned by the Greek Cypriots and then passing anti-Turkish Cypriot legislation could not come to pass. The Supreme Court would consist of three Greek Cypriots, three Turkish

Cypriots and three non-Cypriots, to avoid the possibility of deadlock and to ensure that the Supreme Court was able to exercise the tie-breaking function allocated to it in the event of the other institutions becoming deadlocked.

On security a number of amendments were proposed to the Treaties of Guarantee, strengthening it by extending its scope to cover the territorial limits and constitutional order of the component states, and of Alliance, specifying the equal number of Greek and Turkish troops that could remain on the island (four asterisks only at this stage, signifying a figure between 1,000 and 9,999). Neither treaty was diluted or time limited and the unilateral right of intervention remained. All Cypriot forces were to be disbanded and their arms removed from the island. A legally binding arms embargo was to be established. A UN-mandated international military presence was to be deployed island-wide and for an open-ended period of time, only to be terminated by common agreement; it was to underpin but not enforce the settlement.

The territorial adjustment proposed consisted of two alternative maps, each providing for a transfer to the Greek Cypriots of a bit less than 9 per cent of the island (the scale of the adjustment in the Boutros-Ghali proposals of 1992). One map gave the tip of the Karpas Peninsula (the 'panhandle' deep in the Turkish Cypriot north) to the Greek Cypriots, the other, by making adjustments elsewhere, did not. The drawing of the line was somewhat more sophisticated than in 1992, enabling more Greek Cypriots to return and fewer Turkish Cypriots to be displaced but, inevitably, ending up with an even more irregular line.

On property, elaborate provisions were made for mutual compensation, to be administered by a Property Board. All Cyprus settlement proposals up to and including the Set of Ideas had equated property rights with the right of return to those properties, a right that all accepted would have to be limited. The Annan Plan marked a departure from this, instead separating out the property question from the right of residence, which equated more nearly with the EU freedoms. By placing limitations on the right of residence, the UN did not prejudge whether a Greek of Turkish Cypriot was returning to his own property, to another property in the same village (potentially attractive in the case of neglected or abandoned houses), or indeed building an entirely new property in the other component state. It provided a framework for a more normal existence in the future. Decisions on residence could be taken on the same grounds as elsewhere in the world, such as job location, schools, family, and not the backward-looking criterion of inherited property ownership. That said, there would of course be a strong link between applications for restitution of property and applications for residence. The distinction between 'residence' and 'return' is a fine one, and it was not much observed on the island where most people used the terms interchangeably.

The limits on residence and on property restitution were to be established in parallel with agreement on the territorial adjustment (meaning that, if the adjustment was smaller than proposed, the limit on returns to the north would be higher and vice-versa). There was in any case to be a moratorium on any returns for three years in the case of unoccupied property and five years for property occupied.

The issue of how many and which Turks who had come to Cyprus since 1974 should be covered by Turkish Cypriot citizenship was ducked for the meantime and left over for further negotiation. But it was proposed that all Cypriots should be Cypriot citizens and at the same time be entitled to citizenship status in one or other of the component states.

It was stated flatly that the reunited Cyprus would join the European Union, and the referendum question was so phrased as to make it impossible to split the two issues of the settlement and of EU membership. A protocol was included, which the European Union would be asked to adopt, providing for derogations from the right of establishment and the right to buy property, and ruling out military participation by Cyprus in the European Security and Defence Policy. The European Union would be asked to grant substantial financial assistance to begin narrowing the gap in economic development and prosperity between the north and the south. So far as coordinating the Cypriot position for EU decision making was concerned, the Belgian model, suggested by the Turkish Cypriots, was followed.

A reconciliation commission to help heal the wounds of the past and to remedy the antagonistic interpretations of historical events was also proposed.

From Annan I to Annan II

Annan's covering letter to the plan, which he had sent Clerides and Denktash on 11 November, asked them not to react immediately (the Cypriot tendency to shoot from the hip and to indulge in preemptive press briefing being well known) but to give him their reactions within a week. On 18 November Clerides replied saying that he was prepared to negotiate on the basis of the proposals and seeking a number of clarifications. The clarifications were then pursued between de Soto and Pfirter on the UN side and Markides. Getting a reaction from Denktash was a good deal less straightforward. He was still in New York, by now out of hospital again, but still recuperating in his hotel and not fit to travel back to the island. He had so far had no direct contact with the new government in Turkey. All the sounds coming from him and Olgun, who was with him, which trickled out to the press, were thoroughly negative. A preliminary response asking for more time gave no grounds for optimism.

Meanwhile the newly formed Turkish government, with a prime minister, Gül, who did know something about Cyprus from his time as minister for Cyprus in the Erbakan/Ciller government of 1996–97, and a new foreign minister, Yasar Yakis, with no Cyprus experience, was also trying to grapple with the Annan Plan. They rapidly coined quite a promising phrase that was to become the mantra of their policy in the months ahead: 'no solution in Cyprus is no solution'. However, this was not in itself a policy response to the detailed proposals in the Annan Plan, but it was the complete opposite of Ecevit's claim to have settled the Cyprus problem in 1974, so it did signal a change of mind. They certainly did not want Denktash to reject the plan or to filibuster eternally. So Yakis was despatched to New York with a large delegation, including some of Erdogan's advisers, to discuss the matter urgently with Denktash. It was evident that Denktash gave Yakis a hard time, and after two days of inconclusive meetings there was still no response to Annan. Finally, after further pressure from Ankara had been brought to bear, Denktash sent Annan a letter on 27 November saying that he was prepared to negotiate on the basis of the proposals but noting that he had serious elements of concern with them.

Meanwhile Erdogan had set out on a comprehensive tour of European capitals designed to boost the chances of the Copenhagen European Council taking a decisive step forward in the handling of Turkey's EU candidature, and it became known that the new government was, as its first legislative priority, drafting a further package of laws following up those passed in August on Yilmaz's proposal and aimed at filling remaining gaps in Turkey's ability to meet the Copenhagen criteria. Erdogan, despite his lack of any foreign language and his need therefore to work through an interpreter, made a very considerable and broadly favourable impression wherever he went. He pressed hard the case for Turkey to be given a date for the opening of its accession negotiations, arguing that the EU application was the best lever he had to modernize and reform Turkey and to improve its human rights record. He got a mixed reception, positive in London, Rome, Madrid and some other capitals, notably cautious in Paris, Berlin, Vienna and Scandinavia. In every capital, and also when he moved on to Washington at the beginning of December, he was told of the importance his interlocutors attached to reaching a solution to the Cyprus problem and their support for the Annan Plan, but nowhere were the two issues linked in any formal way. His responses on Cyprus were generally positive but lacked any specificity.

By the time of my next visit to Cyprus on 20–22 November the clock was ticking very loudly indeed. The period before Copenhagen was narrowing and still there was no reply from Denktash. It was highly desirable that there should be some process of negotiation with the two sides (although not necessarily directly between them) before Annan produced a revision of his proposals as a final basis for a pre-Copenhagen decision. But at the moment, there was no Turkish Cypriot side with which to negotiate. I discussed all this with a distinctly depressed de Soto as soon as I reached the island on 20 November and, together, we came to the conclusion that the only way to cut this particular procedural Gordian knot was for Annan to invite Clerides to New York where Denktash already was. It should be possible then for de Soto to shuttle between them, for Annan to make some modest and balanced adjustments to his proposals and for a major push to be made to take decisions before Clerides had to head off for Copenhagen.

I sent these recommendations off to London overnight, where they were endorsed, and next morning they were discussed positively with the US delegation in the margins of the NATO Summit meeting going on in Prague. But when de Soto and I spoke to Weston in Washington that night we ran into a barrage of US objections. I pointed out that it was extremely unwise to allow the negotiations to run on into the same time frame as the Copenhagen meeting itself. Previous experience at European Councils with parallel meetings of this sort had not been happy. There was a high risk of confusion and crossed wires. All this was to no avail, since the US team in Washington (which included Marc Grossman, the Under-Secretary for Political Affairs and former ambassador to Ankara who invariably had the last say on matters relating to Cyprus) was pursuing a different approach that involved cutting Denktash completely out of the negotiation and settling matters directly with the new Turkish government. That approach was incompatible with getting Clerides to New York and focusing the final phase of the negotiations there. The trouble was that it turned out to be unrealistic, because the new Turkish government was no more willing, or perhaps able, to sideline Denktash completely than its predecessors had been. By the time all that had become clear, the opportunity had been missed, and Denktash returned from New York to Cyprus on 7 December. By then we were locked into a scenario that involved bringing matters to a head in Copenhagen on 11–13 December at the same time as the European Council met there.

Anyone who might have supposed that Denktash's will to resist had been weakened by his operation and lengthy convalescence was soon to be disappointed by his performance following his return. Despite all de Soto's efforts, he declined to engage in anything approximating to a negotiation on the specifics of the Annan Plan, sticking to negative generalities all too familiar from previous rounds of negotiation. Indeed Annan's post-negotiation report goes so far as to say of this period: 'Regrettably the substantive input from the Turkish Cypriot side was extremely general and largely conceptual – leaving the United Nations to seek inspiration for concrete improvements from concerns publicly voiced by a broad cross-section of Turkish Cypriot civil society.' When Annan invited Clerides and Denktash to Copenhagen to take the decisions necessary for agreement on the Plan, Denktash not only refused to come himself, an absence which could easily have been justified on health grounds, but also refused to be represented, a move tantamount to boycotting the negotiations. The mini-crisis resulting from this move completely absorbed Annan's meeting with Erdogan in New York on 10 December, which could have been more usefully devoted to discussing the Annan Plan. In the end the Turks told Denktash he must be represented in Copenhagen, and he conceded, late and unwillingly. However, he had the last laugh because he sent to Copenhagen Ertugruloglu, the Turkish Cypriot foreign minister, who could be relied upon to say no to anything the UN might put forward. Denktash himself retired to Ankara for a medical check-up and was installed in a guest-house of the president of Turkey where he was fêted by all of Ankara's not inconsiderable number of rejectionists. It was against this unpromising background that Annan tabled a revised version of his Plan (known as Annan II) and decided, rightly in my view, not to travel to Copenhagen himself.

Annan II

Annan sent his revised proposals to Clerides and Denktash on 10 December, two days before the meeting of the European Council in

Copenhagen. The major part of his 11 November proposals, its structure and most of the content, were left untouched, but a number of modest changes were put forward in response to points made to de Soto in the intervening month. As he had promised in his covering letter of 11 November these changes reflected a careful balance between the interests of the two sides. The main changes proposed (there were in addition a good number of minor, drafting amendments) were the following:

(i) Political rights at the common state level, i.e. participation in elections to the parliament of the common state, would be exercised on the basis of internal component state citizenship status, i.e. a Greek Cypriot who went to reside in the north would only get a vote to determine the Turkish Cypriots elected to the parliament of the common state if he or she had opted for and received Turkish Cypriot citizenship status and renounced Greek Cypriot citizenship status (since holding both was not allowed). This change responded to a Turkish Cypriot concern that, when Greek Cypriots allowed to reside in the north reached a critical mass, they would be able to influence the outcome of parliamentary elections and thus to undermine bi-zonality.

(ii) There could be a four-year moratorium on Greek Cypriots going to reside in the north (as Turkish Cypriots in the south). Thereafter there could be a cap of 8 per cent on such residents in a village or municipality between the fifth and ninth years and 18 per cent between the tenth and 15th years, with a 28 per cent cap beyond that and a review after 25 years. This change gave something to both sides.

(iii) The transitional presidency (when the two signatory presidents would be co-presidents) was reduced from three years to 30 months: a concession to the Greek Cypriots who wanted this transitional period to be further reduced, fearing as they did that Denktash would work to undermine and destabilize the new Cyprus.

(iv) A specific bracket of 2,500–7,500 for the residual Greek and Turkish troop presence (but agreement on a single figure was left for negotiation between Greece and Turkey): a narrowing of the bracket helpful to the Greeks and Greek Cypriots.

(v) In addition to Greece and Turkey the component states also had to give their consent to any international military operations in the new Cyprus: a Greek Cypriot request reflecting their dislike of being cut out of such decisions.

(vi) The management of natural resources was made a common state responsibility. This change responded to Turkish Cypriot concern that the Greek Cypriots, once back in control of Morphou, might tamper with the groundwater resources needed by the Turkish Cypriots' orchards in the region which would remain in Turkish Cypriot control.

(vii) The basic articles of the constitution could not be amended: an additional safeguard for the Turkish Cypriots against the hijacking of constitutional amendments which they believed had happened in 1963.

(viii) The definition of citizens of Cyprus would include those who held such citizenship in 1960, anyone who had resided in Cyprus for seven years, anyone who married a Cypriot and had been there two years, minor children of the above, and, in addition, a list of 33,000 to be handed to the UN. This set of definitions would have allowed most of the Turks who had come to the north since 1974 to remain and be citizens of Cyprus and of the Turkish Cypriot component state.

(ix) Financial assistance of not less than 10,000 Euros was promised for anyone not being given permanent residence and having to be repatriated: a change for the particular benefit of Turks in the north.

(x) One-third of Cyprus's European Parliament seats (two out of six) would go to the Turkish Cypriots. This was helpful to the Turkish Cypriots since a division based on population or a strict proportional representation could have resulted in less.

(xi) One map only was proposed for the territorial adjustment, that giving the tip of the Karpas to the Greek Cypriots. This was what the Greek Cypriots wanted and what the Turks and Turkish Cypriots did not (although they failed to make that clear in the run-up to Annan II by flatly refusing to engage in any discussion of the territorial issue).

(xii) A relocation board was proposed to help those displaced as a result of the territorial adjustment, with direct involvement of the United Nations in the process. Grants of not less than 10,000 Euros were also provided: an addition requested by the Turkish Cypriots.

(xiii) There would be a cap on property restitution of 9 per cent in either component state and 14 per cent in any given village or municipality (but figures could be varied if negotiation over the territorial adjustment led to changes).

(xiv) The notice to be given to the UN for troop movements of their residual contingents was raised to 14 days: a change helpful to the Turks.

(xv) European Union safeguard measures would be available for the Turkish Cypriot component state for three years, rather than one year: a change to meet Turkish Cypriot concerns over the weakness of their economy.

Copenhagen: so near, and yet so far

It would be an exaggeration to say that the Danish EU presidency welcomed the fact that crucial negotiations about the Cyprus problem were likely to take place in Copenhagen in parallel with the meeting of the European Council. Like almost everyone else they had hoped it would be possible to reach agreement in advance of the European Council and for that meeting simply to have to cope with a clearcut situation over admission of a reunited island. They were particularly concerned that the highly sensitive inter-related issues of Turkey's EU candidature and of Cyprus would in some way distract or even divert the meeting from its main task of settling and agreeing terms of accession for the ten first-wave candidate countries in central, eastern and southern Europe. These concerns were especially strongly felt by the Danish prime minister, Anders Fogh Rasmussen, and led to some tension between his team and the foreign minister and his officials. Be that as it may, in the event the Danish presidency performed the necessary juggling act impeccably. In the early stages of their presidency, at the Brussels European Council in October and after the Annan Plan had been tabled on 11 November, they worked successfully to reinforce the messages contained in the Seville European Council conclusions and to give the European Union's full support to Annan's proposals. When it was clear that the cup was going to pass to Copenhagen they set out with a will to make the necessary administrative arrangements. The European Council itself was meeting in a conference centre out by the airport. A suite of offices for the Cyprus negotiations was provided in an elegantly refurbished warehouse next to the foreign ministry and a safe four or five miles and 20 minutes' drive away from where the European Council was meeting.

I arrived in Copenhagen late on 11 December and joined de Soto and Weston for dinner. Who would attend for the Turkish Cypriots and what mandate he would have was still obscure. The only certain thing was that no one had yet turned up, although the Greek Cypriots, Greeks and Turks were already in town in force, even though the European Council was not due to meet until dinner time on 12 December. We agreed on the priorities for the next day, which focused mainly on the Turks and on the

Greek Cypriots. We were joined after dinner by Pat Cox, the recently elected president of the European Parliament, who had already made an important contribution by shifting the parliament's traditional role of uncritical and unquestioning support for the Greek Cypriots to a more even-handed stance and was to continue to do so throughout the Copenhagen meeting.

The 12th of December began for me with a meeting at the Turkish delegation's hotel, out near the airport and the European Council conference centre, with Ziyal (permanent under-secretary equivalent), Ilkin (deputy under-secretary equivalent) and Apakan (former Turkish ambassador to the TRNC and assistant under-secretary equivalent). They told me gloomily that Ertugruloglu would be representing the Turkish Cypriots but would not arrive until the next day. I shared their gloom and said this was an unhappy choice if the objective was to reach an agreement. We went carefully over the ground of Annan II and I pointed out all the significant improvements in it over Annan I from the Turkish and Turkish Cypriot point of view. They did not dispute that the plan had improved but were very upset by the map and the UN decision to propose that the tip of the Karpas Peninsula should go to the Greek Cypriots. I said I was not surprised, since I had always told the UN (as had the US) that we believed the Karpas to be the wrong side of a Turkish red line and suggested that it was not too late to take this up with de Soto. But what the Turks were most concerned about was what was going to happen about their EU candidature later in the day. They made no bones about the fact that that would determine what they could do on Cyprus. I said that their proclaimed objective (for which they had been pushing for some time) of getting accession negotiations going in 2003 or even before enlargement on 1 May 2004 was unattainable, not least given that President Chirac and Chancellor Schroeder had publicly called for the decision to be put off until 2005 or later. On the other hand those who supported their EU candidature, as Britain did, were determined to get a decision taken on opening accession negotiations in 2004 and not to have everything pushed back to 2005 or beyond. It would be a close-run thing as resistance to this sort of timetable was strong. Later in the day Ziyal and Ilkin had a long meeting with de Soto and continued to give the impression that their main problem with Annan II was over the map. De Soto told them the territorial adjustment remained negotiable, and sent them away with a number of alternative maps that did not include the Greek Cypriots getting back any of the Karpas Peninsula.

My own next call was on Clerides and his delegation, including most of the members of the National Council. The small hotel room was packed, the Greek Cypriots in a mood of extreme nervousness as they saw their objective of EU membership almost, but not quite yet, within their grasp. There was not much talk of Annan II, which the Greek Cypriots seemed to be taking very calmly. I had decided in advance that I would not ask Clerides in front of a lot of witnesses, not all of whom were friendly, whether or not he would sign Annan II. Instead I told him that it was the working hypothesis of de Soto, Weston and myself that if the Turks and Turkish Cypriots would sign, so would he. Looking at me with a characteristic twinkle in his eye he said, 'Well, that is your working hypothesis', and there the conversation ended. On the way out I met Papandreou who said that he had brought with him to Copenhagen a military team so that they could settle the numbers of Greek and Turkish troops to remain on the island if that became possible. I fear they must have had a frustrating few days.

In the evening I went to the airport to brief the prime minister on his plane and we all then went straight to see Erdogan and Gül at their hotel before the prime minister went to join his EU colleagues over dinner to discuss Turkey's candidature. The meeting with Erdogan and Gül went well. Tony Blair assured them of our strong support for their candidature but warned them they would not get everything they wanted. Nevertheless he believed that what was achievable would represent a major step towards membership. On Cyprus he urged the need to strike a deal there and then on the basis of Annan II. The Turks stuck to generalities in what they said. What was already clear was that among the mob of advisers, diplomats and politicians crammed into their hotel and the meeting room it was not going to be easy to come to quick and clear conclusions the next day.

The next few hours were spent with everyone kicking their heels waiting for the heads of government to emerge from their dinner, which, as time went on, was clearly not proving plain sailing. Finally, shortly before midnight, Blair returned to the hotel. A formula had been agreed under which the European Union would open accession negotiations with Turkey if, in December 2004, it decided that the Copenhagen political criteria had been fulfilled. It had been a difficult discussion, with many, the French president in particular, wanting a slower timetable and a lesser degree of commitment. It had been the best obtainable. He agreed that I should telephone Ziyal and give him the formula, some flavour of the discussion, and the prime minister's judgement that this was an important breakthrough and the best result obtainable. This I duly did. Ziyal telephoned back at 3.00am to say on behalf of Erdogan and Gül that it would be very helpful if, when the formula agreed over dinner came for approval to the European Council in the morning, the prime minister could argue for a bit more immediacy. I said I would pass the message on, which I did, and Blair, with support from the German chancellor, managed to add the words 'without delay' to the commitment to open negotiations. At that stage, during the night, there was no hint of the dramas to come.

The following morning, however, all was turmoil and chaos in the Turkish delegation. News reports indicated that Erdogan and Gül were taking the outcome of the previous night's dinner-table discussion very badly. There was much talk of rejection and betrayal. The half-full glass was being described as having no water in it at all. Not for the first time Turkish diplomacy was falling victim to the excessive expectations it had built up for itself. Throughout the morning telephone calls and meetings between members of the European Council and the Turkish leaders were used to bring home to them that what had been achieved was both positive and substantial. Further discussion in the European Council showed that there was no stomach for reopening the hard-fought compromise of the night before, apart from the minor addition of the words 'without delay'. By the early afternoon the Turkish leaders had decided to proclaim victory and to present the outcome, correctly, as a considerable success. But by then any chance of getting their attention to take difficult decisions on Cyprus had long since passed, nor was the success so clearcut that they felt able to afford a showdown with Denktash who was in Ankara issuing defiant denunciations of the Annan Plan. All through the morning de Soto tried to get hold of Ziyal and failed; nor was any other Turkish official prepared to say where Turkey stood over Cyprus. Finally in mid-afternoon Ertugruloglu turned up for the first and last time at the foreign ministry conference centre, accompanied by a middle-ranking Turkish diplomat, to say that the proposals were unacceptable in too many ways for him to be able to enumerate and that there was nothing to negotiate about.

At this point any hope of a settlement being reached in Copenhagen finally evaporated. The European Council was moving towards the final stages of agreeing the terms of accession for the ten candidates. Among these was a still divided Republic of Cyprus. It was time to switch to the alternative approach which, fortunately, had been extensively discussed with the Danish presidency and Commission. This consisted in accepting the candidacy of a divided island, in line with the Helsinki commitment. But, in addition, the European Council made clear that it still hoped to welcome a reunited island by the time the Accession Treaty was signed in Athens in April. It called for a continuation and conclusion of negotiations on the Annan Plan by 28 February, which had always been the cut-off date in the plan for the end of negotiations, and repeated its commitment to 'accommodate' a UN settlement. A number of dispositions were made for handling one of two scenarios in the months ahead, either a settlement or failure to reach one and signature of the Accession Treaty by a divided island. The texts adopted by the European Council on Turkey and Cyprus were as follows:

- As the accession negotiations have been completed with Cyprus, Cyprus will be admitted as a new Member State to the European Union. Nevertheless the European Council confirms its strong preference for accession to the European Union by a united Cyprus. In this context it welcomes the commitment of the Greek Cypriots and the Turkish Cypriots to continue to negotiate with the objective of concluding a comprehensive settlement of the Cyprus problem by 28 February 2003 on the basis of the UNSG's proposals. The European Council believes that those proposals offer a unique opportunity to reach a settlement in the coming weeks and urges the leaders of the Greek Cypriot and Turkish Cypriot communities to seize this opportunity.

- The Union recalls its willingness to accommodate the terms of a settlement in the Treaty of Accession in line with the principles on which the EU is founded. In case of a settlement, the Council, acting by unanimity on the basis of proposals by the Commission, shall decide upon adaptations of the terms concerning the accession of Cyprus to the EU with regard to the Turkish Cypriot community.

- The European Council has decided that, in the absence of a settlement, the application of the *acquis* to the northern part of the island shall be suspended, until the Council decides unanimously otherwise, on the basis of a proposal by the Commission. Meanwhile, the Council invites the Commission, in consultation with the government of Cyprus, to consider ways of promoting economic development of the northern part of Cyprus and bringing it closer to the Union.

- The European Council recalls its decision in 1999 in Helsinki that Turkey is a candidate state destined to join the Union on the basis of the same criteria as applied to the other candidate states. It strongly welcomes the important steps taken by Turkey towards meeting the Copenhagen criteria, in particular through the recent legislative packages and the subsequent implementation measures which cover a large number of key priorities specified in the Accession Partnership. The Union acknowledges the determination of the new Turkish government to take further steps on the path of reform and urges in particular the government to address swiftly all remaining shortcomings in the field of the political criteria, not only with regard to legislation but also in particular with regard to implementation. The Union recalls that, according to the political criteria decided in Copenhagen in 1993, membership requires that a candidate country has achieved stability of institutions guaranteeing democracy, the rule of law, human rights and respect for and protection of minorities.

- The Union encourages Turkey to pursue energetically its reform process. If the European Council in December 2004, on the basis of a report and a recommendation from the Commission, decides that Turkey fulfils the Copenhagen political criteria, the European Union will open accession negotiations with Turkey without delay.

- In order to assist Turkey towards EU membership, the accession strategy for Turkey shall be strengthened. The Commission is invited to submit a proposal for a revised Accession Partnership and to intensify the process of legislative scrutiny. In parallel, the EC–Turkey Customs Union should be extended and deepened. The Union will significantly increase its pre-accession financial assistance for Turkey. This assistance will be from 2004 and be financed under the budget heading 'pre-accession expenditure'.

Discussion of this text was uncontentious. And the atmosphere was somewhat improved by the news that, following some hectic shuttling by Javier Solana throughout the day, the Greek Cypriots had agreed that they would not participate in the military provisions of the European Security and Defence Policy; Turkish objections to that policy had been overcome; and the North Atlantic Council, meeting in Brussels, had settled the terms of cooperation between NATO and the EU on defence matters. As so often before, the Cyprus problem was left with the role of Cinderella on an otherwise outstandingly successful and significant occasion.

11

2003: Extra Time

T he failure to get agreement on a comprehensive settlement either before or at Copenhagen was clearly a setback. The moment at which both sides were, for quite different reasons, under the greatest pressure to show flexibility, with a clear deadline set to concentrate minds, and when reaching an agreement would have brought equivalent benefits, had been allowed to slip away. But no irretrievable damage had been done to the structure of the package that Annan had originally put forward in November; some clever legal drafting could take care of the telescoping of the pre- and post-Copenhagen phases provided for in the original proposals. The working groups on international obligations and domestic legislation, to which Denktash had agreed in early October and then prevented for two months from meeting, had now finally been staffed and were ready to start work; they could run in parallel with further negotiations between Clerides and Denktash, and did in fact do so from the beginning of January 2003. Moreover Clerides, who had hitherto given the impression that he would be unable to negotiate beyond Christmas because of the imminence of the presidential election in the south, showed no signs of disengaging or of being unable to sustain his end of the negotiations. And Denktash, who had by now returned to the island, while continuing to make negative statements about the Annan proposals, showed no signs of unwillingness to continue either.

Moreover the pressures on Denktash were mounting considerably. A spontaneous demonstration of Turkish Cypriots took place in north Nicosia on the day of the Copenhagen Summit, demanding acceptance of the Annan Plan and membership of the European Union. This was followed in January by further massive demonstrations. Estimates of their size varied, but 80,000, a remarkably high proportion of a total population of north Cyprus of fewer than 200,000, was generally regarded as close to the mark. Despite many forebodings, the demonstrations passed off peacefully, but there was no doubting the real anger at Denktash's torpedoing of the chances of a settlement at Copenhagen and there were even unprecedented open signs of criticism and discontent at the role Turkey was playing. Nor was attendance at the demonstrations confined to supporters of the opposition parties and business interests; rather it stretched right across Turkish Cypriot society, including many regarded as members of the establishment, usually solid supporters of Denktash, and also Turks from the mainland, often dismissed as a group hostile to a settlement.

Opinion polls showed strong support for the Annan Plan and surprisingly this was even true of polls taken in Morphou, a town due to be handed back to the Greek Cypriots as a result of the territorial adjustment and whose inhabitants therefore faced displacement yet again. The demonstrations and the rising support in the north for a settlement also had a positive spin-off in the south. Greek Cypriots who had tended to regard Turkish Cypriots as giving uncritical and unquestioning support to Denktash realized that a real shift was under way. The noises coming out of Ankara, particularly from the new government and its supporters, while confused and not very clear, were very different from the usual unquestioning support for Denktash. High-level Turkish visitors who streamed through northern Cyprus in the weeks following Copenhagen gave mixed signals. The speaker of the Turkish National Assembly struck a note of nationalist defiance, as did some military visitors. But others, like the prime minister, Gül, and Erdogan, put the accent on finding a solution and were evidently ill at ease with the aggressive tone of Denktash's press statements. The tension between these visitors and Denktash was impossible to conceal.

One new element had begun to emerge right at the end of 2002. Denktash began to speak publicly and to his visitors of the need for a referendum in the north before he, as the TRNC negotiator (or someone else if he could not bring himself to accept the task), signed any commitment at all to a settlement. From the outset it was clear that the referendum Denktash now had in mind was quite separate and different from the simultaneous referendums in the north and the south to approve (or reject) any settlement that the two leaders had signed and submitted to them. This latter approach had been and remained an integral part of every UN plan since the 1992 Set of Ideas. The latest idea fitted into an easily recognizable pattern of Denktash thinking, which consisted of always finding a new procedural obstacle just when negotiations were reaching the home straight – at no point previously had he mentioned this obstacle, although it was now asserted that it formed part of the TRNC constitution. The assumption was that he was expecting to be able to manipulate any such advance referendum so that it produced a negative result and thus give him a firmly democratic excuse for refusing to sign an agreement. As opinion swung in the north towards strong support for the Annan Plan and EU membership, this assumption began to look less and less viable; and, as it swung, so did Denktash's enthusiasm for the idea evaporate, as we shall see. But he had planted a seed. And thought began to be given by the UN as to how, in the necessary task of telescoping the various stages of the original Annan Plan to take account of the passage of time, more prominence could be given to the role of the referendums and less to the up-front legal commitment of the leaders to the outcome of the negotiations.

A presidential election in the south

The Copenhagen European Council brought to an end the semi-truce in Greek Cypriot domestic politics, which, to general surprise, had prevailed through the whole of 2002. With the election only two months away, the members of the National Council returning from Copenhagen headed for the hustings. Clerides, after much agonizing and under pressure to do so from his own party (which had no real desire to support the candidacy of Omirou, the leader of the small socialist party they had backed earlier in the year in an attempt to split DIKO leader Tassos Papadopoulos's coalition) decided to run again. Within 24 hours, despite some frantic arm twisting, his own attorney-general, Markides, who had been heavily involved in the talks process, also threw his hat into the ring as an independent, thus further splitting the centre-right vote and also undermining Clerides's main appeal, right across the political spectrum, as the indispensable negotiator who could be trusted in the final phase of the negotiations to secure a settlement. Unfortunately for Clerides, every word spoken by Denktash belied the picture of a negotiation in its final phase and thus further undermined this appeal. Whether Denktash intended to have this effect it is hard to say; he was certainly not going to put himself out to help Clerides, and he could see the tactical benefits he would be able to draw from the election of someone like Papadopoulos who could be depicted as a rejectionist.

The campaign did not in fact focus much on the negotiations for a settlement or on the Annan Plan. Unlike 1992–93, when Clerides had stood against Vassiliou and had opposed Boutros-Ghali's Set of Ideas,

Papadopoulos resisted any temptation to launch an open onslaught on Annan's proposals. He did not really need to. Every Cypriot voter knew that Papadopoulos was less committed to the success of the negotiations and thus would tend to be less flexible than Clerides; so those who did not like the Annan Plan knew whom they should vote for. And the one-third of the electorate that was in the gift of AKEL was concentrating much more on returning to office than on the settlement negotiations. The opinion polls from the outset gave Papadopoulos a strong lead, with Clerides trailing and Markides well behind that, other candidates being nowhere. By early February the only real question was whether Papadopoulos would win on the first round, thus avoiding a run-off a week later in which Clerides might have hoped to pick up most of Markides's vote. On 16 February Papadopoulos won on the first round.

The negotiations resume

The resumption of the negotiations in the second week of January, while taking place in an atmosphere which fell well short of the euphoria briefly aroused when the face-to-face talks had started exactly a year before, was business-like and practical. The working groups established to draw up the international obligations and domestic legislation of the new Cyprus were at last at work and, while they faced an enormous task in bureaucratic terms, it seemed unlikely that they would throw up any insuperable political problems. Progress was agonizingly painstaking, but progress there was. At the same time, Clerides and Denktash agreed that Annan should conduct competitions for the flag and anthem of a reunited Cyprus and could approach potential candidates for appointment to the transitional Supreme Court which would need to be ready to operate as soon as a settlement came into effect. A total of 1,506 flag designs and 111 suggested anthems were submitted by entrants from 50 different countries. But there were plenty of less positive indicators, among which Denktash's public statements about the Annan Plan were prominent. He put out a series of estimates of the implications of the proposals, designed to scare the Turkish Cypriots and bearing no relation whatsoever to the careful estimates the UN itself had made, based on TRNC census figures, before putting the proposals forward. He alleged that 70,000 Turkish Cypriots would be displaced by the territorial adjustment, while the UN calculations gave figures between 42,000 and 45,000. He gave estimates of the combined effect of the territorial adjustment and the limited and delayed right of residence for Greek Cypriots in the north which implied more than 100,000 Turkish Cypriots (over half the population) would be displaced. He spoke apocalyptically of the Turkish Cypriots being wiped out within a few years. Faced with this steady drip of disinformation, the UN and its backers could do little. The UN was bound by its own news blackout, as were the rest of us. The UN, in any case, as the facilitator of the negotiations, could not go out and proselytize for a particular set of proposals that had not yet been accepted by either side, and reducing to scale Denktash's various estimates was not likely to sound good to a Greek Cypriot electorate that was in the midst of the presidential campaign. Fortunately the credibility of Denktash's propaganda among ordinary Turkish Cypriots seemed low.

The position that Clerides took up when the talks resumed was that there were certainly aspects of the Annan II proposals with which he took issue and would like to see changed. These he and his collaborators discussed with de Soto, trying as far as possible to proceed on the basis of 'clarifications' rather than putting forward actual changes themselves. Conscious that some further changes were almost certain to be made to meet points being raised by the Turks and Turkish Cypriots, in particular the map, they were determined that they too should get changes that would make any further revision of the Annan Plan a balanced one. But Clerides's position, constantly reiterated, was that, if Denktash would accept Annan II and sign it, so would he.

From the Turkish side there trickled out a series of non-papers, three in fact, all called 'Basic requirements for a settlement in Cyprus' and all different from each other. The first, rather general paper was given to de Soto by the Turks themselves and was dated 10 January. It contained five points:

(i) **Territory**. The present (Annan II) map was not acceptable. They were ready to negotiate 'in a substantial manner'.

(ii) **Right of return to property**. Strong preference for compensation only. Bi-zonality must be preserved if there were to be returns. A ten-year moratorium and/or permanent restrictions would be needed.

(iii) **Security**. The Treaty of Guarantee must stand. The UN peace force should not have an enforcement role. There must be no hierarchy between the troops of the guarantor powers and those of the UN. There should be no Cypriot participation in multilateral operations without the agreement of the guarantor powers.

(iv) **Turks in the TRNC**. The settlement should not impose provisions that would result in the repatriation of persons legally resident in Cyprus.

(v) **Status/sovereignty**. A strong plug for 'constituent' states and two 'peoples' and for sovereignty to 'emanate' from the two sides.

Several of these points were already dealt with partially or completely in either Annan I or Annan II; others were going to be more difficult.

The second version of 'Basic requirements' emerged from the Turks on 27 January. It had now grown to seven points and contained actual redrafts of parts of Annan II. The main changes from the 10 January paper were:

(i) **Territory**. As before.

(ii) **Property**. Moratorium now nine years. Returns by Greek Cypriots to be capped at 750 per year thereafter, rising to a total of 11,250 in the 15th year.

(iii) **Turks in Cyprus**. 50,000, plus those already having permanent residence for five years to be able to stay. No forced repatriation of Turks legally in Cyprus.

(iv) **Aliens**. Neither Turks nor Greeks should be allowed to make up more than 5 per cent of the population of the island.

(v) **Governance**. Drafting changes giving effect to the proposals in the first version of the 'Basic requirements' paper. One-third of senators from each constituent state needed for an affirmative vote. Thirteen senators' votes needed for matters requiring a special majority.

(vi) **Status**. Drafting changes giving effect to partnership, 'peoples', non-domination.

(vii) **Security**. Drafting changes to give effect to the ideas in the earlier paper: 14 days' notice of any troop movements.

While some of the precise drafting in this second version was certainly not going to be negotiable, the substance had not changed much nor got much more difficult and the increased specificity on some points made subsequent negotiation more straightforward.

The third version of the 'Basic requirements' paper was handed over by Denktash to Clerides on 3 February. It was unchanged from the second version. But it was accompanied by a copy of Denktash's speaking notes that day, which raised a number of additional issues, namely:

(i) **Property**. A plug for a global exchange of property and no restitution. Restitution would be a 'recipe for disaster ... which will take us back to pre-1974, even to 1963'.

(ii) **An obscure reference requested to the Treaty of Establishment** (which set up the Sovereign Base Areas) to make it clear that that Treaty was only relevant with respect to the SBAs, i.e. avoiding any reconfirmation of the 1960 constitution of the Republic of Cyprus.

(iii) **Debt**. All debts prior to entry into force of the agreement to be the responsibility of the constituent states.

(iv) **European Union**. A plea for simultaneity of entry by Turkey and the TRNC; but acceptance this would not be so, and some consequential amendments.

(v) **Economic aspects**. Request for concrete measures harmonizing the economies of the two constituent states.

(vi) **Signature**. Agreement to be signed by the presidents of the two constituent states.

The additional points from Denktash, not all of which were impossible to accommodate, were added on to nine pages of drafting amendments to the Foundation Agreement handed over by Denktash to Clerides on 15 January. This would all have been a lot more discouraging to the UN team if it had not been made clear within days by the Turks that Denktash had acted without authorization. The only points that needed to be addressed were those in their own 'Basic requirements' paper, i.e. the document of 27 January.

By this stage neither side was really trying very seriously to negotiate with the other. Both were concentrating their efforts on what everyone knew was coming down the road, a further revision by Annan of his proposals. So most attention was focused on the bilateral meetings each had with de Soto, and on de Soto's contacts in Ankara and Athens which were continuing in parallel at a hectic pace.

In late January and early February I visited the regional capitals for the first time since the Copenhagen meetings. The auguries were hard to read. In Athens, Foreign Minister Papandreou (since 1 January taking his turn as the EU president) remained as determined as ever to do what he

could to get a settlement before the 28 February deadline, and Karamanlis, the leader of the opposition, was supportive too. Papandreou was
frustrated that all his efforts to get a Greek–Turkish dialogue going over
Cyprus, and in particular over the outstanding issue of the number of
Greek and Turkish troops to be stationed on the island after a settlement,
had so far come to nothing and evoked no response from the Turks except
to say that they were not yet ready. He undertook to keep pushing for a
meeting to discuss the troops question. He also agreed that the process of
seeking the consent of the European Parliament to the Treaty of Accession, which was in full swing, should be handled in such a way as not to
prejudge whether it would in the end be a divided island or a reunited one
whose representatives would be signing the new Treaty in April. This
meant, rather awkwardly, sending forward two options to the European
Parliament, which deeply upset the legal purists in the Commission and
fluttered some dovecotes in Athens and Nicosia, but which passed off
eventually without causing any problems.

In Nicosia Clerides was in the last three weeks of the election campaign with hope of victory ebbing away, the main doubt being whether
he would be beaten in the first round (16 February) or the second (23
February). Up to then, he said he would continue to negotiate, but, once a
clear result was known, he would pass the responsibility to his successor
even though the formal installation of the new president was not due to
take place until 28 February. Papadopoulos and his coalition partner
Christofias were predictably bullish about their chances of victory but
cautious to the point of total obscurity as to their intentions for handling
the Cyprus problem thereafter. They were offering no rejectionist hos-
tages to fortune. The negotiations were still in the hands of Clerides and
they supported the way he was managing them. On the other side of the
city Denktash, whom I was seeing for the first time since his operation
the previous October, seemed cheerful and reasonably fit, having clearly
lost a bit of weight. As usual he showed no interest in engaging in a serious discussion of the main issues in the negotiations (it was before he had
tabled the 'Basic requirements' paper with his own additions, and it was
never wise to reveal knowledge of Turkish positions to Denktash since he
was only too likely then to try to alter them for the worse). I taxed him
with the disinformation he was spreading about the Annan Plan, going
carefully through those of his public statements widest of the mark, and
pointed out that the conclusion most observers drew was that he was
determined to scupper any chance of a settlement. He showed no sign of

contrition, nor of mending his ways. The one dog that did not bark was that Denktash never mentioned the idea of a pre-signature referendum, from which I deduced (correctly, as it turned out) that the state of public opinion in the north had caused the attractions of this option to pall.

In Ankara I was brought face to face with the reality that the looming war in Iraq and the need for the Turks finally to give a definitive response to the US and UK requests to allow their troops to transit Turkey was gradually drowning out all other issues in the consciousness of both politicians and the bureaucracy. The Turks had been tossing this hot potato from hand to hand ever since Erdogan's visit to Washington in early December when Bush had believed that Erdogan had given him a green light over transit and Erdogan believed he had been completely non-committal. In the eyes of the Americans, at least, the answer was long overdue and the pressures to put the matter to the test in the Turkish parliament were mounting daily. The immediate consequence, so far as my own visit was concerned, was that Ziyal, who was in the lead on Iraq too, had to pull out of the talks at the last moment, and I had to deal with Ilkin and Apakan. Normally this was not a particularly fruitful process but on this occasion it was less discouraging, although not without its oddities. The Turks pressed hard the case for a pre-signature referendum, undeterred by my telling them that Denktash appeared to have lost interest in one. Apart from pointing out that it might seem a little strange to most Turkish Cypriots to vote in two referendums on virtually the same question within a few weeks, I was careful not to rubbish the idea, making clear that this was a matter for the Turks and Turkish Cypriots. The rest of the talks consisted of working through their 'Basic requirements' paper, pointing out what was likely to fly, what was not and what could perhaps be achieved by approaching matters somewhat differently. It was made clear by then that if Turkey secured enough of the points in their paper (not all of them), they would hope to support a new revision of the Annan Plan and to persuade Denktash to do so also. Separate meetings with some of Erdogan's advisers and members of parliament from the governing AK party were even more encouraging. They were quite open about their desire to see the Cyprus problem resolved, about their understanding of how failure to settle now would weigh heavily on the main objective of their foreign policy, getting into the European Union, and about how Erdogan and Gül would have to give a clear lead if Denktash was to be brought along. They pressed eloquently for a concession on the sovereignty issue, but seemed to realize that this was unlikely to be negotiable and that Annan's approach provided the substance of what they were seeking, if not the label.

The UN prepares the final throw

The window through which the UN had to squeeze if the negotiations were to be concluded by 28 February was a remarkably narrow one. It had been accepted from Copenhagen onwards that matters could not be brought to a head until the Greek Cypriot presidential election was over. Having refrained from making proposals during the Turkish election period the previous autumn, the UN could not behave differently towards the Greek Cypriots. While it might be possible to allow a few days' slippage beyond 28 February, it was crucial not to say so in advance, and, in any case, very few extra days were available if the whole timetable of completing the process before the signature of the Treaty of Accession on 16 April and thus making possible the accession of the newly reunited Cyprus were not to be jeopardized. On 13 February Annan called de Soto back to New York to take stock, and, rather unusually, he invited Weston and me to attend as well.

Not surprisingly, since we had all been working together closely for over three years, there was effectively a consensus over our analysis of the situation and our prescriptions for action. We believed that the chances of reaching a settlement hung in the balance. It could go either way. But the only way to find out was to fire the last shot in the UN locker and put the matter to the test, what had been known up till then as the 'do or die scenario'. Delay would not only mean losing many of the positive pressures derived from the EU timetable, but there was also no certainty that the distracting storm clouds massing over Iraq would be rapidly dissipated or would leave behind a Turkey more capable and willing to take the necessary decisions. Annan then informed us that he intended to visit the region in the last week of February, going first to Ankara, then to Athens and ending up in Nicosia, where he would aim to get the agreement of the Greek Cypriots and Turkish Cypriots to a second revised version of his plan which he intended to circulate ahead of time. He agreed himself to press the Greek and Turkish governments to meet ahead of his visit and try to settle the issue of residual troop numbers. Weston and I said that our governments at the highest level gave their full support to this approach and would do all they could during the period ahead to back up Annan's efforts.

One new element was introduced at this stage. The British government had from the outset given its full backing to the UN. In recent months consideration had been given in London to whether anything more could be done. Since the size and configuration of the British Sovereign Base Areas had been settled in 1960 and set out in the Treaty of Establishment, which, along with the Treaties of Guarantee and Alliance, laid the foundations for the independence of Cyprus, their role and purpose had evolved constantly. The 99 square miles of territory originally defined was not all needed for current or prospective military and associated purposes. Could we contemplate offering to give up some of this territory in the context of a settlement of the Cyprus problem? Ministers agreed that we could. About 45 of the 99 square miles could be offered: those areas from the Western Sovereign Base Area going entirely to the Greek Cypriot component state, which surrounded it, those areas from the Eastern Sovereign Base Area going mainly to the Greek Cypriots but with a small parcel of land going to the Turkish Cypriots, which thus left their component state still contiguous to the Base Area, an important point for the Turkish Cypriots. This offer would change the parameters within which the single most hotly debated of the core issues would be settled, providing a little more slack in what had become a very tight situation. And while it did not affect the linked question of the return of Greek Cypriots to their properties in the north, it would bring considerable economic and commercial benefits to the recipients since it would result in the lifting of the ban on commercial development, which was an integral part of the Treaty of Establishment. The offer included a stretch of valuable coastal land. Annan and his team were grateful for this unexpected new trump card added to their hand. In due course we handed over the maps and the draft amendments to the Treaty of Establishment required to give effect to the offer. Astonishingly there was no leak until the secretary-general tabled the second revision of his plan (Annan III). And even more astonishingly neither side in Cyprus was able to identify any perfidious motives behind the British offer.

Annan's latest reminder to the Greek and Turkish governments of the need for them to discuss residual troop numbers finally bore fruit, and a meeting duly took place in Ankara on 21 February. Unfortunately it made no progress and reached no agreement. So de Soto, who had gone to Ankara to be briefed on the outcome and who, at Turkish insistence, had to be given separate briefings on the same meeting by Greek and Turks, was left without an agreed figure to put in the revised plan.

Annan III

De Soto's shuttling between the different capitals had continued up to the eve of Annan's own arrival in the region. This left precious little time to incorporate the fruits of his consultations into the new revised proposals and to get these to all concerned ahead of Annan's arrival. So it was decided to circulate to them over the weekend of 22–23 February an informal paper setting out the main changes being made to Annan II. The full text of Annan III, which took the UN team several sleepless nights to complete, was tabled on 26 February.

There were two important, general points about Annan III. The first of these was that the two-page 'Comprehensive Settlement of the Cyprus Problem' which had formed the first stage of the rocket designed to put Annan I and Annan II into orbit, had now been changed into a two-page 'Commitment to submit the Foundation Agreement to approval at separate simultaneous referenda in order to achieve a comprehensive settlement of the Cyprus problem'. In other words the leaders were no longer asked to bind themselves at the outset to anything beyond putting the package to their electorates. Should the results of the referendums on 30 March both be positive they were then bound, as were the three guarantor powers, to implement the package the following day. But should the result of either referendum be negative, then all agreements were null and void and no binding obligations remained. In a sense therefore the two referendums idea, with which Denktash had toyed, would be telescoped into one; but, before he was required to implement anything that was legally binding and enforceable, there would have been an affirmative vote by the Turkish Cypriots, which is what he argued was a legal requirement under the TRNC constitution. The second point was that Annan III introduced an entirely new text of Article 1 of the Constitution which in one sentence renamed Cyprus, described the form of the central government and banished the old placebos of 'common' state and 'component' states. It read as follows: 'The United Cyprus Republic is an independent and sovereign state with a single international legal personality and a federal government and consists of two constituent states, namely the Greek Cypriot State and the Turkish Cypriot State.' This judgement of Solomon balanced extremely important concessions to both sides: the Greek Cypriots getting the federal label on which they had always insisted, the Turkish Cypriots getting the concept of constituent states and a very attractive name for their own state. It could be said that parthenogenesis had been achieved.

In addition to these two general points, Annan III proposed a considerable number of changes that had emerged from the negotiations and, even more, from the consultations which de Soto had had in the final six weeks. I have grouped them for ease of understanding into those made in response to Turkish and Turkish Cypriot representations and those made in response to Greek and Greek Cypriot representations. The Turkish and Turkish Cypriot points were as follows:

(i) The Karpas Peninsula was to remain Turkish Cypriot, leaving the Turkish Cypriots with 29.2 per cent (an increase on Annan II) of the Republic of Cyprus (Denktash having said since 1992 that he would accept 29-plus per cent).

(ii) Constituent states were given discretion to decide on internal citizenship. So Greek Cypriots returning to the north would not vote as part of the Turkish Cypriot state in federal elections. It also meant the limits were absolute.

(iii) The moratorium on Greek Cypriot right of residence in the north went up to six years (not the nine years the Turks had asked for). The steps following the moratorium became shallower (down to 7 per cent from the end of the moratorium until year 10; down to 14 per cent from 18 per cent for years 10–15; final cap at year 15 down from 28 per cent to 21 per cent).

(iv) Greece and Turkey's consent for any international military operations in Cyprus would be needed as well as that of the constituent states (a reversion to Annan I).

(v) Religious sites were redefined to include only buildings and immediate surroundings (to banish Turkish Cypriots' fear that a wider definition would mean substantial repossession of property in the north by the Greek Cypriot Church which had in many cases possessed land for many miles around religious sites).

(vi) A simple list of 45,000 former Turkish citizens to have the right to Cypriot citizenship (probably less in gross terms than the 33,000 plus different categories in Annan II but easier to operate).

(vii) Students and academic staff exempted from limitations on residency and immigration controls (important for the Turkish Cypriots given the growth of higher-education English-language establishments in the TRNC catering for the Middle East market).

(viii) Most favoured nation status for Turkey.

(ix) Debts taken over by respective constituent states (a Denktash point).

(x) 6,000 Turkish and Greek troops to stay (nearer the top end of the Annan II 2,500–7,500 bracket).

(xi) Period of notice required for military movements reduced from 14 days to two (for ordinary movements) and three (for exercises) (a constantly reiterated Turkish request).

(xii) Request for the European Union and the Council of Europe to endorse the settlement (a safeguard against court action and Loizidou clone cases being pursued).

(xiii) Federal economic policy to pay special attention to harmonization of the economies of the constituent states (a Denktash point).

(xiv) The European Union to be asked to summon a donor conference to raise funds for costs of displacement resulting from the territorial adjustment and other changes.

The Greek and Greek Cypriot points were as follows:

(i) Increase in the territorial adjustment from 71.5 per cent in Annan II to 71.8 per cent (when Sovereign Base Area offer of which Greek Cypriots got over 90 per cent included). Some coastline near Morphou and two historical sites added. 2,300 more returns to the adjusted territory than under Annan II.

(ii) Increase in overall property reinstatement limit from 9 per cent to 10 per cent, and per village from 14 per cent to 20 per cent.

(iii) Returns by Greek Cypriot property owners to four villages in the Karpas unlimited. Karpas villagers to have responsibility for their own cultural and educational affairs.

(iv) Immediate voting for European and local elections by Greek Cypriots resident in the Turkish Cypriots' constituent state.

(v) Greek Cypriots over 65 to have only a two-year moratorium on return to property in the north and no quantitative restrictions.

(vi) Nine years' permanent residence required to acquire Cypriot citizenship as opposed to seven in Annan II (a point designed to reduce the number of Turks able to claim Turkish Cypriot citizenship).

(vii) Non-Cypriot Supreme Court judges only to have a say if Cypriots cannot agree (a point to which Clerides attached importance).

(viii) A Court of First Instance to be created (another Clerides point).

(ix) Rules on entry and residence rights for Turks to be compatible with the Schengen agreement.

(x) Resolution of missing persons (from 1974) issue given constitutional force.

(xi) The referendum question redrafted to modify the reference to EU accession (to make it clear that a negative vote in the referendum would not invalidate EU accession which had already been decided).

The Turks had also pressed hard for some provisions to be linked to Turkish accession to the European Union, thus giving the Greek Cypriots and, indeed, other member states an incentive to work for that outcome. So Annan III proposed the removal of the residual Greek and Turkish troops from the island when Turkey acceded, the removal of the agreement of Greece and Turkey to international military operations, and also the removal of limits on Greek Cypriot residence in the north.

Three visits and no result

Annan's visit to Ankara, his first port of call, seemed at the time to have gone well. The paper setting out the changes to Annan II having only been in the hands of the Turks for a few hours, it was not reasonable to expect a definitive response from them and, in any case, it remained important for reasons of Turkish domestic politics that it should be Denktash who gave the answer first. But, at a working dinner with Erdogan, Ziyal gave an entirely fair presentation of the proposed changes and Erdogan seemed pleased with them. In Athens it was all plain sailing, with the Greeks making it clear that anything the Greek Cypriots could accept they could accept too.

On the island Annan had to face up to the fact that, since Clerides/Papadopoulos and Denktash had only just received the full text of Annan III he could not expect them to sign up to the commitment to a referendum on it there and then. Moreover Papadopoulos, who was not yet in office, had had only ten days since his election to catch up with all the details of the proposals. During that time de Soto had conducted several long teach-ins with the president-elect, who had kept his cards close to his chest. He had been equally cagey when I saw him after my arrival on the island on 22 February. So Annan decided to avoid a failed effort to get agreement when he saw the leaders on 27 February and instead went straight for a short extension of the timetable. He therefore invited Papadopoulos (whose presidential inauguration was to take place the next day) and Denktash to meet him again in The Hague on 10 March. He told them he would ask each of them formally then whether they were prepared to sign the text committing them to putting the proposals to a referendum on 30 March, making it clear that if they said they were so prepared, he would expect them to campaign for a 'yes' vote. He reminded them he was also waiting for their reactions to the names he had given them for appointments to the transitional Supreme Court which he asked for by 3 March. He pointed out that each side needed to give him the draft constitutions for their constituent states which had to be consistent with the Foundation Agreement. He wanted their decisions on a flag and an anthem. He drew attention to the massive amount of work remaining to be done by the working groups on international obligations and domestic legislation. Papadopoulos's response was to say that he would come to The Hague as requested, ready to reply. Denktash grumbled. He called Papadopoulos a 'bloody nuisance' for agreeing to go, but then agreed to go too. Later it emerged that he had stopped participation of his representatives in the working groups on international obligations and domestic legislation. Meanwhile in north Nicosia another huge demonstration had taken place, calling for acceptance of the Annan Plan and accession to the European Union.

That evening Annan invited Weston and me to dinner at the Nicosia Hilton Hotel, partly to thank us for the help we had given the UN throughout the negotiations and also to look ahead. We agreed that everything hinged on Ankara's considered reaction to the proposals in Annan III. Denktash himself was never spontaneously going to accept any proposals. As to Papadopoulos, it was already clear that his enthusiasm for pressing on was a good deal less than that of Clerides, but he was showing every sign of believing that he could not afford to back out. If Denktash, willingly or not, signed up, he was likely to do so too. We also discussed the eventuality of Denktash saying no or continuing to filibuster. We agreed that in either of those circumstances it made no sense to go on beyond The Hague. Once any realistic prospect had gone of a settlement being reached before 16 April, when the Treaty of Accession was to be signed, it would be better to pull the plug on the negotiations and leave Denktash and the Turks to face the consequences. But even the slenderest chance of getting a settlement in that time frame should be seized. Annan asked me to try to find an additional legal drafter to reinforce his hard-pressed team. We produced a name within a few days but were never taken up on it for reasons which soon became clear, including the fact that Denktash had stopped the working groups.

The run-up to The Hague and the last chance

There was only one working week between the Nicosia meeting and that in The Hague and during it nothing of significance happened in the negotiations themselves. The UN was anxious to avoid even the slightest hint that there could be an Annan IV set of proposals; they had used up all the flexibility and scope for manoeuvre on Annan III, and the meeting in The Hague was in any case not designed to negotiate further but to take a political decision on whether or not to put Annan III to referendums in the north and south.

But three major developments did occur during that week, all of them in Turkey, and, although two of them did not directly involve Cyprus, all affected the background and climate against which the decisions on Cyprus had to be taken. The first and least significant was the by-election in south-eastern Turkey which elected Erdogan to the National Assembly and thus opened the way to his becoming prime minister and not, as he had been up to then, merely prime minister in waiting; it also opened the way to a change at the foreign ministry, with Gül, up to then prime minister, replacing Yakis as foreign minister. The campaigning for the by-election and the air of change and upheaval in ministerial ranks reduced the time and appetite for grappling with difficult, complex issues like Cyprus.

The second development was far more damaging. On 1 March, after weeks of anguished internal debate and haggling with the US over the accompanying economic aid package, the Turkish government put to the parliament a proposal authorizing US troops to move through Turkey into northern Iraq in the event of hostilities in that country. While the government's measure was supported by more votes than those against it, there were sufficient abstentions from the ranks of the government's own supporters to mean that it did not get the necessary majority and thus failed. This event and its knock-on consequences were to dominate Turkey's international policy making for the months ahead. It did not, to put it mildly, encourage the government to grasp the Cyprus nettle, which would also have involved a considerable political effort to sell to its parliamentary supporters. Moreover throughout the parliamentary saga over Iraq, the military had stayed quiet, allowing the impression to be created that they did not favour the government's proposal to give a green light to the USA. When they explained in the aftermath that they did actually favour that policy it was too late and rubbed salt in the wound. So relations between the new government and the military were tense, unsatisfactory and not propitious to dealing with another issue that concerned them both, Cyprus.

The third development was directly Cyprus-related. Denktash went to Ankara and conferred with Erdogan, Gül, President Sezer and many others. And he emerged from these consultations with full Turkish support for his policy, which as usual put a lot more emphasis on defiance than on conciliation. Erdogan himself was by the end of the week singing a quite different song than before, no longer emphasizing the desirability of a solution but rather the shortcomings (unspecified) of the Annan Plan. What happened in Ankara to bring about this shift still remains something of a mystery. Ziyal at The Hague said it was as much a mystery and a surprise to him as to those outside the Turkish decision-making machine and he offered no explanation for it. Whether the shaky parliamentary position, an intervention by the military, perhaps with the encouragement of President Sezer, or Denktash's undoubted powers of advocacy were responsible it is difficult to say – probably a combination of all three. Suffice it to say that Denktash emerged not just with Turkish support but with a blank cheque for whatever he chose to do in The Hague. Ziyal was sent off with him, deprived of any leverage or scope for manoeuvre. There is some indication that Denktash misled the Turks over his willingness to have a referendum. He seems to have indicated such willingness in Ankara, but on the day of The Hague meeting the government parties in the TRNC blocked an attempt to introduce referendum legislation by depriving the Assembly of a quorum.

De Soto, Weston and I foregathered in The Hague on 9 March and lunched together at the British ambassador's residence. The outlook was not promising, given the negative sounds coming out of Ankara. But we agreed that the priority remained to push as hard as possible for a positive decision on calling referendums on Annan III and, if that could not be achieved immediately, to explore any fall-back which preserved the timetable we were all working to and still offered realistic hope of a settlement within it. I then called on Papadopoulos, who was somewhat incongruously ensconced in a seaside resort hotel at Scheveningen. The

sun shone pallidly, but the wind blew coldly off the North Sea. Papadopoulos was nervous and cagey. He would not confirm flatly that he
intended to agree the next day to putting Annan III to a referendum but
he gave the impression that he would, while speaking vaguely of the
plan's shortcomings and the shortage of time to prepare for a referendum.
Denktash declined to see either me or Weston, pleading a bad cold (which
did not stop him later alleging that we had refused to see him and were
ganging up to isolate him). Late that night I saw Ziyal. He was tired and
depressed. We agreed that the biggest risk the next day was that Denktash
and Papadopoulos, like drunken men emerging from a pub, would prop
up each other's negative positions. Ziyal's message was clear: if there was
to be any chance of a positive outcome, Papadopoulos would have to pull
away first. I said I thought that could be achieved. But could he manage
the other half? He grimaced and smiled wanly. I breakfasted early the
next morning with Dimitri Droutsas, Papandreou's adviser, and told him
how things stood, pressing the need for Papadopoulos to respond positively to Annan's question about a referendum and taking him through
the possible scenario for a last-ditch effort. His response was helpful on all
points.

The secretary-general's meetings on 10 March were to take place in
the Peace Palace, the home at The Hague of the International Court of
Justice, which had been made available to the UN and the other delegations. Dating architecturally from a period at the beginning of the
twentieth century not renowned for its style, an uneasy compromise
between neo-classical grandeur and Dutch homeliness, it was far from
being an ideal conference centre. Delegations were either shut away in
their own rooms for most of the 19 hours of talks, or they roamed the
corridors. Fraternization there was none. Papadopoulos said his answer to
Annan's basic question was yes, although he argued for more time before
the referendum was held, clearly wanting to push it beyond the 16 April
signature of the Treaty of Accession and thus strengthen the Greek
Cypriots' tactical position and reduce their vulnerability. He was willing
not to reopen negotiations on Annan III if Denktash reciprocated. It was
clear at the time, and later when Annan reported in writing to the Security Council, that Annan believed he could, if necessary, have overcome
Papadopoulos's reservations about the timing of the referendums.
Whether Papadopoulos (and Christofias) would then have campaigned for
a 'no' vote, as they were to do a year later, cannot be stated with any
certainty. But I doubt it. The imminence of the date for signing the

Accession Treaty would have weighed heavily in the balance. But, given Denktash's response, that was never put to the test. Denktash gave Annan a flat no to the request that he put Annan III to a referendum. He proposed that the negotiations begin again from scratch with an open-ended discussion of principles.

In the light of this unpromising opening the rest of the talks were devoted to exploring a basis for continuing the process on a realistic and time-limited basis. Overnight I had put certain suggestions to the UN for a crash work programme to complete the negotiations and all the ancillary work by the end of March, and to slip the referendum a further week, until 6 April. This chimed very much with their own thinking. A consolidated draft of this programme was then put to Papadopoulos, Denktash and the representatives of the three guarantor powers. It read as follows:

1. The two leaders have agreed to an intensified work program for the technical committees to finish their work by 28 March 2003.

2. They are committed to negotiations on the basis of the 26 February 2003 revision of my plan with a view to agreeing on any changes by 28 March and to putting the finalized Foundation Agreement to simultaneous referenda on 6 April.

3. They will nominate the members of the committees on the flag and anthem competitions, which have been launched with the agreement of the two sides, by March 14. They will also strive to reach agreement on the nomination of the members of a future transitional Supreme Court, the Registrar and Deputy Registrars and the members of the transitional Board of the Central Bank, failing which they have asked me to contact persons who would fill those posts in case of approval of the Foundation Agreement.

4. They committed to table draft constituent state constitutions no later than 25 March 2003.

5. They will immediately put in hand preparations necessary and to be completed by 28 March so that the holding of referenda on 6 April will depend only on a political decision to that effect.

6. They will notify the UN SG by 28 March whether they are ready to hold separate simultaneous referenda on 6 April.

7. The guarantor powers endorse this procedure and undertake to complete whatever internal procedures are necessary in order for them to send

an irrevocable written commitment not later than 31 March that they agree with the holding of separate referenda and would sign the suggested 'Treaty on matters related to the new state of affairs' upon entry into force of the Foundation Agreement.

8. If agreed by 28 March, separate simultaneous referenda would be held on 6 April 2003.

9. If referenda produce a positive result, the Foundation Agreement would enter into force at 00:00 hours on the day after certification by the United Nations.

The Turks immediately asked for time to submit it to Ankara and also obtained a clarification to the effect that if either referendum returned a negative outcome, the whole plan would be rendered null and void.

When negotiations resumed later in the day it rapidly became clear that Denktash would accept none of this. He was not prepared to let the working groups resume their labours; he was not ready to make any preparations for a referendum until the negotiations were over and a decision to hold one was reached; everything to do with the Supreme Court nominations, the flag and the anthem was premature; he was not ready to table his constituent state constitution. By the time he had finished with it the UN work programme consisted of one single sentence as follows:

The two leaders have agreed to continue negotiations with a view to agreeing on any changes to my 26 February revised plan on 28 March.

In parallel with these problems, the Turks themselves suddenly found that they had insuperable difficulties about committing themselves in advance of the referendums to signing the amendments to the Treaties of Guarantee, Alliance and Establishment immediately after a successful outcome. These amendments would require changes to Turkey's own international obligations and thus could not be promised until the Turkish parliament had approved them, but equally the Turkish parliament would not even look at such changes until there had been a referendum showing that the Turkish Cypriots approved them. It was a perfect Catch 22 situation. Since the tight timetable requiring the guarantor powers to bind themselves to sign the treaty amendments the day after two successful referendums had taken place had been an unchanged feature of Annan I, II and III, it was odd, to say the least, that the Turks only formally raised the problem for the first time on 10 March. The assumption had to be that the failed vote over Iraq in the Turkish parliament had changed everything.

Throughout the late afternoon, the evening and the night Annan and his team wrestled with these two parallel sets of problems. They tried various amended forms of the work programme that made the details less prominent but preserved the essence of it. Each one was rejected by Denktash. They tried to find ways round the Turkish parliamentary problem at two successive meetings with the guarantor powers, but these tended to come up against a Greek (and by implication a Greek Cypriot) objection that they could not be expected to go into the referendums uncertain whether or not Turkey would endorse the outcome and bring the new state of affairs into effect. There was too much of a risk of ending up stuck in a limbo, with the existing Cyprus effectively wiped out, but the new reunited one not brought into being. They pointed out that their parliament too would need to ratify the outcome in slower time, but that need not prevent Greece and Turkey committing themselves to implement their part of the bargain the day after the referendums had voted in favour.

In the late afternoon I went for a walk in the grounds of the Peace Palace and ran into Annan. It was sunny, but bitingly cold as only an early March day can be. We agreed that things looked bad. Annan said he was about to telephone Erdogan and ask for help. I said we were hoping that the prime minister would do the same, and the Americans were working on a presidential call. In the event all these calls went through but they brought about no change in Turkey's or Denktash's positions. Nor did a call to Denktash by Yakis later that night. The talks adjourned for a dinner hosted by the Dutch foreign minister. He had Papadopoulos on his right and Denktash on his left and the two never exchanged a word. Annan had slipped away to see his newly born granddaughter in Haarlem and returned later. The talks went on into the night at the Peace Palace in an air of increasing frustration and exhaustion. Finally, at a meeting in the early hours, Annan said to the representatives of the guarantor powers that he could see no way forward and no sense in continuing the negotiations. Only Turkey disagreed and said the negotiations should go on, but Ziyal was unable to offer anything beyond that.

Nothing remained to be done except to hold the funerary press conferences: de Soto (on behalf of the secretary-general) sad, Papadopoulos smug and Denktash defiant. De Soto described the situation as the end of the road. Negotiations would have continued if there had been a strict work programme, but that had been rejected. Annan would now report to the Security Council. De Soto's own office in Cyprus would be closed. It was by no means clear that another opportunity like the present one would recur any time soon. It was regrettable that Cypriots had been denied the chance to decide their own future. The plan remained on the table. If there were a clear and realistic prospect of carrying it forward to a solution, with the full backing of the motherlands, he would be ready to assist.

I drove directly from the Peace Palace up the road from The Hague to Schipol Airport to catch the first flight to London. It was a cold, grey, dank morning, which matched my mood as I contemplated the ruins of seven years of hard labour. I wrote my report and my assessment of the future prospects on the plane to London. Both report and assessment were bleak.

12

Epilogue: The Curtain Falls

The view of the secretary-general of the United Nations that the negotiations had reached the end of the road and that there was no purpose to be served in trying to conceal that they had broken down at The Hague was contested by no one. Nor was it contested that the responsibility for the breakdown lay at Denktash's door. Even the Turkish government, which would have much preferred it if some process of negotiation had continued, had had the ground cut from under its feet by the pleasure displayed by Denktash at the breakdown and by the intemperance of his constantly reiterated public onslaughts on the Annan Plan, which he delighted in describing as dead and off the table. That was not the view taken by anyone else: the widespread opinion in the international community was that the Annan Plan was the most sophisticated and the most complete attempt ever made to solve the Cyprus problem and that a key objective must now be to rescue it from the shipwreck of the negotiations. And, while comment on the breakdown was overshadowed by the hostilities in Iraq which broke out within a few days of the meeting at The Hague, there was a general feeling of regret that the effort and skill that de Soto and Annan had put into the negotiations had not been crowned with success. It was another piece of bad news in a world where good news was in short supply.

The European Union moves on

The first steps taken after the meeting in The Hague were by the European Union. There was now no longer even the slenderest chance that a reunited Cyprus could be brought into being in time for it to sign the Treaty of Accession on 16 April. So the documentation sent to the European Parliament to deal with that eventuality was withdrawn and the alternative approach of preparing for the admission of a divided island was pursued. A 'Protocol No. 10 on Cyprus' to be incorporated in the terms of accession was approved by the European Parliament and agreed by the member states. The protocol's main provision was to suspend the *acquis communautaire* in the north of the island, thus avoiding a possible confrontation with Turkey and the Turkish Cypriots and also avoiding the Greek Cypriots being held responsible for events in an area over which they had no control, but making it clear that the European Union was in no way recognizing the division of the island. Another provision enabled the EU Council, acting unanimously, to lift that suspension, thus avoiding the need for treaty amendment and ratification in the event of a settlement being reached. At the same time, the protocol committed the European Union to continue its support for Annan's efforts to get a settlement and reiterated its willingness to accommodate the terms of such a settlement. This latter commitment was important in that it was binding on the Greek Cypriots and thus provided some protection against attempts to unpick the derogations provided for Turkish Cypriots in the Annan Plan.

On 16 April, amidst much fanfare and pomp, the heads of state and government of the European Union and of the candidate countries, including those of the three countries (Bulgaria, Romania and Turkey) which were not yet ready for accession, met in Athens and the Treaty of Accession was signed. Erdogan decided not to attend but Gül, now installed as deputy prime minister and foreign minister, did, although he slipped away from the actual signature ceremony, no doubt finding that just too much for Turkish domestic opinion to bear. For all the sound and fury generated by the previous Turkish government about the possible consequences of a divided Cyprus being admitted into the European Union, with speculation that Turkey might annex the north of Cyprus or resort to other (usually unnamed) measures of retaliation, not a bat's squeak was heard. A diplomatic note repeating Turkey's view that Cyprus's accession was illegal passed unnoticed. While it was cold comfort for the UN, which had laboured so hard for a positive outcome, this quiet acceptance of a fait accompli was an unsung triumph of conflict prevention.

A month later the Commission launched proposals to fulfil the remit it had been given at Copenhagen to find ways of bringing the north of Cyprus closer to the European Union. These proposals focused on possible aid projects in the north to be financed with European Union funds and also on ideas for resuming direct preferential trade between the north and the European Union, which had been largely cut off as a result of a ruling by the European Court of Justice. The aid projects proved easier to move forward than those for trade, partly because it was possible for the Commission to enlist the enthusiastic cooperation of the mayors of those Turkish Cypriot municipalities that had fallen to the opposition in the 2002 elections. The ideas for resuming trade were soon entangled in bureaucratic and legalistic difficulties, many of them enthusiastically contributed by the Greek Cypriots. The Papadopoulos administration retained more than a trace of old-style thinking, that squeezing the Turkish Cypriots was a clever policy, and was slow to recognize that, in the new circumstances, this was largely counter-productive.

The United Nations takes stock

Immediately after the meeting in The Hague de Soto and Annan returned to New York and put in hand the drafting of a substantial written report to the Security Council. This was urgently required, since up till then the whole set of negotiations, which had lasted for nearly three and a half years, had been conducted without Annan making any written reports to the Security Council. The justification for this was clear. Written reports from the secretary-general are public documents, every word of which are pored over and often subsequently contested by the interested parties. To have provided such material while the negotiations were under way would have risked a controversy that would have damaged the already fragile structure of the negotiations and would have also risked embroiling the UN with one or other, or perhaps both, of the protagonists, thus reducing its effectiveness as the facilitator of a settlement. Moreover a written report would have required a formal response from the Security Council, at the very least a presidential statement or, more likely, a resolution. The process of negotiating such a formal response would have been fraught with difficulty, given the superior lobbying capability of the Greek Cypriots and the pressure in the Council of a permanent member, Russia, which simply took the Greek Cypriots' brief unquestioningly. The chances were that any text agreed would not only have upset the Turks and Turkish Cypriots, whose ability to keep their end up in the Security Council was invariably less than that of the Greek Cypriots, but would have destabilized the whole negotiation by moving away from the 'no preconditions' text of Resolution 1250 on which the negotiation was based. So Annan and de Soto had briefed the Security Council orally from time to time throughout the negotiations on their progress or the lack of it, but had sent forward nothing in writing; nor had they officially published either the Annan Plan or its two revisions, although those texts were available for studying by members of the Council in de Soto's office and were, of course, effectively in the public domain as a result of press leaks on the island. The Security Council, for its part, had responded on each occasion with a press statement of its current president, which stuck largely to generalities and to supporting the secretary-general's continuing efforts.

The secretary-general's report was tabled on 1 April (S/2003/398) and the full text of Annan III was posted on the UN website. The report was worth waiting for. It gave a coherent and often eloquent account of the negotiations, of the proposals Annan had made and of the process that had led to Annan's conclusion at The Hague that he had reached the end of the road. He justified the decision to launch a new effort to settle the Cyprus problem: there had been 'a unique set of circumstances ... and the potential existed to make a true impact on the attitudes of the protagonists and bring about the required qualitative changes of position'. He reminded the Council of the scale of the negotiating effort – 54 meetings in the proximity phase, 72 meetings in the face-to-face format, more than 150 separate bilateral meetings between de Soto and the two leaders, 30 trips to Greece and Turkey. The cost had been $3,148,500. The proposals ran to 192 core pages plus 250 pages of finalized laws for the reunited Cyprus. Draft laws running to 6,000 pages and 1,954 international treaties and instruments were awaiting approval when Denktash pulled out of the working group exercise. Annan then ran through the issues, the narrative of the negotiations and the content of his successive proposals in terms similar to those set out in earlier chapters of this book and which I will therefore not weary the reader by repeating.

He concluded by describing the breakdown as the last in a long line of missed opportunities. In measured but trenchant terms he set out the responsibility of Denktash for the breakdown: 'in the case of the failure of this latest effort I believe Mr Denktash, the Turkish Cypriot leader, bears prime responsibility', and 'except for a very few instances, Mr Denktash by and large declined to engage in negotiations on the basis of give and take'. He said little that was critical of the Turkish government, expressing the hope that '[it] will soon be in a position to throw its support unequivocally behind the search for a settlement, for without that support it is difficult to foresee one being reached'. For Clerides he had little but praise: 'He did not feel wedded to tried and true formulas; he was quite prepared to explore approaches different from his own ... [he] showed a capacity to accept that his side bore its share of the responsibilities for the bitter experiences of the past.' He warmly thanked Greece for its support, and the United States and the United Kingdom for their backing and advice. As to the future Annan said a window of opportunity had now closed; he did not believe such an opportunity would occur 'any time soon'. But his plan remained on the table. He did not propose to take any new initiative

> unless and until, such time as I am given solid reason to believe that the political will exists necessary for a successful outcome ... a solution on the basis of the plan could be achieved only if there is an unequivocally stated preparedness on the part of the leaders of both sides, fully and deter- minedly backed at the highest political level in both motherlands, to commit themselves (a) to finalize the plan (without reopening its basic principles or essential trade-offs) by a specific date with UN assistance and (b) to put it to separate, simultaneous referenda as provided for in the plan on a date certain soon thereafter.

Faced with such a full and clear report, the Security Council had no great difficulty reaching similar conclusions. As might have been expected, there was plenty of lobbying. The Greek Cypriots in particular put in a frenzied performance which at some moments gave rise to the suspicion that they too wanted to marginalize the Annan Plan and reopen its main proposals. But none of that affected the outcome very much. Security Council Resolution 1475 was adopted by unanimity on 14 April. It com- mended the secretary-general and his team for their conduct of the negotiations and for the proposals he had made. It gave its full support to Annan III, which it described as 'a unique basis for further negotiations'. It regretted 'the negative approach of the Turkish Cypriot leader', which had deprived both Greek Cypriots and Turkish Cypriots of an opportu- nity to decide for themselves on a plan that would have permitted the reunification of Cyprus before the signature of the Treaty of Accession. It asked the secretary-general to continue to make available his Good Of- fices for Cyprus.

Soon after adoption of this resolution de Soto closed his office in the island, and he and his able team were posted to new assignments, he himself to become the UN Secretary-General's Special Representative for the Western Sahara in the autumn of 2003, Pfirter to go to the Swiss embassy in Lisbon and Dann to the secretary-general's own office in New York. But it was made clear that, should circumstances change and should the prospects for a settlement revive, then the team could be reassembled at short notice. I, too, after consultation with ministers in London decided that there was no useful purpose to be served in the short term by continuing my mission. No new appointment was made but Jack Straw told parliament that if the circumstances justified it he would not hesitate to make a further appointment. The message from all this was clear. The international community had given Cyprus its best effort. If negotiations were to be resumed, there would have to be some fundamental shifts in the region.

A barrier crumbles

A few days after the signature of the Treaty of Accession, on 21 April, the Turkish Cypriots, without any advance notice or the usual leaks, announced the lifting of all restrictions on the Green Line, which had for nearly 30 years prevented Greek Cypriots going to the north and Turkish Cypriots to the south. The response was instant and massive. Huge queues formed at the crossing points. A mass two-way exodus began. Pressure mounted for the opening of new crossing points. Tiresome restrictions that prevented Greek and Turkish Cypriots driving their cars on the other side of the line were lifted. The Greek Cypriots, who had at first been caught on the hop by this sudden move, were driven to reciprocate and to desist from the temptation to make a fuss about such issues as those crossing from the south having to show their passports to authorities in the north, although they continued to try to prevent Greek Cypriots spending a night in the north and would not admit to the south anyone whom they considered to be a Turkish 'settler'. Within a few months it was estimated that three-quarters of all Turkish Cypriots had visited the south, many more than once, and that half of all Greek Cypriots had visited the north.

Perhaps more interesting even than the scale of the crossings was the atmosphere in which they took place. It had been part of Denktash's stock in trade over many years to predict that dire consequences would ensue if Greek Cypriots and Turkish Cypriots ever again mingled in an uncontrolled way. He was not averse to dramatic bloodcurdling analogies with the problems between Israelis and Palestinians. And there were extremists in the Greek Cypriot community with similar views. The reality bore no relation to this picture. The mood was festive. There were many touching accounts of reunions between Greek and Turkish Cypriots who had been neighbours before the events of 1974 had driven them apart. There were practically no ugly incidents of any sort, and the few that there were were handled with a light touch by the police on both sides.

For once ordinary people were able to get ahead of the politicians, and they enjoyed it. It gradually dawned, however, that the Green Line was not the Berlin Wall. The mass crossings were not a prelude to the crumbling of the regime in the north. The political obstacles to a settlement, although they were in the broadest sense undermined and weakened by developments on the Green Line, were not removed by them.

A remaining enigma was why Denktash and the authorities in the north took the action they did to open up the Green Line crossings. No doubt part of the explanation was that both Denktash and the Turks felt under great international pressure following the collapse of the talks at The Hague and the blame they were apportioned in bringing that about, and wanted to take some eye-catching initiative that would place them in a more positive light. If so, it somewhat backfired in the sense that the main international reaction was that this validated the thinking behind the Annan Plan and demonstrated that a bi-zonal, federal Cyprus should have a good chance of working. Other baser motives were possibly at work. Denktash may have expected a violent incident or two to strengthen his case. He may have intended to boost the electoral prospects of his son's party in the parliamentary elections due in December. The huge flood of Greek Cypriots coming to the north (which, of course, had not been anticipated) certainly gave a boost to the Turkish Cypriots' ailing economy. And there were some recognition and status crumbs to be lovingly gathered up as Greek Cypriots showed their passports to Turkish Cypriot policemen. But all in all the story is more one of the law of unintended consequences in full operation than of careful planning and foresight.

Negotiating stasis

With the temporary withdrawal of the United Nations from an active role in promoting a Cyprus settlement and with the removal of short-term external pressure in support of their efforts, the scene rapidly reverted to one in which tactical manoeuvre and the playing of the blame game dominated. Papadopoulos, while insisting that he was ready to accept a settlement on the basis of the Annan Plan, developed an eloquent attachment to a mantra called 'a viable and workable settlement'. What this might mean in terms of changes to the Annan Plan was never explained, perhaps fortunately, but it seemed to signal a desire to unpick some of the EU derogations which had formed such a crucial part of the Annan Plan. Denktash, as so often before when he was in a tight corner, tried to change the subject. He launched proposals for bilateral face-to-face meetings with Papadopoulos without the presence of the UN and quite explicitly designed not to negotiate on the basis of the Annan Plan. He also went back to some of the old Confidence-Building Measures of the 1993–94 period, proposing that the ghost town of Varosha could be opened up to the Greek Cypriots. None of the ideas had any attraction to Papadopoulos. In Ankara denunciation of the Annan Plan was eschewed and repetition of the 'no solution is no solution' slogan continued. But there were few signs yet that Turkey was ready to come to terms with the reality of the Annan Plan or was willing and able to rein in Denktash. Indeed the dislocation in Turkey's Cyprus policy was again underlined by the decision on 8 August to form a customs union between Turkey and the TRNC. This move, of little practical significance or benefit to the Turkish Cypriots, was part of the pre-existing agenda of the Ecevit government to match any move to integrate the south into the European Union with similar moves between the north and Turkey. Its main effect was to put Turkey in the wrong in its own dealings with the European Union (since Turkey's Association and Customs Union Agreements with the EU required prior consultation before Turkey entered into any such new commitments), and to undermine the view which the AK government was anxious to propagate that it was still seriously working for a settlement.

13

What Went Wrong, and
Will It Ever Go Right?

No one who has participated in a failed negotiation can duck the question of what went wrong. Indeed they should not do so, because the answers to that question will be needed by the next person or organization to pick up the baton. Nor is it enough to point the finger at one person or country to the exclusion of all others as being responsible for the failure, because things are seldom as simple as that. The Cyprus settlement negotiations may have been many things, but simple they were not. Some readers may think that I have indeed pointed my finger at Rauf Denktash as that one person whose actions explain what went wrong in Cyprus. It is true that I believe he bore the lion's share of the responsibility for frustrating what was the most far-reaching and the most hopeful of the attempts so far made to resolve the Cyprus problem, as he had done earlier ones. But I do not believe it makes sense to demonize him or to overlook the many other factors that contributed to the setback.

Some of the problems the negotiators faced in Cyprus were generic ones, which could have arisen almost anywhere in the world. To get agreement to a territorial adjustment at the negotiating table and not on the battlefield is one of the most difficult challenges for any negotiator and it has not often been successfully achieved. In this case it was made even more problematic by the fact that Turkey, which ultimately had to agree to the adjustment, remained the militarily dominant force in the immediate region and on the island, not seriously challenged even by the frantic and costly armament programmes initiated by successive Greek Cypriot administrations. To get agreement to making the painful compromises necessary for a solution when the status quo was not urgently unsustainable and when the two parties had not been worn down by conflict, was also a challenge. The Greek Cypriots had made a remarkable recovery from the dog days of 1974 and had built a strong economy on the foundations of their tourist and service industries. They were making their way into the European Union in the happy position of being the most prosperous of the ten candidates and the one that needed the least adjustments to meet the requirements of EU membership. The Turkish Cypriots were less comfortably placed, with a weak and dysfunctional economy, but the annual subsidy from Turkey in the region of $200 million – approximately $1,000 for every man, woman and child in the TRNC – and the Turkish troop presence guaranteeing their security, took the edge off their predicament.

And then there was the ineluctable fact that the Cyprus problem was not right at the top of anyone's agenda. So, however many international meetings issued statements calling for a settlement in Cyprus, the harsh reality remained that the leaders making those statements invariably had more urgent things on their minds and more immediate calls on their time. In the event it proved possible on this occasion to enlist a more sustained effort by those principally concerned – the US, the UK and the other main European countries, the UN and the European Commission – than had ever been the case before. But this concentration of effort was fragile and vulnerable to external distractions. The crisis over Iraq gradually overshadowed the final stages of the negotiations and distracted the attention of some of the main players, especially those in Ankara. I am not suggesting that without a crisis in Iraq a settlement would have necessarily been reached in Cyprus in the spring of 2003. This factor was not that important or fundamental. But it certainly was not helpful.

Two other generic problems plagued the Cyprus negotiations: the blame game and the zero-sum game. The blame game was a speciality of the Greek Cypriots and, to a lesser extent in the early years of this negotiation, of the Greeks. They played it day in day out, and they played it well. If there had been an Olympic medal for playing the blame game, they would have won it. The Turks and Turkish Cypriots played it very badly, except in the eyes of their own public opinion which did not signify much in this contest. Their mistake was not to realize how much tactical damage to their position arose from their inability or unwillingness to raise their presentational game. But the really pernicious aspect of the blame game was its incompatibility with a commitment to negotiate effectively and seriously. If you are playing the blame game you pick the most extreme and unreasonable of your opponent's public statements and make the most use of it you can; if you are negotiating seriously you pick the most useable and reasonable of your opponent's statements and try to make something of them. Points scored in the blame game are points lost at the negotiating table. Neither side understood this or, if they did, drew the right conclusions. The Greek Cypriots believed they could play both games at the same time and were unwilling to recognize the damage they caused to the fabric of the negotiation by continuing with the blame game.

Treating the Cyprus settlement negotiations as a zero-sum game was even more endemic and more pernicious. At its simplest this meant that any of one side's problems that the UN successfully addressed was instantly regarded as a loss to the other side and one which had to be compensated for somewhere else. In the final stages of the negotiations, once the UN plan of 11 November 2002 was on the table, there was no escape from zero-sum calculations; there had to be a balance in any revisions proposed, and the UN achieved that balance with considerable skill. But the failure of many, although not all of those concerned, to realize that getting a Cyprus settlement and getting a reunited Cyprus into the European Union was not a zero-sum game at all was a serious handicap. In the security field, it was essential to understand that achieving a feeling of security only at the expense of creating a feeling of insecurity on the other side (as was the effect of the large Turkish troop presence in the north and of the south's sequence of arms purchases) was not a contribution to achieving lasting and sustainable security, which was much more likely to be obtained by lower troop presences and the demilitarization of indigenous forces. In the economic field, all experience with previous enlargements of the European Union had shown that far from being a zero-sum game, bringing less prosperous countries and regions within the scope of the single market and of the European Union's structural funds tended to result in a substantial increase in overall prosperity and the narrowing of gaps between disadvantaged regions and their better-off neighbours. The importance of appreciating these aspects and of getting away from a zero-sum mentality was all the more crucial in Cyprus because the smallness of the island and the duration of the attempts to get a settlement had meant that the negotiating pitch had long since been trampled into a quagmire; only if the pitch could be enlarged and the mentality changed was the will going to be found to make the necessary compromises.

But, when all was said and done, the generic problems were not the most difficult ones the negotiators had to face: the Cyprus-specific problems were even more daunting. I well remember the fate of Holbrooke's efforts to use historical analogies to impress on the Cypriots of both persuasions the need for and the possibility of overcoming their antagonisms and hatreds. To preach this sermon he produced Dick Spring, former foreign minister of Ireland and a man who had played a distinguished role in overcoming the differences between Britain and Ireland over Northern Ireland. Spring spoke eloquently and well. For a brief time his Cypriot audience looked dazed and impressed. And then with one accord they chorused 'Ah, yes. But Cyprus is different.' The truth of that could not be gainsaid by careful academic analysis because it was in the bloodstream of all concerned.

Most fundamental of the Cyprus-specific problems were what I named the two nightmares. The Turkish Cypriot nightmare was that, however many precautions you took, however many counter-provisions you made in the paperwork of a comprehensive settlement, and even with Turkish troops on the island guaranteeing its constitutional provisions, those wily Greek Cypriots would end up dominating a reunited Cyprus and repressing the Turkish Cypriots as they had done in the Cyprus of the 1960 agreements. The Greek Cypriot nightmare was that, however many times you said that secession was banned and that the new Cyprus was an indissoluble union, Denktash would in fact be able to use to his advantage all the concessions made to him, would cause stalemate in the institutional arrangements (as the Greek Cypriot version of the history of the 1960s had it), and, after a brief time, would walk off into the sunset with the independent, sovereign state he had always been determined to achieve. What could be done to banish these nightmares was done by the UN in the successive iterations of the Annan Plan. But it had to be recognized that only the experience of successfully operating the new, reunited Cyprus was going to banish them for ever. So this was one of several Catch 22 elements.

Another Cyprus-specific problem arose from the complexes the various players had about each other. The Turkish Cypriots had an inferiority complex about the Greek Cypriots, who outnumbered them and were thought to be richer and more astute than they were. The Greek Cypriots had an inferiority complex about Turkey because Turkey dominated their island militarily. I once said to Clerides that it looked as if we were going to have bad weather coming from the Taurus Mountains (in Turkey). 'Yes', he said, 'That's where it always comes from.' He was not talking about the weather. Both lots of Cypriots, as I have observed earlier, had complexes about their motherlands. And Greece also had a complex about Turkey. All these interlocking complexes had somehow to be unlocked if there was to be a settlement and if it was to work. But, as with the interlocking complexes in Northern Ireland, between Protestants and Catholics and between them and their motherlands and between Ireland and Britain, that was easier said than done.

In Cyprus these complexes were exacerbated, particularly in the south, by the weird politically correct vocabulary in which all matters relating to Cyprus had to be discussed. The TRNC was the 'pseudo state', its land 'the occupied territories', its people 'the Turkish Cypriot community', its politicians 'so-called ministers' and so on. In the north there were some equally egregious examples, the Turkish military inter-vention of 1974 being invariably referred to as 'the peace operation' and Greek Cypriot harassment referred to as 'genocide'. Turkish Cypriots were slightly less devoted to the textual exegesis of their visitors' state-ments than were the Greek Cypriots. For any British minister going to Cyprus for the first time, the first document in the briefing folder was not a list of objectives for his or her visit but a glossary of the various words and terms to be used or avoided. All this was translated by the politicians on both sides into highly vitriolic political discourse about the others. I used to ask Cypriot audiences (both in London and on the island) whether it might not make more sense to show some respect for the institutions of the other side. After all, the politicians, judges, civil servants and others whom they so freely denounced and denigrated were the self-same peo-ple, and, largely, with name changes, the self-same institutions, that would be running the Greek Cypriot and Turkish Cypriot constituent states of a reunited Cyprus. This thought seemed quite strange and rather heretical to most of them. However, probably the worst and most dam-aging manifestation of these complexes was in the educational curricula on either side of the Green Line. Children are brought up to regard the other side as the 'enemy', taught bigoted songs at nursery and given time off to demonstrate on significant anniversaries. I remember sitting next to a Greek Cypriot businessman flying to Larnaca who said that, as someone who had lived in a mixed community pre-1974, he could never and would never regard Turkish Cypriots as his enemies; but his children all did so automatically. The history syllabus taught to each side is a travesty.

As if all this was not bad enough, there were some astonishing gaps in human contact, let alone political dialogue, between some of the key players. This was partly, but not exclusively, due to the peculiarities of travel arrangements and diplomatic protocol arising from the fact that no one but Turkey recognized the TRNC and that Turkey did not recognize the Republic of Cyprus. But the Turkish Cypriot authorities did their level best to supplement such obstacles and to harass and obstruct bi-communal gatherings. They seemed to feel that, if they could not be fully recognized, they would prefer to be a hermit state, a view not shared by most of their citizens. The worst gap was that between the Turks, the ultimate arbiters of any settlement, and the Greek Cypriots. There was something surreal about sitting in an office in the foreign ministry in Ankara listening to a row of senior Turkish diplomats telling me in great detail about the objectives, intentions and motivation of Clerides, whom none of them had ever met or talked to. I, of course, would have seen him a few hours before, but that did not seem to register. The only Turks who ever did talk to Clerides were journalists like Mehmet Ali Birand of CNN-Turk, to whom he would from time to time give a conciliatory interview, but that did not register either. And indeed what was needed was some discreet dialogue, not necessarily conducted by diplomats or politicians. But then there was the problem of Denktash, who would have regarded any such dialogue as a personal betrayal. So nothing was ever done.

No consideration of what went wrong would be complete without some consideration of the European Union dimension, if only because Denktash invariably tried to cast the European Union as the villain of the piece, without whose involvement all would have been fine. Elsewhere in Europe, even in some quarters of Ankara, the contrary view was taken and the European Union was seen as a catalyst for reaching a settlement and as likely to provide the cement that would hold one together. I am in no doubt myself that the second thesis is closer to the truth than the first. But it was all a bit more complex than this simple black and white choice can make it appear. Cyprus's EU application and the implementation of the *acquis communautaire* in the island were seen by many Greek Cypri-ots as a tactical stroke of genius enabling them to gain points painlessly without the concessions that would be required of them at the UN's negotiating table. Moreover there was much loose talk on the Greek Cypriot side of how the 1960 Treaty of Guarantee would be invalidated by membership of the European Union and of how the emerging European Security and Defence Policy would miraculously turn into a mutual defence commitment between its members. Much persistence and skill was required, mainly from the European Commission, to dissipate these illusions and to establish the sort of adjustments when applying the *acquis communautaire* which would ensure it was compatible with the UN proposals for a settlement. Once this process had been completed, as it was by late 2002, it became clear to most Cypriots, including most Turkish Cypriots, that European Union membership by a reunited island was the keystone of any settlement.

Turkey's own relationship with the European Union was a less unmitigated success story. The ambivalent attitude of many member states towards the prospect of Turkey joining the European Union was an endlessly complicating factor, as were the problems Turkey itself had in meeting the Copenhagen political criteria for membership. Above all the sequencing of Turkey's slow and halting progress towards membership and the Cyprus negotiations presented a virtually insoluble problem. No one much doubted that if Turkey's candidature had been proceeding to a positive conclusion in parallel with Cyprus's and with the negotiations for a settlement, all three would have passed the finishing post together. But that was not on offer. The 1995 commitment to the Greek Cypriots was clear. And Turkey's accession date could not be predicted. Were the Turkish Cypriots' EU aspirations and a Cyprus settlement to be left in limbo until then, as Denktash and many in Ankara wanted? Not only was that bad news in the meantime for the Turkish Cypriots but it was far from clear that they would avoid ending up with the short straw in any such grand deal. The implications for both Turkey and for the Turkish Cypriots of the Greek Cypriots by then being entrenched as a member inside the European Union were seriously negative. To anyone except Denktash, who wanted neither Turkey nor the TRNC to be in the European Union, and who regarded the European Union as some kind of plague sent to trouble him, these concerns would have provided pause for thought.

There was one further European Union complication. A Greek Cypriot business, egged on by their government, had, in the early 1990s brought a case to the European Court of Justice arguing that Turkish Cypriot exports to the European Union should not be admitted or given preferential treatment because they did not have origin and phytosanitary certificates issued in accordance with the EU/Cyprus Customs Union Agreement. Although the case was contested by the British government (most of the exports went to the UK) and by the Commission, the Court found for the plaintiff and so, from 1994, virtually all direct trade between north Cyprus and its natural market in the EU ceased.

This was known to Turkish Cypriots as 'the embargo' and was treated as if the European Union had imposed sanctions on the TRNC. In fact it was partly their own fault since the problem over certificates was compounded by Denktash's declaration of independence. The effect, however, was to damage further the economy of the north and to lend credibility to Denktash's own view that the European Union was hostile to Turkish Cypriots. Unfortunately, although most members of the EU and the Commission believed the 'embargo' was counter-productive, finding a way around the Court's edict was not straightforward. On numerous occasions I tried to persuade Clerides that it made more sense politically to help the Turkish Cypriots resume exports and thus to demonstrate, contrary to what Denktash was saying, the benefits the EU would bring them. Furthermore I pointed out that, contrary to public belief in the south, the 'embargo' did not give them leverage over the north, but simply made Turkish Cypriots feel angry and sorry for themselves. But to him the political cost of a move always outweighed the benefits and nothing was done. Even in 2003, when the Green Line was open and the Commission was trying to find ways in which trade with the north could be resumed, the Greek Cypriots were dragging their feet and making difficulties. It was the epitome of zero-sum calculation.

So far in this chapter I have concentrated on the underlying indirect factors that militated against a successful settlement negotiation and thus contributed to its failure. The more obvious direct factors have been fully described in the narrative chapters on the negotiations themselves and in the account of Annan's analysis of what went wrong. Ought one to be more self-critical? Were there mistakes made by the UN and those who supported its efforts? Of course there were, and I hope they have been identified in those same narrative chapters, the mistake in pushing the negotiations a bit too far, too fast in November 2000 being the most obvious one.

Another major weakness was that it was never possible to synchronize the moments at which both sides were under pressure to settle. When the Greek Cypriots were under the greatest pressure (up to March 2003) the Turks were not ready to handle Denktash. And when they finally were ready (outside the time-scale of this book, in 2004) the pressure on the Greek Cypriots had eased off.

There remains one big question: should the negotiations have been started at all, knowing, as everyone concerned did, that Denktash was fundamentally opposed to any outcome that was even remotely negotiable? The person who would have been happiest if that question had been answered in the negative would have been Denktash. Negotiations put his position in north Cyprus and as the controller of Turkey's Cyprus policy at risk; the absence of negotiations consolidated it. The hard fact was that the UN was never going to find out whether the Denktash roadblock could be circumnavigated without putting it to the test. I am sure they were right to do so.

So much for what went wrong. What about the more difficult and speculative question of will it ever go right? Many of those who have struggled with the Cyprus problem over the years and broken their teeth on it have concluded that it is insoluble. I do not share that view. The problem is soluble, although only with the greatest difficulty given the inherent negative factors discussed earlier in this chapter. Moreover it is in the general interest of those who live in the island, of those who live in neighbouring countries in the region and of the wider international community, that it should be solved. That is not, however, a confident prediction that it will be solved, and certainly not a prediction that it will be solved, in Kofi Annan's phrase, 'any time soon'. Another reason for believing the problem is soluble is that the material for a comprehensive solution is now on the table. The Annan Plan is not the result of a few months or even years of negotiation; it was built up slowly and painstakingly over a period of 20 years which began with Pérez de Cuéllar's work on the island and afterwards when he became UN secretary-general, and which continued through Boutros-Ghali's Set of Ideas and which only reached its final and complete form in the negotiations described in this book. It is not, as Denktash and, later, Papadopoulos have attempted to depict it, yet another externally devised and imposed settlement like that of 1960, into which Cypriots have made no input. On the contrary it has been pieced together in a process that has involved Cypriots at every stage. Clearly it is not perfect, and some balanced changes can still be negotiated. But it is an illusion to suppose that there is some alternative approach out there waiting to be found, which will prove to be both negotiable and viable. As Annan frequently said, the choice is not between this approach and another one, it is between this approach and no solution at all.

However, the negotiations between 1999 and 2003 did, in my view, demonstrate that external pressures and assistance do have their limitations and cannot, unaided, deliver a settlement. On no previous occasion were external pressures applied so consistently and in such a sustained manner; on no previous occasion was the raw material that emerged from the views of the two sides so skilfully blended and merged. And yet all that was not enough to achieve an agreement. The conclusion to be drawn, surely, is that it is not to an increase in external pressure and assistance that one must look in the future, important though those elements will remain, to produce a positive outcome; it is rather to an increased positive input from Cypriots themselves and from the two motherlands. This switch in emphasis would be no bad thing in its own right. One of the most corrosive characteristics of Cypriot politics on both sides is the belief that Cypriots are mere pawns on the international chess board, that 'they' (sometimes defined as Greece and Turkey, sometimes as the 'great powers') will settle matters and impose their preferred solution on the Cypriots. This attitude has encouraged the growth among politicians on both sides of irresponsible politics, of an unwillingness to accept responsibility for the consequences of the policies being promoted. In any case a solution imposed from outside will risk being as unstable and as fragile as the 1960 settlement, which lasted only three years and had few supporters on either side in Cyprus. If, next time, there is to be a durable solution it will surely have to be one for which the majority of Cypriots claim ownership and one which they are prepared to support and to make work.

One further important regional element will be the development of relations between Greece and Turkey. Will the present fragile and incomplete rapprochement between the two countries be consolidated to the extent of resolving all the disputes between them, including the key ones over the continental shelf in the Aegean and the sea and air boundaries there? Or will the rapprochement stall or even fall apart? Whether or not the two governments go further than that will be a key factor for the chances of solving the Cyprus problem. There cannot be a complete resolution of all the disputes between Greece and Turkey without a settlement of the Cyprus problem. So if the two governments put their hands to settling their bilateral disputes, they will need also to put more effort into helping bring about a settlement of the Cyprus problem. But if they leave the Cyprus problem to fester, then the chances of their being able to settle their bilateral disputes will lessen and the risks of regression in their relationship will increase.

Do these regional elements have to fall into place simultaneously? That would indeed be a triumph of hope over experience. A less clearcut outcome is more likely. But each one will affect the prospects for settling the Cyprus problem. Outside the region the most important elements relate to the European Union and the evolution of its policies. The European Union is debarred from becoming itself a facilitator or mediator by the fact that Greece and Cyprus will now be members and Turkey is not yet one. That role remains for the UN. But, as has been said before, the European Union's handling of the Turkish candidature will be vitally important, as will be its continued willingness to 'accommodate' a UN settlement within the terms of accession that will apply to the north of the island. Any weakening of that commitment, and there are plenty on the Greek Cypriots' side who would be happy to see, and even to work for, a weakening of it, would be damaging, perhaps fatally damaging, to the prospects for a settlement. On the contrary the European Union should be working systematically to demonstrate to Turkish Cypriots that they should have no fear about joining ahead of Turkey and that the institutions of the European Union will be there to protect a settlement once reached, not to undermine it.

14

Envoi

I stepped down from my job as the British government's Special Representative for Cyprus at the end of May 2003 with some relief and some regret. I had done the job for seven years. What had started as a part-time retirement post had gradually come perilously close to being a full-time commitment. When, in April 2001, I was appointed to the House of Lords and almost simultaneously became Pro-Chancellor of the University of Birmingham, I had tried to escape, but the Foreign Office would have none of it: John Kerr (the permanent under-secretary) and Emyr Jones Parry (the political director) persuaded me to carry on. Now, with the breakdown of the negotiations, the indicators all pointed the other way. Moreover I had the feeling that I had done what could be done from the outside to help the process forward. The pieces needed to complete the jigsaw were on the table.

It was a relief to be spared the continuing carping criticism of the Cypriot press, in particular in the south. I had grown my extra skin or two and had evolved a technique of never responding even to their wildest fantasies about the plots I was said to be hatching. It was a relief too to be spared the burden of suspicion about British intentions, which was pervasive almost everywhere on the Cyprus circuit. I had started my diplomatic career in Iran and Afghanistan, two countries whose history had left them convinced that the long, hidden hand of British diplomacy could be held responsible for almost anything that happened; but that was a mere aperitif for Cyprus. As I learned more about our role there in the 1950s, 1960s and 1970s, I came to understand better some of the hostility and suspicions towards Britain. We had indeed not covered ourselves with glory during that period. But the prevalence of that same suspicion, so long after the justification for it had disappeared, was saddening and a trifle wearing.

There was also regret. I did not like leaving a job unfinished. If I had believed that continuing would have made a real difference I would have been ready to do so. I felt in a way that I had let down those many Cypriots, Greek and Turkish, who thanked me quietly (no one ever thanked me publicly) for what I and others were doing to get a settlement. Most of all I regretted severing my last official link with my colleagues in Britain's Diplomatic Service with whom I had worked for 44 years and whose professionalism, capacity for hard work and cheerfulness were as notable when I left as the day I joined their ranks in 1959.

15

Postscript

From the breakdown of the negotiations in May 2003 until the Turkish Cypriot parliamentary elections in December of that year, there was a complete absence of activity, let alone of movement, in attempts to resolve the Cyprus problem. The United Nations camped firmly on the position, endorsed by the Security Council in April, that there would need to be a firm commitment of all concerned to work on the basis of the Annan Plan before it could contemplate re-engagement. The Turkish Cypriot scene remained dominated by a weakened Denktash in full rejectionist mode, regularly denouncing the Annan Plan; the Turks retired to lick their wounds and wait for a shift in the political situation in the north of the island; the Greek Cypriots reclined comfortably on their laurels, occasionally repeating a vague mantra expressing willingness to negotiate on the basis of the Annan Plan (while demanding greater 'viability', whatever that might mean) and coasting towards EU accession on 1 May 2004.

All that changed with the Turkish Cypriot parliamentary elections in December. Although the outcome was a dead-heat (25 seats each for parties supporting a resumption of negotiations on the basis of the Annan Plan and for the rejectionists), the result in fact reflected a substantial shift away from the rejectionists and a repudiation of Denktash's dominance of the Turkish Cypriot handling of the settlement negotiations. Difficult negotiations then ensued over the formation of the new government, it being clear from the outset that to achieve any sort of stability or sense of direction, there would need to be a coalition that in some way straddled the differences over the Annan Plan. Eventually a coalition was formed with Mehmet Ali Talat, the leader of the firmly pro-Annan Plan CTP, as prime minister and Serdar Denktash, leader of the less fundamentally rejectionist of the two centre-right parties, as deputy prime minister and foreign minister. More significantly the coalition agreement committed the new government to work for a resumption of the settlement negotiations on the basis of the Annan Plan. This government was accepted and installed with ill grace by Rauf Denktash towards the end of January 2004.

It was clearly the signal for which the Turkish government had been waiting with some impatience, having in the interim, since the breakdown of negotiations in March 2003, resolved its own internal contradictions and concluded that an early settlement on the basis of the Annan Plan offered a potentially acceptable outcome and the only sure way of furthering its major policy objective of getting a green light for the opening of its own accession negotiations with the EU at the end of 2004. The Turkish prime minister moved rapidly, through a series of high-level meetings with the EU, the UN secretary-general and the president of the United States, to indicate that he was anxious for a resumption of the negotiations on the conditions laid down by Annan and that he and the Turkish Cypriots intended this time to negotiate in good faith for a positive result. How the Denktash obstacle was to be removed or circumnavigated remained, however, at this stage unclear.

With both Greek Cypriots and the Greeks continuing to repeat their commitment to a settlement on the basis of the Annan Plan, and with the whole international community, with the US, the UK and the EU in the lead, keen to have one final try to see whether a settlement could be reached in time to enable a reunited Cyprus to join the EU on 1 May, the UN secretary-general called the parties to New York in early February 2004. Three days of difficult and tense negotiations led to agreement on the following:

1. Negotiations between the two Cypriot sides under the aegis of the UN and on the basis of the Annan Plan would resume on the island without delay.

2. If, after a month (by 21 March), these negotiations had not reached a comprehensive agreement, the Greek and Turkish governments would join the negotiations and try to help the Cypriots to reach an agreement within a further week.

3. Should this second phase not succeed, Annan would, on his own responsibility, complete a definitive new version of his plan, which would be submitted to referendums in both parts of Cyprus at the end of April (at first envisaged for 21 April but subsequently shifted to 24 April).

4. Meanwhile the technical work needed to draft legislation for a reunited Cyprus, including its international commitments (begun in the run-up to The Hague meeting in March 2003), would be completed.

The negotiations in New York revealed rifts on both sides. Those between the Turkish government and Talat on the one hand and Denktash on the other were more evident than ever before. Papadopoulos for his part showed increasing signs of unease about the game plan to which he was committing himself, while for the Greek government the shadow of its own general election on 7 March loomed ever closer and limited its scope for manoeuvre and forceful intervention.

The first phase of the resumed negotiations was a pure charade. Neither side negotiated seriously. Papadopoulos and Denktash pressed for long lists of unnegotiable changes to the Annan Plan and showed no interest in negotiating trade-offs. The unholy alliance between them was already taking shape. The second phase, which the UN moved to Bürgenstock in Switzerland, was more serious. For one thing, Denktash declined to participate, thus (not for the first time) reneging on an agreement into which he had himself freely entered. His absence proved, however, to be a positive development, since his potential for spoiling manoeuvres was removed and the Turkish government was relieved of the necessity of taking the initiative to override him. For another, the Turks themselves came to Bürgenstock with a limited number of proposed changes to the Annan Plan and a determination to settle.

On the other side the situation was neither so clear nor so positive. Not only did Papadopoulos reject any of the symbolic gestures that might have demonstrated his belief that he was on the verge of a historic agreement and was working for a positive outcome in good faith (refusing to shake Talat's hand and declining any direct contact with the Turkish government), but, by refusing to prioritize his own list of demands for changes to the Annan Plan, he effectively frustrated any serious negotiation in this phase too. The new Greek government (in office for little more than a week, following the 7 March election, which the opposition New Democracy party won), while making positive noises, clearly felt in no position to bring effective pressure to bear on the Greek Cypriots. So the second phase ended in deadlock too, despite an attempt by Annan to get agreement on a package of amendments (Annan IV) to the earlier versions of the plan.

Annan was therefore compelled to table his own definitive version of the plan (Annan V), which he duly did on the last day of the Bürgenstock talks, and it was this version that was submitted to the 24 April referendums. For all the allegations of both sides (naturally, in a contradictory sense), Annan V did not differ in any fundamental respect from the earlier versions of the plan. The territorial adjustments proposed in Annan III were not changed at all, nor were the basic structures of a bi-zonal, federated state. Some changes strengthened bi-zonality; provisions enabling property to be partially repossessed were included; token Turkish and Greek troop presences, even beyond accession to the EU (the numbers of troops being those in the 1960 Treaty of Alliance), were to be permitted. But if the plan itself was not greatly changed, the reactions were. The Turkish government and Talat embraced and supported Annan V as warmly and vociferously as Denktash, from afar, rejected it. Papadopoulos, while taking a few days before fully declaring his hand, soon moved to outright and emotional rejection. And the new Greek government wrung its hands on the sidelines, concentrating on limiting the damage to Greek–Turkish relations of any eventual rejection by the Greek Cypriots.

Everything now turned on the referendums. The UN, by definition, could not campaign itself, so its plan and the explanations of it were left to the tender mercies of Cypriot politicians. Nor could the international community afford to play too prominent a role; to have done so would only have confirmed the conviction of many Cypriots that this was yet another settlement being imposed on them from the outside. What could reasonably be done was done. But both UN and EU attempts to explain neutrally what the plan meant were countered by Greek Cypriot government obstruction and by the predominantly rejectionist Greek Cypriot press.

The EU made it clear that, whatever rejectionist Greek Cypriot politicians might say, there was nothing in Annan V that could not be accommodated with the *acquis*. A donor conference was held in Brussels at which substantial sums of international aid were pledged to help resettle those Turkish Cypriots who would be displaced by the settlement and to underpin the objective of reducing the economic discrepancies between Greek and Turkish Cypriots. The Security Council would have endorsed the whole package and committed itself to its prescribed role in its implementation had there not been a disgraceful last-minute veto by the Russian Federation, acting at the behest of Papadopoulos who then argued in the closing days of the campaign that it was impossible to have confidence in the settlement because it had not been endorsed by the Security Council.

The two campaigns on either side of the island were sharply contrasted. In the north the outcome was never in much doubt, with the Turkish government's clear support for the Annan Plan a crucial factor. Denktash fought to the bitter end, with support from right-wing allies, but he no longer cast a spell over his compatriots, either on the mainland or the island. The outcome was a 64.9 per cent vote in favour of the Annan Plan. In the south the rejectionists had a field day. When Papadopoulos did declare his hand, in a lengthy, rambling and emotional television presentation, he did not confine himself to the details of the changes in Annan V but rather launched a root-and-branch onslaught on the fundamentals of the UN's approach (which had not in fact changed much over the last 20 years). He thus disposed of any illusion that he might in fact have been negotiating in good faith up to the last moment. Most Greek Cypriot parties, with the exception of Clerides's Democratic Rally and Vassiliou's small liberal party, followed this lead; and the Greek Orthodox Church campaigned vigorously for rejection. The key thus lay with AKEL, the communist party, whose rock-solid one-third of the popular vote could have swayed the outcome either way. With the pusillanimity that had characterized its position under its leader Christofias throughout the last five years, they finally opted for a procedural device, calling for a delay in the vote, which they knew would not be conceded, and, when it was not forthcoming, recommended a 'no' vote. With that decision the outcome was not in doubt. The Greek Cypriots voted 'no' by 75.83 per cent.

So ended a negotiation that had seemed, against all the odds, to offer a real opportunity for an equitable outcome of substantial benefit to all concerned. The Turks and Turkish Cypriots had made a number of serious tactical errors which meant that they missed the best moment to settle when the Cypriot application for EU membership was still in the balance. They could have negotiated something like the outcome proposed in Annan V a year or more earlier if they had got their act together in time. And there would have been a reasonable chance of its being endorsed by both sides. They paid dearly for not doing so. But the Greek Cypriots made a strategic error. Yet again, as in 1963 and 1974, they opted for a narrow, crabbed vision of their future, dictated more by emotional memories of the past than by a rational view of the future. Let down by their leadership, they chose, just when they were on the point of entering the European Union, to demonstrate that they had not under-stood the first thing about the fundamental objectives of that Union. They will now have to live with the consequences of that decision. The Greeks, who eventually spoke out in favour of the plan, had learned yet again that the Cypriot tail had a tendency to wag the Greek dog. As to the international community in general, and the UN in particular, it had nothing to be ashamed of but much to regret. After years of neglect, and then of inadequately supported efforts to get a solution, it had shown commendable ingenuity and determination. But in the last resort it de-pended on rational self-interest overcoming the demons of history and prejudice, and in this instance that was not achievable.

What will happen now? Much will depend on the prospects for Turk-ish accession to the EU. If Turkey's candidature prospers, and as the reality of Turkish accession comes closer, a solution to the Cyprus prob-lem will become a necessity; and it is difficult to see any solution straying far away from the Annan Plan which has been so widely endorsed. But if Turkey's candidature stalls or is blocked, it is not easy to be so sanguine.

Index

247